PRACTICAL NUMERICAL METHODS

PRACTICAL NUMERICAL METHODS
Algorithms and Programs

Michael C. Kohn

McGraw-Hill Publishing Company

New York   St. Louis   San Francisco   Auckland   Bogotá
Caracas   Hamburg   Lisbon   London   Madrid   Mexico
Milan   Montreal   New Delhi   Oklahoma City
Paris   San Juan   São Paulo   Singapore
Sydney   Tokyo   Toronto

1234567890   8965432109

ISBN 0-07-035514-2

Printed in the United States of America.

For more information about other McGraw-Hill materials, call
1-800-2-MCGRAW in the United States. In other countries,
call your nearest McGraw-Hill office.

Library of Congress Cataloging-in-Publication Data

Kohn, Michael C.
  Practical Numerical Methods: Algorithms and Programs

  Bibliography: p. 253
  Includes index.
  1. Numerical analysis — Data processing.   2. Numerical
analysis — Computer programs.   I. Title.
QA297.K587   1986   519.4   86-8461
ISBN 0–07–035514–2

To Lynn

so she can read the "secret writing"

CONTENTS

PREFACE

There are many fine texts on numerical analysis. They generally fall into three categories:

Mathematical treatises with proofs of many theorems

Tutorial surveys of numerical methods

Handbooks describing specific computer program packages

Most of these texts find their greatest use in courses in departments of mathematics or computer science. The handbooks facilitate the use of program libraries, such as IMSL and EISPACK, whose programs are nearly indispensable for the solution of large problems.

Professional scientists and engineers need a reference book for easy and rapid selection of a computational method for the solution of relatively simple problems. They want the underlying concepts and the range of applicability of the numerical methods to be unobscured by rigorous mathematics or excessively complicated examples. Because they do not intend to delve into these complexities, formal citations to the literature of numerical analysis are unnecessary. This text is intended for that group. It is organized into chapters whose constituent sections outline alternative methods for the solution of a single class of problems. Mathematical proofs and derivations have been kept to a minimum. Several methods are illustrated by simple examples from various technical disciplines. The text advises the reader on the limitations of the techniques discussed and the conditions under which each technique is applicable. Instead of citations to the literature a bibliography is provided for further reading.

Fortran and Pascal programs for selected methods are included for the reader's convenience. Although computer scientists have attacked Fortran because it does not force the programmer to write clear, structured code, no other language provides so many easily used tools for mathematical programming. Many of the newer languages suffer from an impoverished mathematical library and primitive input/output functions.

Structured program control can easily be achieved in Fortran; all that is required is discipline.

Although this book is not intended primarily as a text for a course in numerical methods, it evolved from a set of lecture notes for an undergraduate course. Selected chapters have been distributed to the students for several years. The students found that the simplicity and clarity of the presentation made these notes a valuable supplement to their textbook. This book should be useful in similar courses as a supplement to the textbook. The material is suitable for science and engineering students who have previously taken courses in calculus, differential equations, and linear algebra. Each section can be communicated to the students in a fifty-minute lecture period. Examples appearing in this book are taken from homework and examination questions which have proved to be instructive. Homework assignments may be based on the computer programs given in the text. They are suitable for implementation on a microcomputer.

Four motifs run throughout this text:

Several techniques may be used to solve a given problem.

The technique of choice usually depends on the nature of the data.

A method for the solution of a given problem may appear in a modified form in an algorithm for a different problem.

An error analysis is essential to demonstrate that a computed result is reliable.

Experience with the lecture notes that were the prototype for this book indicates that the recurrence of these motifs will give coherence to a lecture course. Such a continuity of ideas should also aid in a self-study course.

This book is divided into seven chapters. The first chapter describes the source of errors in numerical solution of mathematical problems and explains why estimation and control of those errors is important. The second chapter outlines several methods for finding the roots of nonlinear algebraic equations. The concept of an iteration function is introduced here; it is one of the important recurring themes in the book. The third chapter includes methods for solution of simultaneous algebraic equations. Chapter 4 describes least-squares approximation and polynomial interpolation. Interpolating polynomials are employed in chapters 5 and 6, which deal with numerical differentiation and integration and with numerical solution of differential equations, respectively. Some elementary statistical methods are described in chapter 7.

Because this text is intended to provide scientists and engineers with easy to use methods for routine solution of small-scale problems, descriptions of techniques for the solution of more ambitious problems (finding all the eigenvalues and eigenvectors of general matrices, for example) have been omitted. Instead, in the appendix the reader is directed to widely available program packages that have been developed for such problems. A strong motivation in writing this book was to develop numerical techniques from widely familiar concepts, so techniques based on more exotic mathematical objects, such as orthogonal polynomials, have reluctantly been omitted.

A consistent notation is used in the text. Scalars are indicated by plain typeface whereas arrays are denoted by **boldface type**: lowercase for vectors and uppercase for matrices. Array indices are denoted by roman subscripts; iteration numbers and derivative orders are written in parentheses as Arabic and italic numerical superscripts, respectively. This is to avoid confusion between such indices and radixes or exponents. Derivatives of order less than four are indicated by primes. Error terms are always represented by e, and tolerances placed on solution values as convergence criteria are represented by ε. Algorithms are presented in a combination of mathematics and a simplified "pseudocode," rather than in a formal computer language.

Michael C. Kohn

chapter *1*

Origin and Significance of Numerical Errors

1.1 REPRESENTATION OF NUMBERS

Several mathematical problems arise repeatedly in the course of scientific investigations or engineering projects. Among these are:

Solution of single or simultaneous algebraic equations

Approximation of functions

Differentiation and integration of functions

Solution of differential equations

Statistical analysis of data

Some elementary techniques for numerical solution of these problems are outlined in this book.

Why are such problems routinely solved using numerical methods? First, analytical solution may be extremely difficult for a complicated function. Second, even if an analytical solution were available, calculation of the desired quantities may require evaluation of unfamiliar esoteric functions. Third, the mathematical functions involved may not even be analytical; they may, for example, be a table of ordered pairs. Fourth, a symbolic representation is necessary. For example, if computation of the circumference of a circle of radius 3 is required, an exact answer (in terms of π) is 6π. This is awkward. What if the radius were $\sqrt{2}$? The solution would have to be expressed in terms of $\sqrt{2}\pi$. Arithmetic and algebraic techniques must be used for generality. Finally, and most important, every new equation would have to be solved afresh even though it belongs to a family of problems whose members have similar mathematical properties.

To achieve the desired generality most numerical methods approximate the analytical form of the solution. Often the numerical value of the solution is guessed and that guess is refined by iterative recalculation of the approximating function. Because digital computers can perform these numerical calculations much faster than can a human being and are not susceptible to human errors, such as dropping a decimal point or miscopying a number, these machines are ideally suited to handle the tedious calculations. Computerized numerical methods, then, comprise the convenient general techniques that are needed.

This convenience and generality carries a price, however: the introduction of error into the calculation. An obvious source of error is the very act of approximating the analytical form of the solution, but there are more subtle sources of error as well: representation error, round-off error, and propagated error. The first two types of error are ultimately due to the way numbers are stored in a computer. The last type of error arises because the error-containing result of one computation is used in a subsequent computation. In general, all three types of numerical error contribute to the inaccuracy of a computed result even in those cases where no mathematical approximation has been made.

Representation Error

The way we write numbers is actually a shorthand notation for a polynomial in b, the "base" of the number system. In the familiar decimal system $b = 10$.

Example 1.1:

$$396 = 3 \times 100 + 9 \times 10 + 6 \times 1$$
$$= 3 \times 10^2 + 9 \times 10^1 + 6 \times 10^0$$

Any decimal number represented by a string of digits has a similar form.

$$[a_n a_{n-1} \cdots a_1 a_0]_{10} = a_n \times 10^n + a_{n-1} \times 10^{n-1}$$
$$+ \cdots + a_1 \times 10^1 + a_0 \times 10^0$$

In general, for any number represented in base b notation

$$[a_n a_{n-1} \cdots a_0]_b = a_n \times b^n + a_{n-1} \times b^{n-1} + \cdots + a_0 \times b^0$$

This notation can be extended to fractions. In the decimal system a fraction may be represented as

$$[0.a_{-1}a_{-2} \cdots a_{-n}]_{10} = a_{-1} \times 10^{-1} + a_{-2} \times 10^{-2} + \cdots + a_{-n} \times 10^{-n}$$

This can be generalized to any number represented in any base system where the integral and fractional parts are separated by a "radix" point.

$$[a_n \cdots a_0 \cdots a_{-1} \cdots a_{-m}]_b$$
$$= a_n \times b^n + \cdots + a_0 \times b^0 + a_{-1} \times b^{-1} + \cdots + a_{-m} \times b^{-m}$$
$$= \sum_{i=m}^{n} a_i b^i$$

Clearly, any number can be represented equivalently in any integral base system. For computer applications the binary system, $b = 2$, is chosen. Because we are most familiar with the decimal system, our computer programs will generally accept input as decimal numbers, and the computer will have to convert to the corresponding binary representation. To convert a number from its representation in one base β to its equivalent representation in another base b each digit must be represented in base b and the polynomial expansion in base β evaluated in base b arithmetic.

Example 1.2:

Convert $[36]_{10}$ to binary notation.

$$[36]_{10} = 3 \times 10 + 6$$
$$= [11]_2 \times [1010]_2 + [110]_2$$
$$= [11110]_2 + [110]_2$$
$$= [100100]_2$$

The number of digits required to represent the decimal number in binary is greater than the number of digits required in decimal notation. Furthermore, a terminating decimal fraction may be an infinitely repeating string of digits in binary.

Floating-Point Representation

Any n-digit number in base b can be represented in the computer in a standardized form called "floating-point representation."

$$x = \pm [.d_1 d_2 \cdots d_n]_b \times b^e$$

where the string of digits d is called the "mantissa" and e is an integer called the "exponent." The base b is usually 2. If $d_1 \neq 0$, the floating-point number is said to be "normalized."

The length n of the mantissa is typically about 23 bits, and the exponent can vary over the range m to M (often $M = -m$) where b^M is about 10^{37} on most computers. If the number has more than n digits in its binary representation, the least significant digits in excess of n are either "chopped off" or "rounded off," leading to representation error. If this error is denoted by e, then for chopping

$$0 > e \geqslant -b^{1-n}b^e \quad \text{(absolute error)} \qquad \text{or} \qquad -b^{1-n} \quad \text{(relative error)}$$

and for rounding

$$|e| \leqslant 0.5b^{1-d}b^e \quad \text{(absolute error)} \qquad \text{or} \qquad 0.5b^{1-d} \quad \text{(relative error)}$$

A number $x \geqslant b^M$ cannot be represented at all. This situation is called a "floating-point overflow" and results in totally erroneous results if not actual termination of the program. If $|x| \geqslant b^{m-n}$, the result is a "floating-point underflow." In this case the computer will generally represent the number either as zero or as the smallest possible floating point number, 2^{m-n}. Such errors are generally not serious, but if the resulting number is to be used subsequently as a divisor, a serious error will occur. Division by such a result often leads to a floating-point overflow, and division by zero usually produces an error message and termination of the program in most computer languages. Several of the numerical methods described in this book are sensitive to such errors, and the corresponding computer programs supplied in the text explicitly check for attempted division by zero and print out a diagnostic message before the computer can terminate execution of the program.

1.2 PROPAGATION OF ERROR

Round-off Error

Suppose we wish to perform an arithmetic operation on two floating-point numbers, each of which has its own representation error. The result of such an operation is seldom a third floating-point number with the same number of digits as in the original pair.

Example 1.3:

$$x = 0.20 \times 10^1$$
$$y = 0.77 \times 10^{-6}$$
$$z = 0.30 \times 10^1$$
$$x + y = 0.200000077 \times 10^1$$
$$xy = 0.154 \times 10^{-5}$$
$$\frac{x}{z} = 0.6666 \cdots \times 10^0$$

Because the mantissa of a floating-point number is of fixed length, the result of the arithmetic operation may have to be chopped off (or rounded off) to fit the available number of significant digits. This is the round-off error mentioned in the previous section. It may arise even in the absence of representation error in the floating-point numbers being operated on.

If the relative representation error is denoted as e, then the addition of the floating-point representations of the numbers x_1 and x_2 produces a relative error given by

$$x_1(1 + e) + x_2(1 + e) = (x_1 + x_2)(1 + e)$$

Multiplication of these two floating-point numbers produces a relative error given by

$$x_1(1 + e)x_2(1 + e) = x_1 x_2(1 + 2e + e^2)$$

As e^2 is negligible compared to e, the relative round-off error produced by multiplication is of the same order of magnitude as the representation error in the original numbers. In general, if a mathematical operation Ω is approximated by a floating point operation Ω^*,

$$x \ \Omega^* \ y = (x \ \Omega \ y)(1 + e)$$

An important exception to this generalization occurs when two numbers of nearly the same value are subtracted.

Example 1.4:

Perform the following subtraction $x - y$ on a computer that has eight decimal digits of precision,

$x = 0.76545321 \times 10^1$ (digits which may be in error are underscored)
$y = 0.76544200 \times 10^1$
$z = 0.00001121 \times 10^1 = 0.11210000 \times 10^{-3}$

Note that seven-digit precision has been reduced to three digits of precision after performing the subtraction. Although the absolute error in z is at most the sum of the absolute errors in x and y, the relative error in z may be 10^4 times as great. If it is important to keep the relative error in a calculation small, loss of significance must be anticipated and measures taken to prevent its occurrence. For example, if we must evaluate $1 - \cos x$ for x near 0, there will be a loss of precision on performing the subtraction because $\cos x \to 1$ as $x \to 0$. We can avoid this problem by performing the substitution

$$1 - \cos x = \frac{1 - \cos^2 x}{1 + \cos x} = \frac{\sin^2 x}{1 + \cos x}$$

Because $\sin^2 x \to 0$ as $x \to 0$, this formula can give accurate results.

Propagated Error

Solution of mathematical problems using numerical methods always requires a sequence of such operations. Representation and round-off errors may accumulate step by step in the calculation. This is called "propagated error." In the extreme case, the solution contains so much round-off error that the result is unreliable.

Example 1.5:

Solve $x^2 + 242.14x + 6.2949 = 0$ using a computer which employs five-place floating-point arithmetic and chops past the fifth significant digit.
From the quadratic formula,

$$b^2 - 4ac = 58631 - 25.176 = 58605;$$
$$\sqrt{b^2 - 4ac} = \sqrt{58605} = 242.08;$$
$$x_1 = \frac{\sqrt{b^2 - 4ac}}{2a}$$
$$= -242.4 + 242.08 = -0.03000$$

The true solution to five significant figures is -0.02600. The large relative error occurs because a five-digit mantissa is too short to hold a sufficient number of digits to produce an accurate result when b is subtracted from the square root of the discriminant. If both the numerator and the denominator of the quadratic formula are multiplied by $b - \sqrt{b^2 - 4ac}$, the alternative formula $x_1 = -2c/(b + \sqrt{b^2 - 4ac})$ is obtained. Using five-place arithmetic with this formula yields the correct solution, because 242.14 is added to 242.08 instead of subtracted from it.
A general way to estimate the amount of propagated round-off error in the result of a calculation is to evaluate the computed function $f(x)$ expanded in a Taylor series about x^*, the floating point representation of x.

$$f(x) = f(x^*) + \frac{f'(x^*)}{1!}(x - x^*) + \frac{f''(x^*)}{2!}(x - x^*)^2 + \cdots$$

If $(x - x^*)$ is sufficiently small, then the Taylor series may be terminated after the linear term. The error in computing $f(x)$ as $f(x^*)$ is roughly proportional to the representation error $x - x^*$ with a proportionality factor of $f'(x)$ evaluated at x^*.

Example 1.6:

$$f(x) = e^x/x$$
$$f'(x) = (x e^x - e^x)/x^2$$

$$\text{relative error} = \frac{|f(x) - f(x^*)|}{|f(x)|}$$

$$= \frac{|x\,e^x - e^x|}{x^2} \cdot \frac{|x - x^*|}{e^x/x} = |x - 1|\frac{|x - x^*|}{x}$$

So the relative error in the function value equals the relative error in x times the deviation of x from unity. For a computing machine with eight decimal digits of precision, the relative error in x is 10^{-7} or less. So for moderate values of x the propagation of round-off error is acceptable.

1.3 ESTIMATING ROUND-OFF ERROR

The mathematical theory of errors, which will be used in subsequent sections to derive estimates of the uncertainty in a numerical result, is concerned only with "approximation error," the error arising from the use of a mathematical approximation to the true solution. Because of the propagation of representation and round-off errors in the computer solution of mathematical problems, it is necessary to have an estimate of the upper limit of the round-off error if we are to have any faith in the reliability of the calculations. Unfortunately, an adequate mathematical theory of error estimation is lacking. However, there are several empirical approaches that can provide such information.

Brute Force

Perform the computation with both single- and double-precision arithmetic and compare the results. The difference is an estimate of the error. This may be too costly for a large problem.

Interval Arithmetic

Represent each number in the data and each constant in the equations of the computation by minimum and maximum values to account for representation error. Perform the calculation with each of these estimates. The difference between the results obtained in the two cases is a measure of the accumulated error. This method, like the previous one, more than doubles the amount of computation necessary to solve the mathematical problem.

Significant Digits Calculation

Repeat the procedure used in the previous section to determine the number of significant digits remaining after performing a series of arithmetic operations. In addition to being cumbersome, this approach may overstate the error.

Forward Error Analysis

Subject the initial representation error of the data to the same mathematical operations as the data themselves as illustrated in the previous section. This results in an equation for the accumulated error. Error estimates from this method tend to be excessively conservative, and the analysis is quite tedious.

Backward Error Analysis

The above approaches all try to determine what is the likely or the maximum error in the solution. Backward error analysis attempts to regenerate the original mathematical problem from the solution obtained numerically. That is, it tries to determine the range of data values that could result in the solution actually obtained. If the constants in the regenerated problem are within the representation error of the computer used, the solution is accepted as reliable. The constants in the original equation(s) may be derived from measurements, in which case they would include experimental errors. If the regenerated equation's constants are within the range expected from such errors, the solution can be accepted as reliable.

Example 1.7:

Application of the most common form of the quadratic formula to the equation

$$x^2 + 242.14x + 6.2949 = 0$$

given in the previous chapter yielded the result

$$x = -0.03000$$

Substituting this result into the equation gives a residual of -0.9684, indicating that the above value of x is actually the solution of

$$x^2 + 242.14x + 7.2633 = 0$$

As this value for x produces an equation which differs from the original equation by more than the representation error (10^{-5} in this example), the solution is unreliable (in the preceding section the true solution was calculated to be -0.02600).

Statistical Methods

The significant digits and the forward error analysis methods tend to overestimate the propagated error because individual errors probably do not have the maximum value given by the upper limit of the representation error and because these methods neglect the compensating effect of errors with different signs. There is no way to know how much cancellation will occur after thousands of (or even 100) arithmetic operations. The statistical approach attempts to correct for cancellation of error by considering numerical errors to be random variables drawn from a universal population with a specified probability density function (*pdf*), denoted by $p(x)$.

Suppose the error in representing a quantity q as an r-digit floating-point number is in the range $-0.5 \times 10^{-r} < x < 0.5 \times 10^{-r}$ with a mean value of zero. If the probability of observing an error in this interval is given by a uniform *pdf*, in order for the integral of the *pdf* over this range to equal unity $p(x) = 10^r$ for all x. The variance σ^2 of the error distribution is given by

$$\int_{-e}^{e} x^2\, p(x)dx = e^2/3$$

where the value of e is 0.5×10^{-r}.

If we add two numbers q_1 and q_2 having errors represented by uniform *pdf*'s, the resulting round-off error of the sum varies from $-2e$ to $2e$ with a mean value of zero and a variance of $2e^2/3$. The *pdf* for the round-off error of the sum varies linearly from zero at $x = -2e$ to $1/(2e)$ at $x = 0$, and linearly back to zero at $x = 2e$. After n such additions the error is distributed with a mean of zero and a variance of $ne^2/3$. The *pdf* can be shown to be $\dfrac{\exp(-x^2/\sigma^2)}{\sqrt{2\pi}\,\sigma}$, that is, a normal distribution with a mean of zero and a variance equal to n times the variance of the error propagated by a single arithmetic operation. This distribution predicts that the most probable error is $0.6745\sigma = 0.3894e\sqrt{n}$.

Because round-off error is expected to accumulate linearly with the square root of the number of arithmetic operations, if the representation error e is sufficiently small the solution obtained should be reliable. Of course, it is possible that the round-off error will accumulate more rapidly than expected or that fortuitous cancellation of errors will occur, but such occurrences should be relatively rare for a large number of arithmetic operations. The greatest danger is that a computation may require so many steps that the accumulated round-off error will make the solution unreliable. Therefore, it is important to select the computational method with care.

1.4 ITERATIVE ALGORITHMS AND CONVERGENCE

Iterative Refinement

Because the solution to a mathematical problem is often estimated by an approximating function, it is necessary to improve the estimate until the upper limit of the approximation error is within the tolerance required by the application. A commonly used technique is to add a correction to the current estimate and then compare the maximal approximation error to the required tolerance. If the approximation error exceeds the tolerance, repeat the procedure. After n iterations this process yields a series of approximations $a^{(1)}, a^{(2)}, \ldots, a^{(n)}$. If $a^{(n)}$ approaches the true solution a^* as n increases, the algorithm is said to converge to a^*. When the approximation error is within the desired tolerance, the improved estimate is sufficiently close to the true solution to terminate the iterations.

Unfortunately, there is no guarantee that an iterative algorithm will converge. It is conceivable that for some particular initial estimate the first "improved" estimate, when substituted into the approximating formula, yields the original estimate as the second refinement. (We shall see an example of this when Newton's method for the solution of nonlinear equations is discussed.) Clearly, this behavior leads to an infinitely repeating cycle and no convergence. Even worse, an algorithm may, in certain cases, actually produce a poorer estimate of the solution with each additional iteration. Therefore, if a reliable solution is to be obtained, the iterated approximating function must have some special properties.

Sensitivity and Condition

In the preceding section, application of the statistical method of error estimation indicated that round-off error is expected to increase linearly with the square root of arithmetic operations. The actual rate of increase can be estimated from the truncated Taylor expansion for the error, which was presented in section 1.2. The sensitivity of the function value to errors in the independent variable is given by the derivative $f'(x)$ in the Taylor expansion.

When error growth is linear and slow (i.e., when the sensitivity is small), the approximating function is said to be "well-conditioned." In some cases round-off error increases as a constant raised to the power of the number of arithmetic operations. Such a rapid growth of error can produce totally meaningless numerical results and is usually indicative of a fundamental flaw in the algorithm used.

Stability

A procedure which exhibits exponential growth of round-off error is said to be "unstable." In the extreme, the error may rapidly grow so large as to render the solution obtained meaningless.

Example 1.8:

The discrete function $f^{(n)}(x)$ is given by the recurrence relation

$$f^{(n+1)}(x) = (n + 1)f^{(n)} - (x)^{n+1}$$

where $f^{(0)}(x) = e^x$. Using five decimal place precision and $x = 1$ we obtain:

n	$f^{(n)}(n)$
0	0.7183
1	0.71830
2	0.43660
3	0.30980
4	0.23920
5	0.19600
6	0.17600
7	0.23200 (correct value = 0.15991)

The underscored digits are in error because of loss of precision in performing the arithmetic. By $n = 7$ there are no significant digits of accuracy left.

The above recurrence relation is for the function

$$f^{(n)}(x) = n!\left(e^x - 1 - \frac{x^2}{2!} - \cdots - \frac{x^n}{n!}\right)$$

which does yield the correct solution to five decimal places when five-place arithmetic is used. This difference in behavior is due to the fact that the analytical form of the function is a unique function whereas the recurrence relation does not have a unique solution. To be stable, an algorithm with multiple solutions must have one solution approach the true solution as the number of iterations increases while all other solutions approach zero.

Example 1.9:

The difference equation

$$y^{(n+1)} = 5y^{(n)} - 6y^{(n-1)}$$

is the recurrence relation for the sequence 1, 2, 4, 8, 16, . . . , which has the general solution

$$y^{(n)} = c_1 2^n + c_2 3^n$$

This is a linear combination of the two solutions to the equation. From the first two members of the series the coefficients c_1 and c_2 may be determined as 1.0 and 0.0, respectively.

If a computer were programmed to print out the first 200 numbers in the sequence as given by the recurrence relation, the numbers would be correct to eight decimal places for a while. Thereafter, the solution would rapidly get too large. The reason for this behavior is that represen-

Error

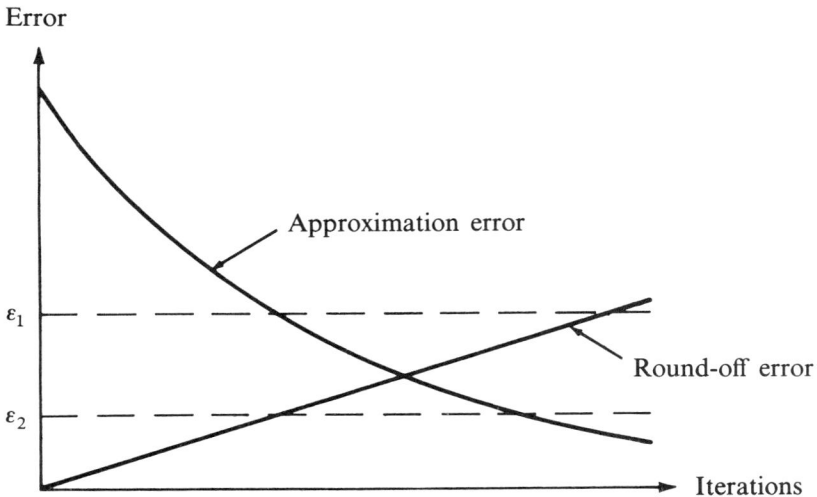

Fig. 1.1.   Efficiency of convergence of an algorithm; ε_1 and ε_2 are examples of the required tolerance of the numerical solution.

tation error may result in the values for $y^{(0)}$ and $y^{(1)}$ being 0.99999999 and 1.99999999 instead of exactly 1 and 2, requiring c_2 to be nonzero, though small. At small values of n the solution is dominated by the first term in the general solution; at large values of n the second term dominates. That is, the sequence is given by the first solution to the equation, whereas the error follows the second solution. This second solution is called a "parasitic solution." Because it does not approach zero with increasing n, the recurrence relation is an unstable algorithm for computation of the members of the sequence.

Efficiency of Convergence

The series of numbers $a_1, a_2, \ldots, a_n$ given by

$$a_n = 1 - \sum_{j=1}^{n} \frac{2}{16j^2 - 1}$$

approaches $\pi/4$ as n approaches ∞, with an approximation error of $1/(4n + 3)$. Suppose we wish to calculate π to a tolerance of 10^{-6}. Solving the equation

$$\frac{1}{4n + 1} = 10^{-6}$$

gives $n = 250,000$ terms in the series to be evaluated. But after so many iterations, the accumulated round-off error is likely to be greater than

10^{-6}. This algorithm converges too slowly to be used to compute the value of π.

An efficient algorithm for machine calculation must converge faster than round-off error accumulates if the result is to be reliable. Fig. 1.1 shows the expected decrease in approximation error and increase in round-off error with each successive iteration. If the required accuracy in the result of a computation is given by ε_1, the algorithm will converge while round-off error is still acceptably small. If the required accuracy is given by ε_2, however, round-off error will be unacceptably high before the algorithm converges.

chapter 2

Solution of Nonlinear Algebraic Equations

2.1 METHOD OF BISECTION

The solution of an arbitrary equation $f(x) = 0$ is commonly called the "root" of the function $f(x)$. More specifically, if $f(x)$ is continuous on an interval $[a, b]$ and the signs of $f(a)$ and $f(b)$ differ, then for some x in $[a, b]$, $x = z$, $f(z) = 0$, and z is a root of the function. This latter definition is the basis of a group of methods for the iterative solution of nonlinear algebraic equations. These methods all seek a value for the independent variable x that satisfies the properties:

$$f(x) = 0$$
$$f(x + dx) > 0$$
$$f(x - dx) < 0$$

for some nonzero dx.

Weierstrass' Method

Suppose it is known that a function $f(x)$ is positive at $x = a$ and negative at $x = b$. Divide the interval into ten equal parts and find the first sub-interval over which the sign of the function changes. The value of the low endpoint gives the first decimal place of the solution. Then repeat the process by dividing the subinterval identified above into ten smaller sub-

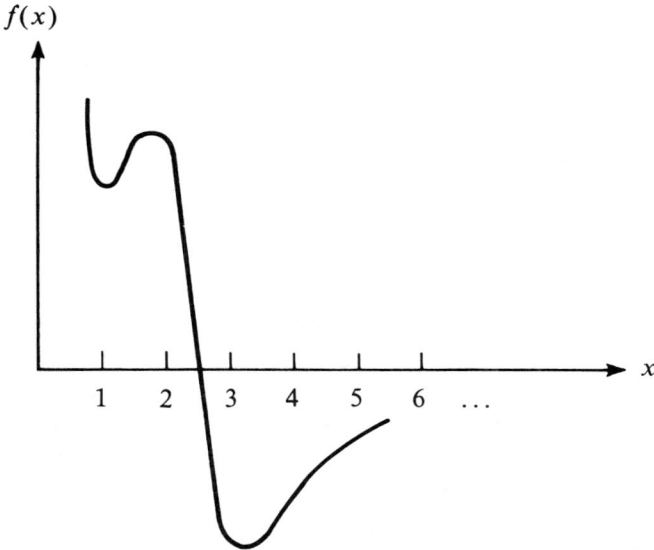

Fig. 2.1. Weirstrass' method. In this example the root of $f(x)$ lies between 2 and 3.

intervals. Again, look for the first of these subintervals over which the sign of the function changes. This step gives the second decimal place of the solution. Repeat the process, dividing the last interval obtained into ten ever smaller subintervals until the desired degree of precision is achieved. That is, when the width of the subinterval is within a preset tolerance, stop the iterations.

Because there are ten subintervals at each step in the algorithm, on the average the Weierstrass method requires six function evaluations per iteration. If the relative error must be $\leq 10^{-6}$, about 42 function evaluations would be necessary. This may be too costly if the function is complicated.

The algorithm can be simplified by dividing the interval at each step into two rather than ten subintervals. This is the method of bisection. It requires only one function evaluation per iteration. To complete the algorithm we must also specify:

Where to start the search for the root

When to stop

When bisection gives significant round-off error

The algorithm starts when an interval over which the function changes sign is found. The iterations cease either when the function value is within some tolerance ε_1 deemed sufficiently close to zero or when the width of the current subinterval is within some tolerance ε_2.

$f(x)$

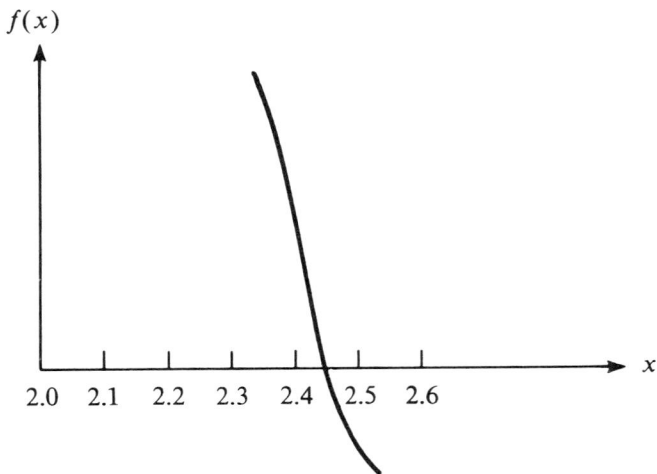

Fig. 2.2. Weirstrass' method. Subdivision of the interval [2, 3] yields 4 for the first decimal place of the fractional part of the root.

Suppose that at one step of the bisection algorithm one endpoint is $a = 0.???...101$ (in binary), and the other endpoint is $b = 0.???...111$ (in binary), differing only in the penultimate digit. Because of the limited precision of the mantissa on the computer used, the midpoint of the interval is

$$m = \frac{a + b}{2} = 0.?...101 + 0.?...111 = 0.?...101$$

and the procedure can cycle indefinitely. The use of the tolerance ε_2 prevents this from occurring.

Algorithm for Bisection

if $f(a^{(0)})f(b^{(0)}) \leq 0$, stop
for $n = 0, 1, 2,...$ until satisfied do
    if $|f(a^{(n)})|$ or $|f(b^{(n)})| \leq \varepsilon_1$, set x to $a^{(n)}$ or $b^{(n)}$ and stop
    else $m = \dfrac{a^{(n)} + b^{(n)}}{2}$
    if $|a^{(n)} - b^{(n)}| \leq \varepsilon_2$, set $x = m$ and stop
        else if $f(a^{(n)})f(m) \leq 0$, $a^{(n+1)} = a^{(n)}$, $b^{(n+1)} = m$
            else $a^{(n+1)} = m$, $b^{(n+1)} = b^{(n)}$

Example 2.1:

$$f(x) = x^3 - 2 = 0, \; \varepsilon_1 = \varepsilon_2 = 10^{-4},$$
$$a^{(0)} = 1, \; b^{(0)} = 2, \; f(a^{(0)}) = -1, \; f(b^{(0)}) = 6$$

Iteration	a	b	m	f(m)
1	1	2	1.5	1.375
2	1	1.5	1.25	−0.4688
3	1.25	1.5	1.375	0.5996
4	1.25	1.375	1.3125	0.2610
5	1.25	1.3125	1.2813	0.1033

After 13 iterations the solution to four decimal places is $x = 1.2599$.

Convergence

How many iterations will it take for the method of bisection to converge? Let the newly selected endpoint at the nth iteration be $z^{(n)}$ and the true

$$|z^{(n)} - x^*| \le \varepsilon_2 \ge \frac{b^{(0)} - a^{(0)}}{2^{n+1}}$$

Solving for n

$$n \ge \frac{\log \left[(b^{(0)} - a^{(0)})/\varepsilon_2\right]}{\log 2 - 1}$$

If the function value is fortuitously within ε_1 at an earlier iteration, the algorithm will converge more rapidly than indicated by this equation. For $f(x) = x^3 - 2 = 10^{-4}$

$$n \ge \frac{\log (10^4)}{\log 2 - 1} = 12.29$$

which agrees with the actual 13 iterations required for convergence.

2.2   REGULA FALSI METHOD

In searching for a root of an equation by the method of bisection the current interval is always divided in half. However, the root is more likely to lie near the end of the interval which corresponds to the smaller value of the function. That is, if $|f(a)| > |f(b)|$, the root is more likely to lie closer to b than to a. Instead of being bisected, the interval $[a, b]$ can be divided proportionally by weighting a by $f(b)$ and b by $f(a)$. This is called the "regula falsi" (false position) method, and it is illustrated graphically in Fig. 2.3.

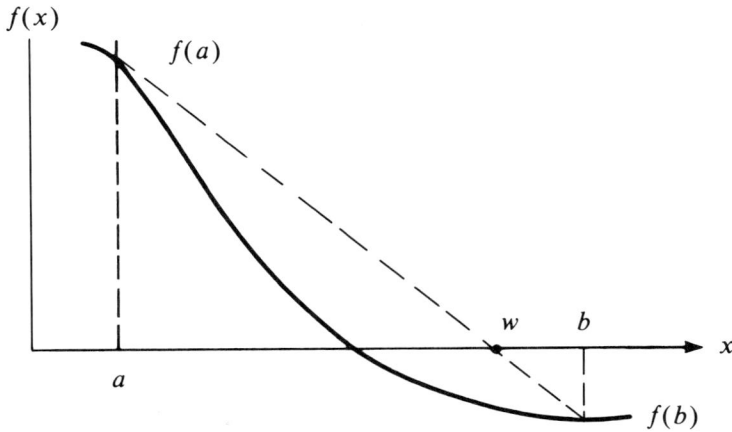

Fig. 2.3. Regula falsi method.

Regula Falsi Algorithm

Given $f(x)$ on $[a^{(0)}, b^{(0)}]$ and tolerances ε_1 (maximum deviation of $f(x)$ from zero) and ε_2 (maximum interval width), find the root lying in the interval:

> check that $f(a^{(0)})f(b^{(0)}) < 0$; else there is no root on interval
> for $n = 0, 1, 2,\ldots$ do
> $$w = \frac{f(b^{(n)})a^{(n)} - f(a^{(n)})b^{(n)}}{f(b^{(n)}) - f(a^{(n)})}$$
> if $f(w) \leq \varepsilon_1$, output solution w and stop
>> else if $f(a^{(n)})$ and $f(w)$ have opposite signs, replace "b" endpoint:
>> $a^{(n+1)} = a^{(n)}$
>> $b^{(n+1)} = w$
>>> else replace "a" endpoint:
>>> $a^{(n+1)} = w$
>>> $b^{(n+1)} = b^{(n)}$
> if $(a^{(n+1)} - b^{(n+1)}) \leq \varepsilon_2$, output solution w and stop

The straight line joining the endpoints of the interval is called a "secant." The slope of this secant line is $[f(b^{(n)}) - f(a^{(n)})]/b^{(n)} - a^{(n)}$. As $f(x)$ must equal zero at the root, the required change Δf in the function value relative to the "a" endpoint is $f(a^{(n)})$. From the equation for the secant line:

$$x\text{-intercept} = a^{(n)} + \frac{\Delta f}{\text{slope}} = \frac{f(a^{(n)})(b^{(n)} - a^{(n)})}{f(b^{(n)}) - f(a^{(n)})}$$

$$= \frac{f(b^{(n)})a^{(n)} - f(a^{(n)})a^{(n)} - f(a^{(n)})b^{(n)} + f(a^{(n)})b^{(n)}}{f(b^{(n)}) - f(a^{(n)})}$$

which is the regula falsi formula for w. Just as in the method of bisection, the root is bracketed at every step of the regula falsi method.

Example 2.2:

$$f(x) = x^3 - 2, \ \varepsilon_1 = \varepsilon_2 = 0.0001, \ [a^{(0)}, b^{(0)}] = [1, 2]$$

n	a(n)	b(n)	f(a^{(n)})	f(b^{(n)})	w	f(w)
0	1.0	2.0	−1.0	6.0	1.1429	−0.5071
1	1.1429	2.0	−0.5071	6.0	1.2097	−0.2298
2	1.2097	2.0	−0.2298	6.0	1.2389	−0.0987
3	1.2389	2.0	−0.0987	6.0	1.2512	−0.0412
4	1.2512	2.0	−0.0412	6.0	1.2563	−0.0172
5	1.2563	2.0	−0.0172	6.0	1.2584	−0.0071
6	1.2584	2.0	−0.0071	6.0	1.2593	−0.0030
7	1.2593	2.0	−0.0030	6.0	1.2597	−0.0012
8	1.2597	2.0	−0.0012	6.0	1.2598	−0.0003
9	1.2598	2.0	−0.0003	6.0	1.2607	0.0039
10	1.2598	1.2607	−0.0003	0.0039	1.2599	−0.0003
11	1.2599	1.2607	−0.0003	0.0039	1.2600	0.0002
12	1.2599	1.2600	−0.0003	0.0002	1.2600	0.0002

The algorithm terminates here because the width of the interval is 0.0001, the desired tolerance. Note that four-decimal-place precision is insufficient to satisfy the tolerance on the function value; the algorithm is caught in an infinitely repeating loop. Fortuitously, the interval contracted sufficiently just when this loop was entered. However, there is no guarantee that this will always occur, so it is wise to always set a limit on the number of iterations allowed.

Whereas bisection of the interval yields one additional binary digit of precision, regula falsi yields a fixed number of additional binary digits (generally > 1) at each step. The exact number of digits of increased precision of the root depends on the steepness of the function. The root of the function in the above example was found in only one fewer iteration with regula falsi than with bisection. How can convergence of the algorithm be accelerated?

Extrapolated Regula Falsi Algorithm

$F = f(a^{(0)})$

$G = f(b^{(0)})$

$w^{(0)} = a^{(0)}$

for $n = 0, 1, 2,...$ do

$$w^{(n+1)} = \frac{Ga^{(n)} - Fb^{(n)}}{G - F}$$

if $f(w^{(n+1)}) \leq \varepsilon_1$, output solution w_{n+1} and stop

if $f(a^{(n)})$ and $f(w^{(n+1)})$ have opposite signs, replace "b" endpoint:

$a^{(n+1)} = a^{(n)}$

$b^{(n+1)} = w^{(n+1)}$

$G = f(w^{(n+1)})$

if $f(w^{(n)})$ and $f(w^{(n+1)})$ have same sign, $F = F/2$

if $f(b^{(n)})$ and $f(w^{(n+1)})$ have opposite signs, replace "a" endpoint:

$a^{(n+1)} = w^{(n+1)}$

$b^{(n+1)} = b^{(n+1)}$

$F = f(w^{(n+1)})$

if $f(w^{(n)})$ and $f(w^{(n+1)})$ have same sign, $G = G/2$

if $|a^{(n+1)} - b^{(n+1)}| \leq \varepsilon_2$, output solution $w^{(n+1)}$ and stop

Again, an iteration counter should be used to prevent cycling due to loss of precision.

This algorithm accelerates the convergence of regula falsi by testing if the current interpolated estimate of the root is on the same side of the true root as the previous iteration's estimate. If it is, the slope of the secant line is halved by halving the function value of the endpoint that does not change. This is illustrated in Fig. 2.4.

The result is that the extrapolating line intersects the x axis at a point closer to the root than it would have reached without acceleration. Although the extrapolating line is no longer a secant, the root is still bracketed by the new endpoints. This behavior is illustrated in Fig. 2.5.

2.3 ITERATION TO A FIXED POINT

In Chapter 1 of this book the concept of iteration was defined as the sequential refinement of an approximate formula's estimate of the solution to a mathematical problem. The formula that approximates the solution is called an "iteration function"; it gives the refined estimate of the solution as a function of the previous estimate. In the method of bisection the refined estimate is given by the midpoint of the interval. In the regula

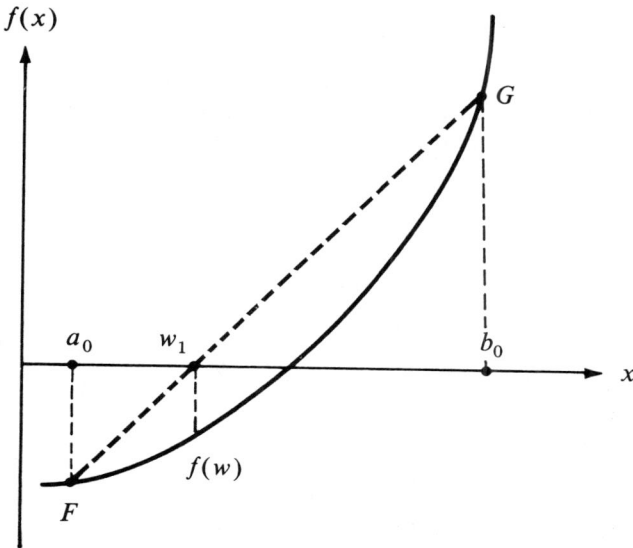

Fig. 2.4. Extrapolated regula falsi method. As $f(w)$ has the same sign as F, the slope G should be halved.

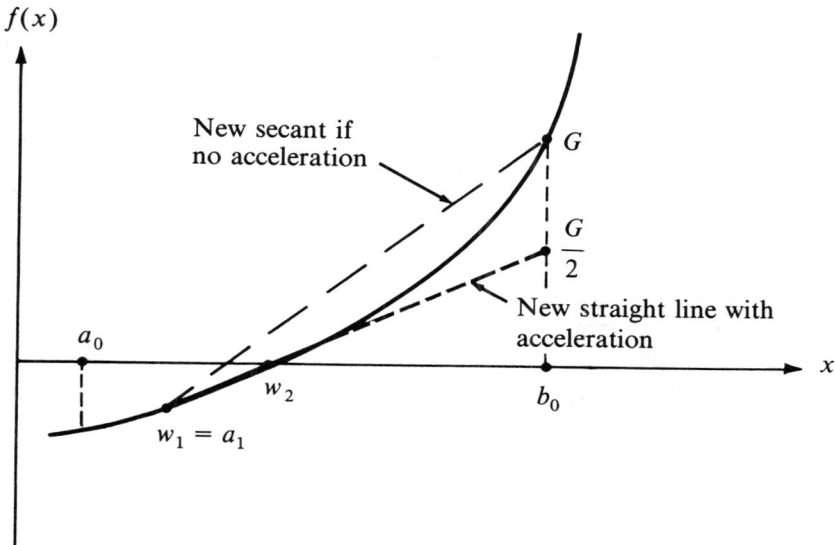

Fig. 2.5. On the next iteration w_2 will fall closer to the root than it would without acceleration. Note that the root is still bracketed.

falsi method the refined estimate is given by the weighted division of the interval. There are many other iteration functions that can be used to find roots of nonlinear equations. This section gives a general approach.

Suppose it is possible to transform the equation $f(x) = 0$, whose root is sought, into the form $x = g(x)$. A root of $f(x)$ is that value of x which will satisfy the latter equality.

Example 2.3:

The function $f(x) = x^2 - x - 2$ transforms to

$$x = g(x) = x^2 - 2 \quad \text{or}$$
$$x = g(x) = \sqrt{x + 2} \quad \text{or}$$
$$x = g(x) = 1 + 2/x \quad \text{or}$$
$$x = g(x) = x - \frac{x^2 - x - 2}{m} \quad \text{for } m \neq 0$$

This behavior can be shown graphically by plotting $y = x$ and $y = g(x)$ on the same set of axes (Fig. 2.6). The point where the two lines intersect is the root. Because substitution of the corresponding x value into the function $g(x)$ does not alter the function value (i.e., x does not change), the intersection of the two lines is called a "fixed point" of $g(x)$. Thus the iteration function for refinement of the estimate of the root at the ith iteration is

$$x^{(i+1)} = g(x^{(i)})$$

Starting from an initial estimate, calculate $y = g(x)$. As this is the refined value of x, it corresponds to the x value of $y = x$ at the same ordinate

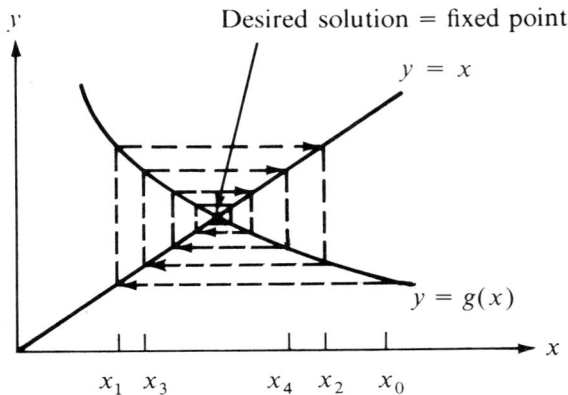

Fig. 2.6. Iteration to a fixed point. The depicted behavior is termed "spider web" convergence.

value. The graphical representation of this method shows how the fixed point is gradually approached.

Fixed-Point Iteration Algorithm

for $n = 0, 1, 2,...$ do

$$x^{(n+1)} = g(x^{(n)})$$

if $|g(x^{(n+1)})| \leq \varepsilon_1$ or $|x^{(n+1)} - x^{(n)}| \leq \varepsilon_2$, output solution and stop

This algorithm will converge only if the following assumptions are satisfied.

1. There is an interval $[a, b]$ on which for any x, $g(x)$ is also on $[a, b]$. This means that each new iterate for x remains in the original interval, i.e., the algorithm does not diverge.
2. The function $g(x)$ is continuous on $[a, b]$. Thus iterative calculation of $x^{(n)}$ will proceed smoothly to the convergence point. This is not always true, however.
3. To avoid this divergent behavior, $g'(x)$ must exist on $[a, b]$ and for $0 < K < 1$, $|g'(x)| \leq K$ for all x in $[a, b]$.

Example 2.4:

$f(x) = x^2 - x - 2$; $x_0 = 2$ (initial estimate of root). Let

$$g(x) = x^2 - 2$$
$$g'(x) = 2x$$

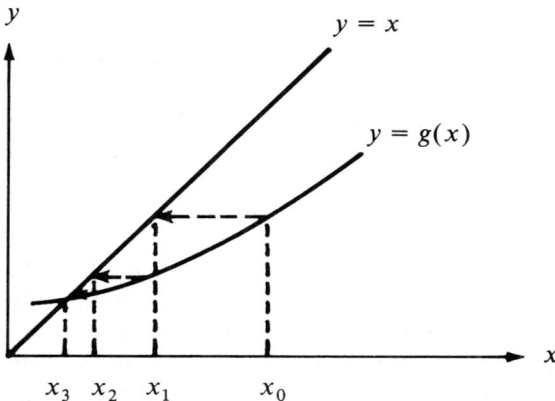

Fig. 2.7. Convergence of fixed-point iteration. This behavior is termed "staircase" convergence.

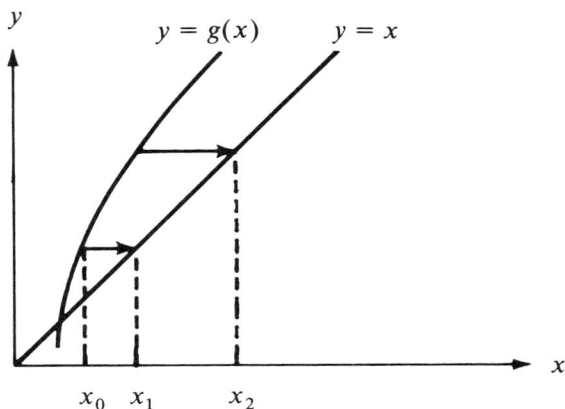

Fig. 2.8.   This example of fixed-point iteration does not converge.

If $x^{(0)} = 2$, then $g'(x^{(0)}) = 4 > K$. So $g(x) = x^2 - 2$ cannot be used as an iteration function. However, for

$$g(x) = \sqrt{x + 2}$$

$$g'(x) = \frac{1}{2\sqrt{x + 2}}$$

at $x_0 = 2$, $g'(x_0) = 0.25 < K$. So this function will work.

Example 2.5:

$$f(x) = x - 2\sin(x)$$
$$g(x) = 2\sin(x)$$

The curves $y = x$ and $y = g(x)$ intersect on the interval $[\pi/3, 2\pi/3]$. On this interval, $g(x)$ varies from $\sqrt{3}$ to 2 and $g'(x)$ varies from -1 to 1. As long as the initial guess is within the interval $(\pi/3, 2\pi/3)$, the algorithm will converge.

Error Estimate for Fixed-Point Iteration

In the bisection and regula falsi methods the width of the final interval of operation is an estimate of the approximation error of the solution because the root is known to lie within that interval. For fixed point iteration, if $g'(x) < 0$ over the interval of operation, the algorithm shows "spider web" convergence and two successive iterates for x will bracket the root. In this case the approximation error of the solution is given by

$$e^{(n+1)} = |x^{(n+1)} - x^{(n)}|$$

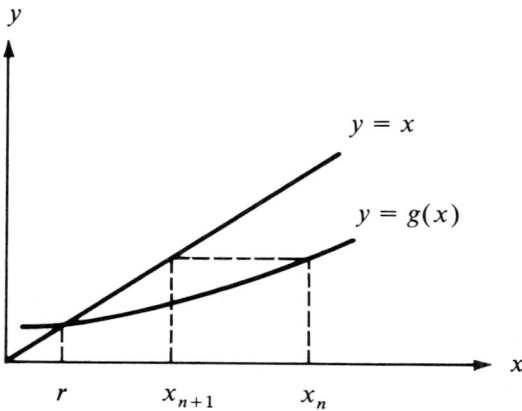

Fig. 2.9.   Error calculation for staircase convergence.

If $g'(x) > 0$ over the interval of operation, the algorithm shows "staircase" convergence and the root is not bracketed. A more general way to estimate the approximation error is needed.

Let p = the average ratio of the deviations from the true root, r, in two successive iterations.

$$p = e^{(n+1)}/e^{(n)} = \frac{|x^{(n+1)} - r|}{|x^{(n)} - r|}$$

From the accompanying graphs

$$|x^{(n)} - r| \leqslant |x^{(n+1)} - x^{(n)}| + |x^{(n+1)} - r|$$

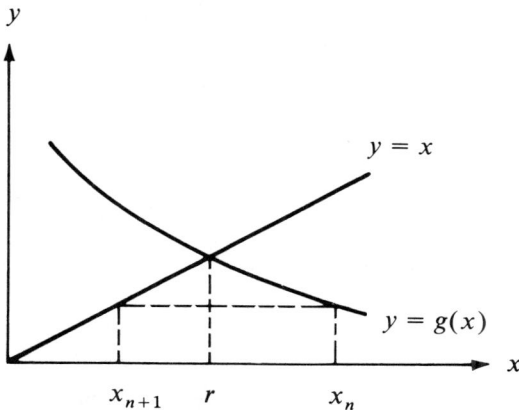

Fig. 2.10.   Error calculation for spider web convergence.

Substituting into the equation for p,

$$p \geq |x^{(n+1)} - r|/(|x^{(n+1)} - x^{(n)}| + |x^{(n+1)} - r|)$$

Solving for $e^{(n+1)}$ yields

$$|x^{(n+1)} - r| \leq |x^{(n+1)} - x^{(n)}|p/(1 - p)$$

Example 2.6:

$$f(x) = x^2 - x - 2$$
$$g(x) = \sqrt{x + 2}$$

n	$x^{(n)}$	
0	0.00000	
1	1.41421	
2	1.84776	
3	1.96157	
...	....	
15	2.00000	(the true root)

At $n = 3$ the approximation error is given by

$$p = |x^{(3)} - x^{(2)}|/|x^{(2)} - x^{(1)}| = 0.12/0.43 = 0.35$$
$$e^{(3)} = |x^{(3)} - r| \leq 0.12 \times 0.35/0.65 = 0.06$$

which is the case as illustrated by the above table.

2.4   NEWTON'S METHOD

Rate of Convergence

If the root of an equation is r, then the error after $n + 1$ fixed-point iterations is

$$e^{(n+1)} = |x^{(n+1)} - r| = g'(z^{(n)})e^{(n)}$$

for $z^{(n)}$ between r and $x^{(n)}$. Because

$$\lim_{n \to \infty} z^{(n)} = r$$

($z^{(n)}$ is close to r after the first couple of iterations) and

$$\lim_{n \to \infty} g'(z^{(n)}) = g'(r)$$

where $0 \leq g'(z^{(n)}) < 1$, the approximation error is linearly decreasing with the number of iterations n. This behavior is called "linear convergence."

If the iteration function $g(x)$ is twice-differentiable, the expression for the approximate solution can be expanded in a Taylor series about r and truncated after the second term:

$$e^{(n+1)} = |x^{(n+1)} - r| = |g(x^{(n)}) - g(r)|$$
$$= g'(r) (x^{(n)} - r) - g''(z^{(n)}) (x^{(n)} - r)^2/2$$

for some $z^{(n)}$ between $x^{(n)}$ and r. If $g''(x)$ is continuous at $x = r$ and $g'(r) = 0$, the maximal rate of convergence is achieved.

$$e^{(n+1)} = g''(r)e^{(n)}$$

and error decreases as the square of the number of iterations. This behavior is called "quadratic convergence."

If a function $f(x)$, whose root is sought, is twice differentiable on an interval containing the root r, then an iteration function which shows quadratic convergence is

$$g(x) = x - f(x)/f'(x)$$

This formula is the basis of Newton's method.

Algorithm for Newton's Method

for $n = 0, 1, 2,...$ do
$$x^{(n+1)} = x^{(n)} - f(x^{(n)})/f'(x^{(n)})$$
if $f(x^{(n+1)}) \leq \varepsilon_1$ or $|x^{(n+1)} - x^{(n)}| \leq \varepsilon_2$, output solution and stop.

Note that the algorithm employs the same tolerances as the previous methods. As always, a computer program implementing an iterative algorithm should include an iteration counter to guard against repetitive cycling of the estimate of the root.

Example 2.7:

$$x^3 - 2 = 0$$
$$f'(x) = 3x^2$$
$$\varepsilon_1 = \varepsilon_2 = 10^{-4}$$
$$x^{(0)} = 2$$

n	$x^{(n)}$	$f(x^{(n)})$	$f'(x^{(n)})$	$x^{(n+1)}$
0	2.0	6.0	12.0	1.5
1	1.5	1.375	6.75	1.2963
2	1.2963	0.7829	5.0412	1.2609
3	1.2609	0.00482	4.7699	1.2599
4	1.2599	3.863×10^{-6}	4.7622	1.2599

Newton's method converges within four iterations whereas the linearly converging bisection and fixed-point iteration methods took 12 to 15 iterations, approximately the square of the number of iterations required here.

Several problems may arise using Newton's method.

1. If $|f'(x^{(n)})|$ is very small near the root, $|f'(x^{(n)})/f'(x^{(n)})|$ can be very large and errors in computation of $x^{(n+1)}$ and $f(x^{(n+1)})$ will be magnified. In such cases good accuracy is difficult to obtain. This may happen if the function has a double root.
2. Depending on the initial estimate of the root of a function with more than one root, one or another of the roots may be found by the algorithm. It may be that only one of the roots has physical significance, so it may be important to begin the iterations close to the desired solution. The method of bisection is often useful in identifying separate intervals containing each root.
3. It is possible for the computation to be caught in an infinitely repeating loop (the reason for the iteration counter!). This often happens when the root is near an inflection point in the curve of $f(x)$ as shown in Fig. 2.11.

Example 2.8:

$$f(x) = x - x^3$$

The values $x = \pm 1/\sqrt{5}$ are called the double points of the iteration function $x^{(n+1)} = x^{(n)} - f(x^{(n)})/f'(x^{(n)})$. If $x^{(n)}$ equals one of these values, $x^{(n+1)}$ will equal the other value and the algorithm will shuttle between the two double points until the maximum number of iterations has been reached.

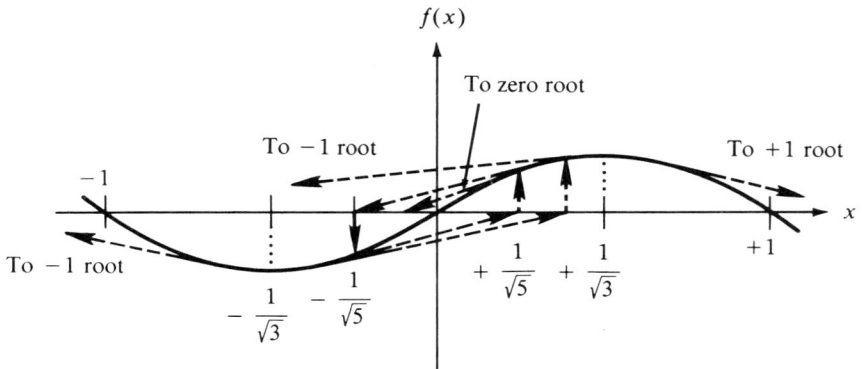

Fig. 2.11. Convergence or infinite recycling of the iterations for Newton's method depending on the initial estimate.

4. The function $f(x)$ may be very difficult (or impossible) to differentiate. In such cases $f'(x^{(n)})$ is often approximated by a secant

$$f'(x^{(n)}) = \frac{f(x^{(n)} + \Delta x) - f(x^{(n)})}{\Delta x}$$

where Δx is a small increment in $x^{(n)}$.

Origin of Newton's Method

Newton's method is based on linear extrapolation like the regula falsi method. However, instead of constructing a straight line between the endpoints of an interval and locating the x intercept, a line tangent to the curve of $f(x)$ at $(x^{(n)}, f(x^{(n)}))$ is constructed and its x intercept is located. The equation of the tangent line is

$$g(x) = f'(x^{(n)}) x + f(x^{(n)}) - x^{(n)}f'(x^{(n)})$$

To find the x intercept set $g(x)$ to zero and solve for x. This yields Newton's formula.

2.5 COMPARISON OF LINEAR EXTRAPOLATION METHODS

The regula falsi method locates a root of a nonlinear function by iterative linear interpolation on an interval known to contain the root. Newton's method locates a root by iterative linear extrapolation from the most recent estimate of the root. These two methods are actually members of a family of linear extrapolation techniques, where the equation of the extrapolating line is

$$y = \text{slope} \cdot x^{(n)} + y \text{ intercept}$$
$$= Kx^{(n)} + f(x^{(n)}) - K x^{(n)}$$

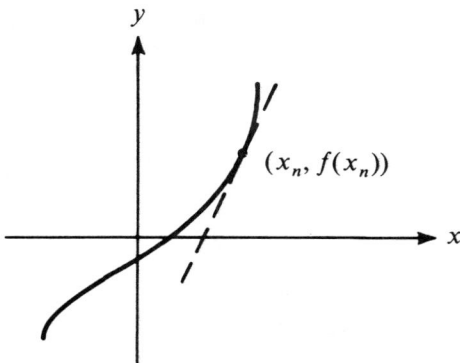

Fig. 2.12. Graphical representation of Newton's method.

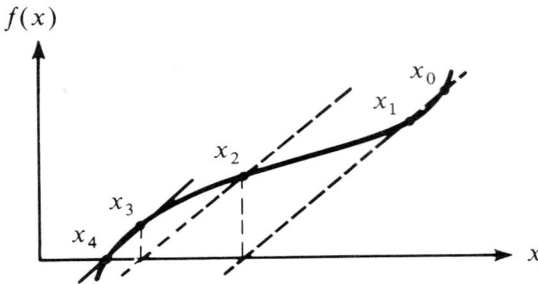

Fig. 2.13. Fixed-secant method.

where K is the slope of the line and $f(x)$ is the nonlinear function whose root is sought. Solving for the x intercept (the estimate of the root) gives the iteration function

$$x^{(n+1)} = x^{(n)} - f(x^{(n)})/K$$

One way to evaluate K is to hold it constant; another way is to reevaluate it at every iteration.

Fixed-Slope Methods

Let $x^{(0)}$ and $x^{(1)}$ be two estimates of the root. If a constant value is chosen for the slope

$$K = [f(x^{(1)}) - f(x^{(0)})]/(x^{(1)} - x^{(0)})$$

the method is called the "fixed secant" method. This method is useful when function evaluations are costly; it is not necessary to recalculate K at each iteration. A disadvantage is that convergence may be slow because the extrapolation does not adjust to the changing slope of $f(x)$ as the estimate of the root changes. If K is held constant at $f'(x^{(0)})$, the method is called the "fixed-tangent" method. If the derivative is a very complicated function, this method avoids its costly reevaluation.

Variable-Slope Methods

If the slope of the extrapolating line is recalculated at every new iteration by using the new estimate of the root as one endpoint of the secant, the method is called the "variable-secant" method.

$$K = [f(x^{(n+1)}) - f(x^{(n)})]/(x^{(n+1)} - x^{(n)})$$

If $x^{(n)}$ and $x^{(n+1)}$ always bracket the root, this is the regula falsi method. If

$$K = f'(x^{(n)})$$

the method is the "variable-tangent" (Newton's) method.

$f(x)$

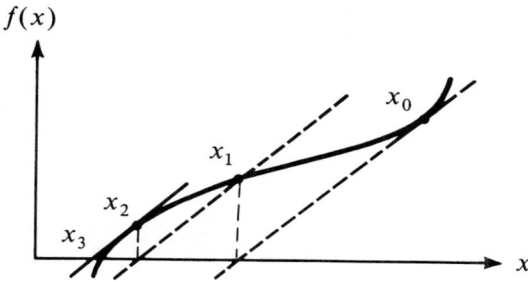

Fig. 2.14. Fixed-tangent method.

Convergence Properties

Let the root of the function $f(x)$ be given by r. Then the estimate of the root after n iterations is

$$x^{(n)} = r + e^{(n)}$$

where e is the error. For the variable secant method

$$x^{(n+1)} = x^{(n)} - y^{(n)}\frac{(x^{(n)} - x^{(n-1)})}{(y^{(n)} - y^{(n-1)})} = \frac{x^{(n-1)}y^{(n)} - x^{(n)}y^{(n-1)}}{y^{(n)} - y^{(n-1)}}$$

Substituting the above expression for $x^{(n+1)}$ and solving for $e^{(n+1)}$

$$e^{(n+1)} = \frac{e^{(n-1)}f(r + e^{(n)}) - e^{(n)}f(r + e^{(n-1)})}{f(r + e^{(n)}) - f(r + e^{(n-1)})}$$

Expanding this error term in a Taylor series gives

$$e^{(n+1)} = e^{(n-1)} e^{(n)} f''(r)/2 f'(r) = Ce^{(n-1)} e^{(n)}$$

It is more convenient to express the rate of convergence as a function of only one previous iteration. Let

$$e^{(n)} = A[e^{(n-1)}]^m$$

where A is a constant. The error at the previous iteration is

$$e^{(n-1)} = A^{-1/m}[e^{(n)}]^{1/m}$$

Then the error at the next iteration is

$$e^{(n+1)} = C e^{(n)} A^{-1/m} [e^{(n)}]^{1/m}$$

Absorbing all constant factors into a single constant C',

$$e^{(n+1)} = C'[e^{(n)}]^{1 + 1/m} = C[e^{(n)}]^m \qquad \text{(from the initial assumption)}$$

Because only the power to which the error is raised is of interest here, we may ignore the fact that $C \neq C'$ and solve for m setting m equal to $1 + 1/m$. This yields $m = 0.5 + \sqrt{5/2} = 1.618$. So the regula falsi method converges more rapidly than linearly in n, the number of iterations, as is the case for iteration to fixed point, but not as rapidly as Newton's method.

For Newton's method

$$e^{(n+1)} = \frac{e^{(n)}f'(r + e^{(n)}) - f(r + e^{(n)})}{f'(r + e^{(n)})}$$

Expanding the error after $n + 1$ iterations in a Taylor series and truncating after the second term gives

$$e^{(n+1)} = \frac{f''(r)}{2 f'(r)} \times [e^{(n)}]^2 = C[e^{(n)}]^2$$

which is the quadratic rate of convergence previously obtained by a different approach.

2.6   DEFLATION OF POLYNOMIALS

If a function $f(x)$ has more than one zero on an interval of interest, the method of bisection could be adapted to find several subintervals over which the function changes sign. Then each subinterval contains one root, and Newton's method can be used to estimate it. For the special case where $f(x)$ is a polynomial in x there is a more efficient approach: deflation.

Suppose one root of a polynomial of degree n

$$p(x) = \sum_{i=0}^{n} a_i x^i$$

is known to be $x = r_1$. Dividing $p(x)$ by $x - r_1$ yields a quotient polynomial $q(x)$ of degree $n - 1$. We can then find a root of $q(x)$, $x = r_2$, and repeat the procedure until all roots have been found. This approach is equivalent to factoring the original polynomial.

$$p(x) = (x - r_1)\, q(x)$$
$$= (x - r_1)\, (x - r_2)\, \cdots\, (x - r_n)$$

Newton's Method for Polynomials

Using the above strategy and root finding by Newton's method, all the real roots of a polynomial can be found. In this case the iteration function for Newton's method is

$$x^{(m+1)} = x^{(m)} - p(x^{(m)})/p'(x^{(m)})$$

and the derivative $p'(x)$ must be known as well as $p(x)$ itself. If z is an approximation to a root of $p(x)$,

$$p(x) = (x - z)\, q(z) + R$$

where R is the remainder. By the product rule of differentiation,

$$p'(x) = q(z) + q'(z) (x - z)$$

When $x = z$,

$$p'(z) = q(z)$$

So rather than actually differentiating $p(x)$, Newton's method for polynomials computes the derivative from the quotient polynomial.

Horner's Method

Suppose the polynomial whose real roots are to be found is of degree 22. Evaluating $p(x)$ generally requires raising x to the 1st through the 22nd powers, and evaluating $q(x)$ generally requires raising x to the 1st through the 21st powers. Even if the powers of x computed in the evaluation of $p(x)$ were stored for use in the evaluation of $q(x)$ rather than recomputed, this involves a lot of calculation at each iteration. However, $p(x)$ can be factored into the form

$$p(x) = [(a_n x + a_{n-1}) x + a_{n-2}] x + \cdots + a_0$$

whose calculation does not require evaluation of powers of x. This technique is Horner's method.

Algorithm

$$b_n = a_n$$
for $k = n-1, n-2, \ldots, 0$ do
$$b_k = a_k + b_{k+1}x$$

The value of b_0 equals $p(x)$. If $x = r$, simply substitute r for x in this algorithm.

Synthetic Division

With $x^{(m)} = r$ as the estimate of one of the roots of $p(x)$, how can $q(x)$ be obtained? Adapting the technique of long division from arithmetic to the evaluation of $p(x)/(x - r)$ gives the following result for the first three steps.

$$
\begin{array}{r}
(a_n)x^{n-1} + (a_{n-1} + ra_n)x^{n-2} + (a_{n-2} + ra_{n-1} + r^2a_n)x^{n-3} + \cdots \\
\hline
x - r)\, \overline{a_n x^n \qquad + a_{n-1} x^{n-1} \qquad\quad + a_{n-2}x^{n-2} \qquad\qquad\quad + \cdots} \\
\underline{a_n x^n \qquad - ra_n x^{n-1}} \\
(a_{n-1} + ra_n)x^{n-1} + a_{n-2}x^{n-2} \\
\underline{(a_{n-1} + ra_n)x^{n-1} - r(a_{n-1} + ra_n)x^{n-2}} \\
(a_{n-2} + ra_{n-1} + r^2a_n)x^{n-2}
\end{array}
$$

Note that the coefficients of the quotient polynomial are in the form obtained by multiplying out the factored form of a polynomial as is done in Horner's algorithm.

A more compact way of obtaining the same result is to construct a table as follows.

Coefficients of $p(x)$

$$\frac{\text{Factors obtained by multiplying previous term in quotient by } r}{\text{Term-by-term sum gives the coefficients of } q(x)}$$

We compute the term-by-term sum because r is negated in the divisor and the next coefficient is obtained by subtraction of the product of the previous coefficient and $-r$.

There is no factor in the first column of the second row because the coefficient of x in the divisor is one. The diagonal arrows correspond to the multiplication of the previous coefficient of $q(x)$ by r. The coefficients of $q(x)$ are the quantities b_i calculated by Horner's method, and the remainder term b_0 is the value of $p(x)$.

Newton's method for polynomials takes advantage of these properties to simultaneously compute both $p(x)$ and $q(x)$ and use them in the iteration function. Clearly, the remainder is zero at the root; this can be used as one of the convergence criteria for the iterations.

Algorithm

Let the maximal permissible deviation of the remainder from zero be ε_1 and the desired precision of the solution be ε_2.

$$b_n = a_n$$
$$c_n = a_n$$

for $m = 0, 1, 2,...$ do

    $z = x^{(m)}$

    for $k = n-1, n-2,..., 1$ do

        $b_k = a_k + z b_{k+1}$ (evaluate coefficients of q)

        $c_k = b_k + z c_{k+1}$ (evaluate $q(z) = c_1$)

        $b_0 = a_0 + z b_1$ (calculate $p(z) = $ remainder)

        $x^{(m+1)} = x^{(m)} - b_0/c_1$

        if $|b_0| < \varepsilon_1$ or $|x^{(m+1)} - x^{(m)}| < \varepsilon_2$, output root and stop.

2.7 NEWTON'S METHOD FOR POLYNOMIALS

Newton's method adapted to polynomial functions uses synthetic division (deflation) to find the quotient polynomial $q(x)$ resulting from the division of the polynomial $p(x)$ by $(x - z)$, where z is an approximation to the root. This is a very efficient algorithm because the quotient polynomial is at once the derivative $p'(x)$ evaluated at z required by Newton's method and the function of reduced degree which is the subject of the next application of Newton's method. The strategy, therefore, is to find one root of $p(x)$, using the algorithm of the previous chapter, decrement n, the degree of the polynomial, and apply the same algorithm to the deflated polynomial $q(x)$. The process is repeated until the quotient polynomial is of first degree, $a_1 x + a_0$, at which point the last root is $-a_0/a_1$.

Algorithm

> while $n > 1$ do
> > $b_n = a_n$
> > $c_n = b_n$
> > for $m = 0, 1,...$ do
> > > $z = x^{(m)}$
> > > for $k = n-1, n-2,...$ do
> > > > $b_k = a_k + zb_{k+1}$
> > > > $c_k = b_k + zc_{k+1}$
> > > $b_0 = a_0 + zb_1$
> > > $x^{(m+1)} = x^{(m)} - b_0/c_1$
> > > if $|x^{(m+1)} - x^{(m)}| < \varepsilon_1$ and $|b_0| < \varepsilon_2$, output root and exit loop
> > for $k = 0, 1,..., n-1$ do
> > > $a_k = b_{k+1}$ (use the coefficients of q in deflated p)
> > $n = n - 1$ (decrease degree of p)
> $x = -a_0$ (calculate final root)

Example 2.9:

$$p(x) = x^2 + 3x - 4; \ x_0 = 0; \ \varepsilon_1 = \varepsilon_2 = 10^{-4}$$

m	b_1	b_0	c_1	$x^{(m+1)}$	
0	3.0	-4.0	3.0	1.3333	
1	4.3333	1.7776	5.6666	1.0196	
2	4.0196	0.0984	5.0392	1.0001	
3	4.0001	0.0004	5.0002	1.0000	(ε_1 satisfied)
4	4.0000	0.0000	5.0000	1.0000	(ε_2 satisfied)

The quantity b_0 is the remainder after synthetic division by $x - x^{(m)}$ and is the value of $p(x^{(m)})$. It equals zero at the root $x = 1$. The column c_1 is the value of $q(x^{(m)}) = p'(x^{(m)})$. Note that b_2 is always equal to 1, the coefficient of the squared term of $p(x)$. After the root $x = 1$ has been found, the root of the deflated polynomial of first degree must be found. As a_1 now takes the value of b_2 and a_0 takes the value of b_1, the second root is -4.

Conditioning

The values found for the roots of a polynomial are very sensitive to small errors in the values of the coefficients. So steps must be taken to minimize the accumulation of round-off error in the deflation of the polynomial to one of lower degree. Because in synthetic division the nth coefficient of $q(x)$ is multiplied by r and the product added to the n-1st coefficient of $p(x)$, the larger the value of r is, the more any error in the coefficients will be magnified.

Example 2.10:

$$(x - 1)(x - 2)(x - 20) = x^3 - 23x^2 + 62x - 40 = p(x)$$

Suppose we first computed the root $x = 20$ to a tolerance of 0.01 percent and obtained the value 20.02. Deflation of the cubic proceeds as follows.

1.0000	− 23.0000	62.0000	− 40.0000
	20.0200	− 59.6596	46.8548
1.0000	− 2.9800	2.3404	6.8458 (= remainder)

The first problem is that the remainder is not close enough to zero even though the solution has acceptable precision. Of course, this problem could be minimized if a stricter tolerance were placed on the solution. More seriously, when the three coefficients of the quotient polynomial are substituted into the formula for the roots of a quadratic polynomial, the result is $x = 1.49 \pm i$ (it is complex instead of real). This result is clearly incorrect and, in any case, could not be found by this version of Newton's method.

   Suppose instead that we first computed the root $x = 1$ to a tolerance of 0.01 percent and obtained the value of 0.999. Synthetic division then gives the following result.

1.0000	− 23.0000	62.0000	− 40.0000
	0.9990	− 21.9790	40.0170
1.0000	− 22.0010	40.0210	0.0170 (= remainder)

Now the remainder is much closer to zero, and the roots of the quotient polynomial are 2.001 and 20.000 from the quadratic formula. So round-off error is minimized if the roots of $p(x)$ are found in ascending order of absolute value.

2.8 COMPUTER PROGRAMS

```
              SUBROUTINE BISECT (A, B, TOLER, ZERO, MAXIT, MIDPT)
C*********************************************************************
C* Root finding by the method of bisection.  A and B are the       *
C* endpoints of the interval.  TOLER is the maximum width of       *
C* the interval at convergence of the algorithm.  ZERO is the      *
C* maximum deviation of the function value from zero at the        *
C* estimate of the root.  MAXIT is the maximum number of iter-     *
C* ations.  MIDPT is the midpoint of the interval and contains     *
C* the estimate of the root on return to the calling program.      *
C* The user must supply a function subprogram named FUNC(X) to     *
C* evaluate the function whose root is sought.                     *
C*********************************************************************
C
      WRITE 1000
1000  FORMAT('1       Root Finding by the Method of Bisection'/)
C
C -- Check that function changes sign on interval [A, B]
C
      F = FUNC(A)
      G = FUNC(B)
      IF (SIGN(1., F) .EQ. SIGN(1., G)) GO TO 200
C
C -- Check for root at one endpoint
C
      IF (F .GE. G) GO TO 10
        MIDPT = A
        V = F
        GO TO 20
10    MIDPT = B
      V = G
20    IF ((V .LE. ZERO) .OR. (ABS(A - B) .LT. TOLER)) GO TO 100
      ITER = 0
      WRITE 2000
2000  FORMAT(' ITER',5X, A',10X,'F(A)',9X,'B',10X,'F(B)',1
     9X,'M',10X,'F(M)'/)
C
C -- Begin iteration loop
C
30    ITER = ITER + 1
      MIDPT = (A + B)/2.0
      V = FUNC(MIDPT)
      WRITE 3000, ITER, A, F, B, G, MIDPT, V
3000  FORMAT(I4,1X,6(1X,1PE11.4))
C
C -- Check for convergence
C
```

```
      IF ((V .LE. ZERO) .OR. (ABS(A - B) .LE. TOLER) GO TO 100
      IF (SIGN(1.,F) .NE. SIGN(1.,V)) GO TO 1
C
C -- Replace endpoint A by MIDPT
C
      A = MIDPT
      F = V
      GO TO 2
C
C -- Replace endpoint B by MIDPT
C
1     B = MIDPT
      G = V
2     IF (ITER .GE. MAXIT) GO TO 300
      GO TO 30
C
C -- Convergence achieved
C
100   WRITE 4000, ITER, MIDPT, V
4000  FORMAT(/5X,'Convergence achieved after',I3,'iterations',
     1 /5x,'Root = ',1PE12.4)
      GO TO 40
C
C -- Error Section
C
200   WRITE 5000
5000  FORMAT(/' ***Error***No change in sign of function on',
     1 ' starting interval')
      GO TO 40
300   WRITE 6000, MAXIT, MIDPT, V
6000  FORMAT(/'  ***Error***No convergence in',I3,'iterations'/
     1 5X,'Current approximation to root =',1PE12.4,
     2 ' with a function value of',1PE12.4)
40    RETURN
      END

procedure bisect(a,b,toler,zero: real; maxit: integer;
             var midpt: real);
{
***********************************************************************
*  Root finding by the method of bisection. a and b are the        *
*  endpoints of the interval.  toler is the maximum width of       *
*  the interval at convergence of the algorithm.  zero is the      *
*  maximum deviation of the function value from zero at the        *
*  estimate of the root.  maxit is the maximum number of iter-     *
*  ations.  midpt is the midpoint of the interval and contains     *
*  the estimate of the root on return to the calling program.      *
*  The user must supply a function subprogram named func(x) to     *
*  evaluate the function whose root is sought.                     *
***********************************************************************
}
type
  flag = (continue, converge, no_root, error);
```

```
var
  f, g, v: real;
  iter: integer;
  status: flag;

function samesign(x, y: real): boolean;
begin
  samesign := false;
  if ((x < 0.) and (y < 0.)) or ((x > 0.) and (y > 0.))
    then samesign := true
end;

begin
  status := continue;
  writeln('          Root Finding by the Method of Bisection';);
writeln;

{Check that function changes sign on interval [a, b]}

f := func(a);
g := func(b);
if samesign(f, g)
  then begin
    status := no_root;
    writeln('***Error***No change in sign of function on',
      ' starting interval')
  end
  else {check for root at one endpoint}
    begin
      if (f < g)
        then begin
          midpt := a;
          v := f
        end
        else begin
          midpt := b;
          v := g
        end
      if (v < zero) or (abs(a - b) <= toler)
        then status := converge

      {initialize iteration loop}

      if (status = continue)
        then begin
          iter := 0;
          writeln(: iter      a          f(a)      b',
            '               f(b)           m          f(m)');
          writeln
        end
    end;

  {Begin iteration loop}
```

```
    while (status = continue) do
      begin
        midpt := (a + b)/2.0;
        v := func(midpt);
        writeln(iter:4,' ',a:11,'  ',f:11,'  ',b:11,'  ',g:11,'  ',
          midpt:11,'  ',v:11);
        if (v <= zero) or (abs(a - b) <= toler)
          then status := converge
          else
            if samesign(f, v)
              then begin {replace endpoint a}
                a := midpt;
                f := v
              end
              else begin {replace endpoint b}
                b := midpt;
                g := v
              end;
        iter := iter + 1;
        if (iter >= maxiter) then status := error
      end; {of while loop}
    case status of
      converge:
        begin
          writeln;
          writeln('    Convergence achieved after',iter:3,
            ' iterations');
          writeln('    Root = ',midpt:12,
            ' with a function value of',v:12)
        end;
      error:
        begin
          writeln;
          writeln('***Error***No convergence in ',maxit:3,
            ' iterations');
          writeln('    Current approximation to root =',
            midpt:12,' with a function value of ',v:12)
        end
      end {of case}
end;
          SUBROUTINE REGULA(A, B, TOLER, ZERO MAXIT, W)
C*******************************************************************
C* Root finding by the extrapolated regula falsi method.  A      *
C* and B are the endpoints of the interval.  TOLER is the max-   *
C* imum width of the interal at convergence of the algorithm.    *
C* ZERO is the maximum deviation of the function value from      *
C* zero at the estimate of the root.  MAXIT is the maximum       *
C* number of iterations.  W is the point found by linear inter-  *
C* polation on the interval and contains the estimate of the     *
C* root on return to the calling program. The user must supply   *
C* a function subprogram named FUNC(X) to evaluate the           *
C* function whose root is sought.                                *
C*******************************************************************
```

```
      WRITE 1000
1000  FORMAT('       Root Finding by the Regula Falsi Method'/)
C
C -- Check that sign of function changes on interval
C
      F = FUNC(A)
      G = FUNC(B)
      IF (SIGN(1.,F) .EQ. SIGN(1.,G)) GO TO 200
C
C -- Initialize search for root
C
      IF (F .GE. G) GO TO 10
        W = A
        V = F
        GO TO 20
10    W = B
      V = G
20    IF ((V .LE. ZERO) .OR. (ABS(A - B) .LE. TOLER)) GO TO 100
      WRITE 2000
2000  FORMAT('ITER',5X,'A',10X,'F(A)',9X,'B',10X,'F(B)',9X,'W',
     1 10X,'F(W)'/)
      ITER = 0
C
C -- Begin iterations
C
30    ITER = ITER + 1
      W = (G * A - F * B)/(G - F)
      V2 = FUNC(W)
      WRITE 3000, ITER, A, F, B, G, W, V2
3000  FORMAT(I4,1X,6(1X,1PE11.4))
      IF ((V2 .LE. ZERO) .OR. (ABS(A - B) .LE. TOLER)) GO TO 100
      IF (SIGN(1.,F) .NE. SIGN(1.V2)) GO TO 1
C
C -- Else replace endpoint A by W
C
        A = W
        F = VS
        IF (SIGN(1.,V2) .EQ. SIGN(1.,V)) F = F/2.0
        GO TO 2
C
C -- Then replace endpoint B by W
C
1     B = W
      G = V2
      IF (SIGN(1.,V2) .EQ. SIGN(1.,V)) G = G/2.0
2     V = V2
      IF (ITER .GE. MAXIT) GO TO 300
      GO TO 30
C
C -- Convergence achieved
C
100   WRITE 4000, ITER, W, V2
```

```
4000  FORMAT(/5X,'Convergence achieved after ',I3,' iterations'/
     1  5X,'Root = ',1PE12.4,' with a function value of',1PE12.4)
       GO TO 40
C
C -- Error Section
C
200   WRITE 5000
5000  FORMAT(' ***Error***No change in sign of function on',
     1  ' starting interval')
       GO TO 40
300   WRITE 6000, MAXIT, W, V2
6000  FORMAT(/' ***Error***No convergence in',I3,' iterations'/
     1  5x,'Current approximation to root =',1PE12.4,
     2  ' with a function value of',1PE12.4)
40    RETURN
      END
```

```pascal
procedure regula (a,b,toler,zero: real; maxit: integer; var w:
                  real);
{
**********************************************************************
* Root finding by the extrapolated regula falsi method.  a        *
* and b are the endpoints of the interval.  toler is the max-     *
* imum width of the interval at convergence of the algorithm.     *
* zero is the maximum deviation of the function value from        *
* zero at the estimate of the root.  maxit is the maximum         *
* number of iterations.  w is the point found by linear inter-    *
* polation on the interval and contains the estimate of the       *
* root on return to the calling program. The user must supply     *
* a function subprogram named func(x) to evaluate the             *
* function whose root is sought.                                  *
**********************************************************************
}
type
  flag = (continue, converge, no_root, error);

var
  f, g, v, v2: real;
  iter: integer;
  status: flag;

function samesign(x, y: real): boolean;
begin
  samesign := false;
  if ((x < 0.) and (y < 0.)) or ((x > 0.) and (y > 0.))
    then samesign := true
end;


begin
  writeln('     Root Finding by the Regula Falsi Method');
  writeln;
  status := continue;
```

```
{Check that sign of function changes on interval}

f := func(a);
g := func(b);
if samesign(f, g)
  then begin
    status := no_root;
    writeln('***Error***No change in sign of function on',
      ' starting interval')
  end
  else {check endpoint for root}
    begin
      if g > f
        then begin
          w := a;
          v := f
        end
        else begin
          w := b;
          v := g
        end;
      if (v <= zero) or (abs(a - b) <= toler)
        then status := converge;

      <initialize iteration loop>

      if (status = continue)
        then begin
          writeln(' iter    a              f(a)          b',
            '           f(b)           w           f(w)');
          writeln;
          iter := 0
        end
  end;
{begin iteration loop}

while (status = continue) do
  begin
    w := (g * a - f * b)/(g - f);
    v2 := func(w);
    writeln(iter:4,' ',a:11,' ',f:11,' ',b:11,' ',g:11,' ',
      w:11,' ',v2:11);
    if (v2 <= zero) or (abs(a - b) <= toler)
      then status = converge
      else begin
        if samesign(f, v2)
          then
            begin  {replace endpoint a by w}
              a := w;
              f := v2;
              if samesign(v, v2) then f := f/2.
            end
```

```
            else
              begin  {replace endpoint by w}
                b := w;
                g := v2;
                if samesign(v, v2) then g := g/2.
              end;
          iter := iter + 1
          if (iter > maxit) then status := error
        end
    end; {of while loop}

  {Output results}

  case status of
    converge: begin
      writeln;
      writeln('   Convergence achieved after ',iter:3,
        ' iterations');
      writeln('   root = ',w:12,' with a function value of ',
        v2:12)
    end;
    error: begin
      writeln('***Error***No convergence in ',maxit:3,
        ' iterations');
      writeln('    Current approximation to root =',w:12,
        ' with a function value of ',v:12)
    end
  end {of case}
end;
              SUBROUTINE NEWTON(X, ZERO, MAXIT,TOLER)
C*********************************************************************
C*                                                                  *
C* This routine finds a root of a nonlinear equation by Newton's    *
C* method.  X is the initial estimate of the root and contains      *
C* the best approximation to the root on return.  ZERO is the       *
C* maximal value the function may have at the solution. TOLER       *
C* is the maximal difference between successive iterates of the     *
C* estimate of the root at convergence.  The user must supply       *
C* the functions FUNC and DERIV, which compute the value of the     *
C* nonlinear function whose root is sought and the value of its     *
C* derivative, respectively.                                        *
C*                                                                  *
C*********************************************************************

      DATA SMALL/1.E-30/

      WRITE 1000
1000  FORMAT(5X,'Root Finding by Newton's Method'/)
      F = FUNC(X)
      IF (F .E. ZERO) GO TO 100
      WRITE 2000
2000  FORMAT('iter',5X,'x',10X,'F(x)',7X,'f''(x)',7X,'x-new'/)
      ITER = 0
```

```
C -- Begin iteration loop

10      ITER = ITER + 1
        FPRIME = DERIV(X)
        IF (FPRIME .LE. SMALL) GO TO 200
          XNEW = X - F / FPRIME
          WRITE 3000, ITER, X, F, FPRIME, XNEW
3000      FORMAT(I4,2X,4(1PE11.4,1X))
          F = FUNC(XNEW)
          IF (F .LE. ZERO .OR. ABS(X - XNEW) .LE. TOLER) GO TO 100
          X = XNEW
          IF (ITER .GE. MAXIT) GO TO 300
          GO TO 10

C -- Convergence achieved

100     WRITE 4000, ITER, X, F
4000    FORMAT(/5X,'Convergence achieved after ',I3,' iterations'/
       1 5X,'Root =',1PE12.5,' with a function value of',1PE12.5)

C -- Error Section
C    Slope of function is too small

200     WRITE 5000, X, F, FPRIME
5000    FORMAT(/' ***Error***Slope of function is too small'/5X,
       1 'Currency approximation to root =',1PE2.5,
       2 ' with a function value of',1PE12.5/5X,
       3 'and a derivative value of',1PE12.5)
        RETURN

C -- Maximum iterations exceeded

300     WRITE 6000, MAXIT, X, F
6000    FORMAT(/' ***Error***No convergence in ',I3,' iterations'/
       1 5X,'Current approximation to root =',1PE12.5,
       2 ' with a function value of',1PE12.5)
        RETURN
        END
procedure Newton(var x: real; zero, toler: real; maxit: integer);
{
*********************************************************************
*                                                                   *
* This routine finds a root of a nonliner equation by Newton's      *
* method. X is the initial estimate of the root and contains        *
* the best approximation to the root on return. ZERO is the         *
* maximal value the function may have at the solution. TOLER        *
* is the maximal difference between successive iterates of the      *
* estimate of the root at convergence.  The user must supply        *
* the real functions func and deriv, which compute the value of     *
* the nonlinear function whose root is sought and the value of      *
* its derivative, respectively.                                     *
*                                                                   *
*********************************************************************
```

```
}
const
  toosmall = 1.E-30;

type
  flag = (continue, converge, small_slope, error);

var
  iter: integer;
  status: flag;
  f, fprime, xnew: real;

begin
  status := continue;
  writeln('      Root Finding by Newton's Method');
  writeln;
  f := func(x);
  if (f <= zero)
    then status = converge
    else
      begin
        writeln(' iter     x            f(x)          f''(x)',
          '           x-new');
        writeln;
        iter := 0
      end;

  {begin iteration loop}

  while status = continue do
    begin
      fprime := deriv(x);
      if (fprime <= toosmall) then status := small_slope;
      if not error
        then begin
          xnew := x - f / fprime;
          writeln(iter:4,'   ',x:11,' ',f:11,'   ',fprime:11,' ',
            xnew:11);
          f := func(xnew);
          if (f <= zero) or (abs(x - xnew) <= toler)
            then status := converge;
      x := xnew
        end;
      iter := iter + 1;
      if (iter >= maxit) then status := error
    end;  {of while loop}

  {output results}

  case status of
    converge:
      begin
```

```
        writeln;
        writeln('     Convergence achieved after',iter:3,
          ' iterations');
        writeln('     Root =',x:12,' with a function value of',
          f:12)
      end;
    small_slope:
      begin
        writeln;
        writeln('***Error***Slope of function is too small');
        writeln('     Current approximation to root =',x:12,
          ' with a function value of',f:12);
        writeln('     and a derivative value of',fprime:12)
      end;
    error:
      begin
        writeln;
        writeln('***Error***No convergence in',maxit:3,'
iterations');
        writeln('   Current approximation to root =',x:12,
          ' with a function value of',f:12);
      end
    end  {of case}
end;
        SUBROUTINE DEFLAT(PCOEFF, X, N, MAXIT, ZERO, TOLER)
C******************************************************************
C*                                                              *
C* Finding all the roots of a polynomial with real roots using  *
C* Newton's method and using synthetic division to deflate the  *
C* polynomial.  PCOEFF is the array of polynomial coefficients;  *
C* maximal degree is 20.  X is the approximation to the root.    *
C* MAXIT is the maximal number of iterations.  ZERO is the maxi- *
C* mal value of the polynomial at the root, and TOLER is the     *
C* maximal difference between successive iterations at conver-   *
C* gence.                                                        *
C*                                                              *
C******************************************************************

        DIMENSION PCOEFF(1), QCOEFF(21)
        DATA SMALL/1.E-30/

        WRITE 1000
1000    FORMAT(5X,'Real Roots of Polynomials by Newton's Method'//)
        NTERMS = N + 1
        DO 10 K = N, 1, -1
          ITER = 0
          WRITE 2000, NTERMS - 1
2000      FORMAT(' Root of polynomial of degree',I3/'iter',5X,'x',10X,
          'p(x)',7X,'q(x)',7X,'x-new'/)
          ITER = ITER + 1

C -- Compute polynomial and derivative value
```

```
         QCOEFF(NTERMS) = PCOEFF(NTERMS)
         DERIV = QCOEFF(NTERMS)
20       DO 30 I = NTERMS-1, 2, -1
            QCOEFF(I) = PCOEFF(I) + QCOEFF(I+1) * X
30          DERIV = QCOEFF(I) + DERIV * X

C -- Calculate value of polynomial and test for convergence

         REMAIN = PCOEFF(1) + QCOEFF(2) * X
         IF (REMAIN .LE. ZERO) GO TO 100

C -- Else extrapolate to new x-value

         IF (DERIV .LE. SMALL) GO TO 200
         XNEW = X - REMAIN / DERIV
         WRITE 3000, ITER, X, REMAIN, DERIV, XNEW
3000  FORMAT(I4,2X,4(1PE11.4,1X))
         IF (ABS)X - XNEW) .LE. TOLER) GO TO 100
         IF (ITER .GE. MAXIT) GO TO 300

C -- Else continue iterating

         X = XNEW
         GO TO 20

C -- Convergence achieved

100      WRITE 4000, ITER, X, REMAIN
4000  FORMAT(/5X,'Convergence achieved after ',I3,' iterations'/
     1  5X,'Root =',1PE12.5,' with a function value of',1PE12.5)
         NTERMS = NTERMS -1
         DO 40 I = 1,NTERMS
40          PCOEFF(I) = QCOEFF(I+1)
10       CONTINUE

C -- Error Section
C    Slope of function is too small

200      WRITE 5000, X, REMAIN, DERIV
5000  FORMAT(/' ***Error***Slope of function is too small'/5X,
     1  'Current approximation to root =',1PE12.5,
     2  ' with a function value of',1PE12.5/5X,
     3  'and a derivative value of',1PE12.5)
         RETURN

C -- Maximum iterations exceeded

300      WRITE 6000, MAXIT, X, REMAIN
6000  FORMAT(/' ***Error***No convergence in ',I3,' iterations'/
     1  5X,'Current approximation to root = ',1PE12.5,
     2  ' with a function value of',1PE12.5)
         RETURN
         END
```

```
procedure deflate(var pcoeff: real_array, x: real; n, maxit:
  integer; zero, toler: real);
{
**********************************************************************
*                                                                  *
* Finding all the roots of a polynomial with real roots using      *
* Newton's method and using synthetic division to deflate the      *
* polynomial.  PCOEFF is the array of polynomial coefficients;     *
* maximal degree is 20.  X is the approximation to the root.       *
* MAXIT is the maximal number of iterations.  ZERO is the maxi-*
* mal value of the polynomial at the root, and TOLER is the        *
* maximal difference between successive iterations at conver-      *
* gence.  The calling procedure must define the data type          *
* real_array as an array[1..n] of real.                            *
*                                                                  *
**********************************************************************
}
const
  toosmall = 1.e-30;

type
  flag = (continue, converge, small_slope, error);

var
  iter, nterms, i: integer;
  qcoeff: real_array;
  remain, deriv, xnew: real;
  status: flag;

begin
  writeln('     Real Roots of Polynomial by Newton's Method');
  writeln;
  nterms := n + 1;
  status := continue;

  while (nterms > 1) and (status = continue) do
    begin
      iter := 0;
      writeln('Root of polynomial of degree',(nterms-1):3);
      writeln;

      {Compute values of polynomial and derivative}

      qcoeff[nterms] := pcoeff[nterms];
      deriv := qcoeff[nterms];
      while status = continue do
        begin
          for i := nterms downto 2 do
            begin
              qcoeff[i] := pcoeff[i] + qcoeff[i+1] * x;
              deriv := qcoeff[i] + deriv * x
            end;
```

```
        {Calculate value of polynomial
         and test for convergence}

        remain := pcoeff[1] + qcoeff[2] * x;
        if remain <= zero
          then status := converge
          else if deriv <= toosmall then status := error;
        if status = continue
          then begin
            xnew := x - remain / deriv;
            writeln(iter:4,'   ',x:11,' ',remain:11,' ',

              deriv:11,' ',xnew:11);
            if abs(x - xnew) <= toler
              then status := converge
          end
      end;  {of inner while loop}
    if status = converge
      then begin {output root}
        writeln;
        writeln('    Convergence achieved after',iter:3,
          ' iterations');
        writeln('    Root =',x:12,' with a function value',
          ' of',remain:12);
        nterms := nterms - 1;
        for i := 1 to nterms do
          pcoeff[i] := qcoeff[i+1]
      end
  end;  {outer while loop}

{Error Section}

case status of
  small_slope:
    begin
      writeln;
      writeln('***Error***Slope of function is too small');
      writeln('    Current approximation to root =',x:12,
        ' with a function value of',remain:12);
      writeln('    and a derivative value of',deriv:12)
    end;
  error:
      begin
        writeln;
        writeln('***Error***No convergence in',maxit:3,
          ' iterations');
        writeln('    Current approximation to root =',x:12,
          ' with a function value of',remain:12)
      end
    end {of case}
end;
```

2.9 EXAMPLE PROBLEMS

Example 2.11: Angular Displacement of a Cam

A machine has a cam that displaces a pushrod according to the equation for the cam radius as a function, $r(\theta)$, of the angular displacement θ of the cam from the pushrod axis.

$$r(\theta) = 1 + 4\exp[-(\theta/\pi)^2]$$

for θ (in radians) on the interval $[-\pi, \pi]$. Using the regula falsi method, find, to three decimal place precision, the angle θ at which $r(\theta) = 3.5$. Let $\varepsilon_1 = \varepsilon_2 = 0.5 \times 10^{-3}$.

Solution

The desired value for the angle of the cam satisfies (it is the root of) the equation

$$f(\theta) = r(\theta) - 3.5 = 0$$

Because the cam is bilaterally symmetrical with $r(0) = 5$ and $r(\pi) = r(-\pi) = 1 + 4/e = 2.4715$, the angular displacement of the cam must lie between 0 and π (or $-\pi$) radians. These values define the initial interval $[a_0, b_0]$ for the regula falsi method's search for the root. The interpolated value for the root is given by the regula falsi formula

$$w = \frac{f(b_n)a_n - f(a_n)b_n}{f(b_n) - f(a_n)}$$

n	a	f(a)	b	f(b)	w	f(w)
0	0.0	1.5	p	−1.0285	1.8637	0.3133
1	1.8637	0.3133	p	−1.0285	2.162	−0.009
2	1.8637	0.3133	2.162	−0.009	2.154	0.0002
3	2.154	0.0002	2.162	−0.009	2.1538	−0.00003

After three iterations $f(w) < \varepsilon_1 = 0.5 \times 10^{-3}$. Therefore, the last value of w, 2.154 radians, is the solution for the angle of the cam that will displace the pushrod by 3.5 units of distance. To check this value, perform another iteration of the regula falsi algorithm. The value for w is still 2.154 radians to three decimal places. Therefore, the criterion that the difference between successive iterates must be less than ε_2 is satisfied.

Example 2.12: Molar Volume of a Gas

Two equations for the molar volume V of a gas in terms of its temperature T and pressure P are the ideal gas equation

$$PV = RT$$

and the van der Waals equation

$$(P + a/V^2)(V - b) = RT$$

where $R = 0.08207$ liter-atmospheres/degree-mole. For carbon dioxide, $a = 3.592$ and $b = 0.04267$. Assume $P = 2.2$ atmospheres and $T = 320°K$.

Find an iteration function for the solution of the van der Waals equation for V. Demonstrate that this iteration function obeys all the requirements for convergence of the iteration to a fixed-point algorithm if a good estimate for V is provided by the ideal gas equation. Using this function and the initial estimate provided by the ideal gas equation, find, to four-decimal-place precision, the molar volume of carbon dioxide under the conditions stated above.

Solution

The van der Waals equation can be rewritten as

$$V = g(V) = \frac{RT}{P} + b + \frac{ab}{PV^2} - \frac{a}{PV}$$

which is the ideal gas equation with a correction added. This function can be used as an iteration function provided that it is continuous on its interval $[a, b]$ of operation, that it maps a V on $[a, b]$ into $[a, b]$, and that its derivative $g'(V)$ is less than 1 in absolute value.

Clearly, the candidate iteration function is continuous for $V > 0$. From the ideal gas equation we calculate the initial estimate of V as

$$V = RT/P = 0.08207 \times 320/2.2 = 11.93745$$

The correction term in the function $g(V)$ is

$$b + \frac{ab}{PV^2} - \frac{a}{PV} = 0.09362$$

This correction is small compared to V and decreases as V increases (the correction is positive). Therefore, there will be an interval around V such that any V in the interval will be mapped into the same interval by $g(V)$. The derivative of the candidate iteration function

$$g'(v) = -\frac{ab}{2PV^3} + \frac{a}{PV^2}$$

equals 0.01144 at the initial estimate $V = 11.93745$. As this value is less than 1 and decreases as V increases, the third criterion for a good iteration function is also satisfied.

The molar volume from the ideal gas equation is used as the initial estimate of V for the fixed-point iteration. As four-decimal-place precision is desired, the convergence tolerance is $\varepsilon = 0.5 \times 10^{-4}$.

n	V	$g(V)$ n
0	11.93745	11.84384
1	11.84384	11.84277
2	11.84277	11.84275

After three iterations, successive values of V differ by less than ε so the desired molar volume to four decimal places is 11.8428.

chapter 3

Systems of Linear Algebraic Equations

3.1 Gaussian Elimination

Suppose we have the set of simultaneous equations

$$x + y + z = 3 \tag{3.1}$$
$$y - 2z = 5 \tag{3.2}$$
$$3z = 21 \tag{3.3}$$

How would we solve for x, y, and z? The obvious procedure is:

1. Solve for z from equation (3.3).

$$z = 21/3 = 7 \tag{3.4}$$

2. Substitute the value for z into equation (3.2) and solve for y.

$$y = 5 + 2 \times 7 = 19 \tag{3.5}$$

3. Substitute the values for y and z into equation (3.1) and solve for x.

$$x = 3 - 19 - 7 = -23 \tag{3.6}$$

This procedure is called "back substitution." Generalizing (x, y, z) to the vector $\mathbf{x} = (x_1, x_2, \ldots, x_n)$, the algorithm for back substitution is:

For $i = n, n - 1, \ldots, 1$ do

$$x_i = \frac{1}{a_{ii}} \left\{ b_i - \sum_{j=i+1}^{n} a_{ij} x_j \right\}$$

The quantities a_{ij} are the coefficients of x_j in equation i. The quantity b_i is the constant on the right-hand side of equation i. The coefficients on the right-hand side constitute a constant vector **b**, and the coefficients on the left-hand side of the transformed equations (e.g., 3.4–3.6) constitute an upper triangular matrix (one whose subdiagonal elements are all zero) **A**.

nonzero elements

↓

$$A = \begin{pmatrix} 0 & \diagdown \end{pmatrix}$$

In matrix notation the system is written in the form

$$\mathbf{Ax} = \mathbf{b}$$

In the above example:

$$\begin{array}{ccc} \mathbf{A} & \mathbf{x} & = & \mathbf{b} \end{array}$$

$$\begin{pmatrix} 1 & 1 & 1 \\ 0 & 1 & -2 \\ 0 & 0 & 3 \end{pmatrix} \begin{pmatrix} x \\ y \\ z \end{pmatrix} = \begin{pmatrix} 3 \\ 5 \\ 21 \end{pmatrix}$$

When the matrix equation is expanded by multiplying **A** by **x**, the original equations are generated.

In general, the simultaneous equations will not correspond to a matrix in upper triangular form. The strategy for solution of the system of equations is to transform the matrix for the system into upper triangular form by adding equations, multiplied by appropriate constants, so that one of the variables drops out in the sum. The process is repeated until only one equation in one unknown remains.

Example 3.1:

$$\begin{array}{lr} x + 2y - z = 2 & (3.7) \\ 3x + y + 2z = 6 & (3.8) \\ x - y + 3z = 3 & (3.9) \end{array}$$

$$\begin{array}{lr} -3 \times \text{equation (1)} + \text{equation (2):} \quad -5y + 5z = 0 & (3.10) \\ - \text{equation (1)} + \text{equation (3):} \quad -3y + 4z = 1 & (3.11) \\ \text{equation (3')} - 3/5 \times \text{equation (2'):} \quad z = 1 & (3.12) \end{array}$$

The triangularized system is:

$$\begin{matrix} \mathbf{A} & \mathbf{x} & = & \mathbf{b} \end{matrix}$$

$$\begin{pmatrix} 1 & 2 & -1 \\ 0 & -5 & 5 \\ 0 & 0 & 1 \end{pmatrix} \begin{pmatrix} x \\ y \\ z \end{pmatrix} = \begin{pmatrix} 2 \\ 0 \\ 1 \end{pmatrix}$$

Equation
(3.13)
(3.14)
(3.15)

This procedure is called "Gaussian elimination."

Algorithm

for $j = 1,\ldots, n$ do
  for $i = j+1,\ldots, n$ do
    (equation i) = (equation i) $- a_{ij}/a_{jj} \times$ (equation j)

Possible Problems

If at some stage of the elimination algorithm $a_{jj} = 0$, the above algorithm could not be continued. This problem may arise if:

1. One equation equals another equation times a constant.
2. One equation is the sum of multiples of two or more equations.
3. All the elements of a row or a column of the matrix $\mathbf{A}$ are zero.

(The next chapter describes a method that may prevent this problem.) If any of these conditions arise, the matrix is said to be "singular." One way of looking at this property of singularity is to view a matrix as made up of rows, each of which is a basis vector in an n-dimensional space, that is, a space defined by n linearly independent vectors.

Example 3.2:

3-space (Euclidean space)
   Any vector in Euclidean space may be represented by the three basis vectors **i, j, k.**

$$\mathbf{i} = (1, 0, 0)$$
$$\mathbf{j} = (0, 1, 0)$$
$$\mathbf{k} = (0, 0, 1)$$

Linear Independence

If there are n vectors $\mathbf{a}_i$ of dimension n such that

$$c_1\mathbf{a}_1 + c_2\mathbf{a}_2 + \cdots + c_n\mathbf{a}_n = 0$$

if and only if all coefficients c_i are zero, then the vectors $\mathbf{a}_i$ are said to be "linearly independent." If there is some nonzero value for one or more of the coefficients that will satisfy the above equality, then one or more of the vectors a_i is a linear combination of others. A vector v is a "linear combination" of vectors w and x if

$$v = c_1 w + c_2 x$$

and neither c_1 or c_2 equals zero. This can readily be extended to n vectors. If there is a vector v of dimension n that is a linear combination of n linearly independent vectors x_i, then the $n + 1$ vectors do not "span" (i.e., uniquely define) the $n + 1$-dimensional space. The vector v duplicates the directions of the other vectors.

3.2 PARTIAL PIVOTING

General Strategy for Gaussian Elimination

Convert the $n \times n$ matrix A to upper triangular form. For each equation i (that is, for each row a_{ij} of the matrix and its associated constant right-hand side b_j), perform the following operation on all rows $j = i + 1,...,$ n.

$$(\text{Equation } j) = (\text{Equation } j) - (a_{ji}/a_{ii})(\text{Equation } i)$$

Then perform the back substitution. Because all matrix elements below the diagonal are zero, the rule for multiplication of such a matrix by a vector may be written as

$$\sum_{j=i}^{n} a_{ij} x_j = b_i = a_{ii} x_i + \sum_{j=i+1}^{n} a_{ij} x_j$$

Solving for x_i gives the formula for back substitution.

$$x_i = \frac{1}{a_{ii}} (b_i - \sum_{j=i+1}^{n} a_{ij} x_j)$$

Algorithm

(Triangularize matrix A)
for $i = 1,..., n\text{-}1$ do   (do not have to work on last row)
  for $j = i+1,..., n$ do   (operate on all lower rows)
    for $k = i+1,..., n$ do   (go over each column $> i$)
      $a_{jk} = a_{jk} - (a_{ji}/a_{ii})a_{ik}$
      $b_j = b_j - (a_{ji}/a_{ii})b_i$ (operate on constant vector)
(Back substitution)
$x_n = x_n/a_{nn}$ (Solve last equation)
for $i = n - 1,..., 1$ do   (Solve remaining equations)
  $x_i = b_i$

for $j = i + 1,\dots, n$ do

$\qquad x_i = x_i - a_{ij} x_j$

$\quad x_i = x_i / a_{ii}$

Example 3.3:

$$\begin{array}{cc} \mathbf{A} & \mathbf{b} \\ \begin{pmatrix} 1 & 2 & -1 \\ 3 & 1 & 2 \\ 1 & -1 & 3 \end{pmatrix} \mathbf{x} = \begin{pmatrix} 2 \\ 6 \\ 3 \end{pmatrix} \end{array}$$

Step 1: Reduce first column

$$\left(\begin{array}{ccc|c} \multicolumn{3}{c}{\mathbf{A}} & \mathbf{b} \\ 1 & 2 & -1 & 2 \\ 0 & 1 - \dfrac{3}{1} \times 2 = -5 & 2 - \dfrac{3}{1}(-1) = 5 & 6 - \dfrac{3}{1} \times 2 = 0 \\ 0 & -1 - \dfrac{1}{1} \times 2 = -3 & 3 - \dfrac{1}{1}(-1) = 4 & 3 - \dfrac{1}{1} \times 2 = 1 \end{array} \right)$$

Step 2: Reduce second column

$$\left(\begin{array}{ccc|c} 1 & 2 & -1 & 2 \\ 0 & -5 & 5 & 0 \\ 0 & 0 & 4 - \dfrac{-3}{-5} \times 5 = 1 & 1 - \dfrac{3}{5} \times 0 = 1 \end{array} \right)$$

This is the result obtained for this system in the previous section.

Step 3: Back substitution

$$x_3 = 1/1 = 1$$
$$x_2 = (1/-5)(0 - 5 \cdot 1) = 1$$
$$x_1 = (1/1)\{2 - (2 \cdot 1 - 1 \cdot 1)\} = 1$$

Because division by the diagonal elements of the triangularized matrix is performed in the back substitution, this algorithm will work as long as no diagonal element becomes zero in the triangularization procedure. Denote the rows of the matrix by the vectors $\mathbf{v}_i = $ row i. If

$$\mathbf{v}_i = \sum_{\substack{j=1 \\ j \neq i}}^{n} c_j \mathbf{v}_j$$

and at least one c_j is nonzero, at least one row of the matrix is a linear combination of other rows. Such a matrix is singular, and at least one of the diagonal elements of the resulting triangular matrix will be zero, making back substitution impossible.

Suppose matrix A is nonsingular. What could thwart this algorithm? As a first example, the system of equations

$$x_2 = 3$$
$$x_1 = 7$$

corresponds to the matrix equation

$$\begin{pmatrix} 0 & 1 \\ 1 & 0 \end{pmatrix} \mathbf{x} = \begin{pmatrix} 3 \\ 7 \end{pmatrix}$$

Clearly the matrix is nonsingular, but the first row already has a zero on the diagonal, making it impossible to solve.

As a second example, suppose that at some step in the elimination procedure a region of the matrix is

$$\begin{pmatrix} - & - & - & - \\ 0 & 0.001 & 1.21 & - \\ 0 & 0.0181 & 21.9 & - \end{pmatrix}$$
$$\downarrow \quad \vdots \quad \vdots \quad \vdots$$

Let us say we are working in four-place arithmetic. To eliminate element $a_{3,2}$ we do for $j = 3,\ldots, n$

$$a_{3,\,j} = a_{3,\,j} - (a_{3,2}/a_{2,2})\, a_{2,\,j}$$

to get the new row.

$$a_{3,3} = 21.9 - (0.0181/0.001)\, 1.21 = 21.9 - 21.90\underline{1}$$

where the underscore indicates a digit lost in rounding to four digits. So the computed result for this diagonal element is zero even though the true value is nonzero.

Both these problems can be avoided by scanning the ith column to be eliminated (converted to zeroes) for the subdiagonal matrix element with the largest absolute value and proceeding as though the corresponding row r were in the ith row. This tactic of interchanging the row in position i with that in position r is called partial pivoting. It prevents accidental zeroes on the diagonal. It minimizes the accumulation of round-off error when performing the subtraction in

$$a_{ik} = a_{ik} - (a_{ij}/a_{jj})\, a_{jk}$$

because division by the largest possible a_{jj} perturbs the values of the matrix elements the least.

Example 3.4:

$$\begin{pmatrix} \mathbf{A} & & & \mathbf{b} & \mathbf{p} \\ 2 & 3 & -1 & 5 & 1 \\ 4 & 4 & -3 & 3 & 2 \\ -2 & 3 & -1 & 1 & 3 \end{pmatrix}$$

The vector $\mathbf{p}$ is the permutation vector. The value of p_i tells which row r was pivoted into the ith position. Instead of literally interchanging a pair of rows, much effort or computer time can be saved by just swapping the values of p_i and p_r.

Step 1: Row 2 has the pivot element. As row 2 should be in position 1, swap the values of p_1 and p_2.

$$\begin{pmatrix} 0 & 1 & 1/2 & \bigm| & 7/2 & \bigm| & 2 \\ 4 & 4 & -3 & \bigm| & 3 & \bigm| & 1 \\ 0 & 5 & 5/2 & \bigm| & 5/2 & \bigm| & 3 \end{pmatrix}$$

Step 2: Row 3 has the pivot; swap the values of p_2 and p_3.

$$\begin{pmatrix} 0 & 0 & 1 & \bigm| & 3 & \bigm| & 2 \\ 4 & 4 & -3 & \bigm| & 3 & \bigm| & 3 \\ 0 & 5 & 5/2 & \bigm| & 5/2 & \bigm| & 1 \end{pmatrix}$$

Step 3: Back substitution; find the rows to be operated on from the $\mathbf{p}$ vector ($p_3 = 1$ indicates that row 1 was pivoted into the position of row 3).

$$0\,x_1 + 0\,x_2 + 1\,x_3 = 3 \qquad x_3 = 3$$

Position 2 is given by $p_2 = 3$.

$$0\,x_1 + 5\,x_2 - 5\,x_3 = 5/2 \qquad x_2 = \{(5/2)\cdot 1 + 15/2\}/5 = 2$$

Position 1 is given by $p_1 = 2$.

$$4\,x_1 + 4\,x_2 - 3\,x_3 = 3 \qquad x_1 = (3\cdot 1 - 4\cdot 2 + 3\cdot 3)/4 = 1$$

The solution is $\mathbf{x} = (1, 2, 3)$. Notice that once the division b_i/a_{ii} is done, b_i is never used again. If Gaussian elimination is being done by computer, the solution values x_i can be stored in the same locations as the b_i values.

3.3 GAUSS-JORDAN ELIMINATION

There are several variations of the Gaussian elimination algorithm that make it more convenient for solution by computer. In some cases, a variant may be computationally more efficient than the algorithm presented in the last section.

Normalization

It is inefficient, when subtracting $(a_{ji}/a_{ii})a_{ik}$ from each a_{jk} of the rows below the pivot, to perform the division anew. Of course, the quotient for row j can be calculated once and stored as a separate variable which is used in the reduction of the appropriate row elements. An even more efficient method is to normalize the row containing the pivot by dividing each row element by the pivot element. In addition to avoiding having to store the quotient for the row being reduced, this technique has the advantage of scaling all the elements of the matrix, which keeps them small and helps prevent loss of significance when performing the subtraction in the row reduction.

Multiple Right-hand Sides

It is often necessary to solve the same set of equations m times with a different **b** vector on the right-hand side each time. For example, the constant vector may be a function of time or spatial position. The m problems may be solved simultaneously by appending to matrix **A** a matrix whose columns are the constant vectors.

$$\left(\mathbf{A} \,\middle|\, \begin{matrix} \mathbf{b}_1 & \mathbf{b}_2 & \cdots & \mathbf{b}_m \\ \vdots & \vdots & & \vdots \end{matrix} \right)$$

The resulting matrix, having n rows and $n + m$ columns, is treated just like the original matrix, except that normalization and row reduction is performed for $j = 1,\ldots, n + m$. All the **b** vectors are transformed at the same time as the matrix is triangularized. Similarly, at each stage in the back substitution, the algorithm is applied to each constant vector, that is, for $k = 1,\ldots, m$. The m solution vectors replace the **b** vectors when this variation is implemented on a computer.

Gauss-Jordan Elimination

The matrix equation $\mathbf{Ax} = \mathbf{b}$ has the solution $\mathbf{x} = \mathbf{A}^{-1}\mathbf{b}$. Gaussian elimination solves the equation without explicitly finding the inverse of **A**, because it is more work to compute the inverse and then multiply by **b**. Sometimes it is necessary to know the inverse matrix. If to **A** we append n constant vectors which are the columns of the identity matrix

$$\left(\mathbf{A} \,\middle|\, \begin{matrix} 1 & & & 0 \\ & 1 & & \\ 0 & & \ddots & \\ & & \cdots & 1 \end{matrix} \right)$$

and perform the Gaussian elimination and back substitution, the solution vectors are the columns of $\mathbf{A}^{-1}$. When, as in this case, the number m of constant vectors is greater than or equal to the number n of rows of **A**, performing the m back substitutions can take a lot of computer time and, hence, be very costly. There is a variant of Gaussian elimination that accumulates the terms in the back substitution at the same time as triangularizing the matrix. This is "Gauss-Jordan elimination." It employs the same pivoting strategy as Gaussian elimination but is more efficient when $m \geq n$.

Algorithm

> for $i = 1,\ldots, n$ do
> $\quad$ f Find pivot row and perform row interchange; $r = p_i$
> $\quad$ for $j = i,\ldots, n + m$ do
> $\quad\quad$ $a_{rj} = a_{rj}/a_{ri}$ (normalize row)
> $\quad$ for $k = 1,\ldots, n$ except for $k = r$ do
> $\quad\quad$ for $j = i,\ldots, n + m$ do
> $\quad\quad\quad$ $a_{kj} = a_{kj} - a_{rj}a_{ki}$ (row reduction)

Note that in this variant all rows not including the pivot element are operated on.

Determinant

The determinant is a crude measure of the "magnitude" of a matrix. That is, a matrix with large elements tends to have a large determinant. (The determinant of a singular matrix, however, equals zero.) The determinant of a triangular matrix $\mathbf{A}$ is given by

$$\det \mathbf{A} = |\mathbf{A}| = \prod_{i=1}^{n} a_{ii}$$

As the matrix $\mathbf{A}$ is triangularized, each factor in the above product can be multiplied by the previous factors, starting with det $= 1$. Each row interchange, however, changes the sign of the determinant.

Algorithm

> for $i = 1,\ldots, n$ do
> $\quad$ find pivot row $r = p_i$
> $\quad$ if $r \neq i$, det $= -$ det
> $\quad$ det $=$ det $\cdot a_{ri}$

After multiplying by the current pivot element, proceed with normalization and row reduction.

Example 3.5:

For simplicity, we'll use only one constant vector, but the columns of the identity matrix will be appended to produce the inverse.

$$\begin{array}{ccc} \mathbf{A} & \mathbf{b} & \mathbf{I} & \mathbf{p}\ \det \end{array}$$

$$\left(\begin{array}{rrr|r|rrr} 2 & 3 & -1 & 5 & 1\ 0\ 0 \\ 4 & 4 & -3 & 3 & 0\ 1\ 0 \\ -2 & 3 & -1 & 1 & 0\ 0\ 1 \end{array}\right) \begin{array}{l} 1 \\ 2\quad 1 \\ 3 \end{array}$$

Step 1: Row 2 has the pivot element for column 1. Interchange p_1 and p_2 to indicate that row 2 should be in the first position. Set det $= a_{2,1}$ det. Normalize the pivot row. Perform row reductions on all other rows from column 1 to column 7.

$$\begin{pmatrix} 0 & 1 & 1/2 \\ 1 & 1 & -3/4 \\ 0 & 5 & -5/2 \end{pmatrix} \left. \begin{matrix} 7/2 \\ 3/4 \\ 5/2 \end{matrix} \right| \begin{matrix} 1 & -1/2 & 0 \\ 0 & 1/4 & 0 \\ 0 & 1/2 & 1 \end{matrix}$$

$$\begin{matrix} \mathbf{p} & \det \\ 2 & \\ 1 & -4 \\ 3 & \end{matrix}$$

Step 2: Row 3 has the pivot for column 2. Interchange p_2 and p_3. Set det $= -a_{3,2}$ det. Normalize the pivot row and perform row reduction on all other rows from column 2 to column 7.

$$\begin{pmatrix} 0 & 0 & 1 \\ 1 & 0 & -1/4 \\ 0 & 1 & -1/2 \end{pmatrix} \left. \begin{matrix} 3 \\ 1/4 \\ 1/2 \end{matrix} \right| \begin{matrix} 1 & -6/10 & -1/5 \\ 0 & 3/20 & -1/5 \\ 0 & 1/10 & 1/5 \end{matrix}$$

$$\begin{matrix} \mathbf{p} & \det \\ 2 & \\ 3 & 20 \\ 1 & \end{matrix}$$

Step 3: There are no rows remaining below position 3, whose entry in the **p** vector now points to row 1, so there is no opportunity to pivot. As $a_{1,3}$ already equals 1, normalization is not needed and det is unchanged when multiplied by the pivot element. Perform the row reductions on rows 2 and 3.

$$\begin{matrix} \mathbf{I} & & & \mathbf{x} & & \mathbf{A}^{-1} \\ \begin{pmatrix} 0 & 0 & 1 \\ 1 & 0 & 0 \\ 0 & 1 & 0 \end{pmatrix} & \left. \begin{matrix} 3 \\ 1 \\ 2 \end{matrix} \right| & \begin{matrix} 1 & -6/10 & -1/5 \\ 1/4 & 0 & -1/4 \\ 1/2 & -1/5 & 1/10 \end{matrix} \end{matrix}$$

$$\begin{matrix} \mathbf{p} & \det \\ 2 & \\ 3 & 20 \\ 1 & \end{matrix}$$

Note that the Gauss-Jordan algorithm has transformed the original matrix into the identity matrix with permuted rows while transforming the original identity matrix into $\mathbf{A}^{-1}$ with permuted rows. The b vector has become the solution vector **x.**

3.4   ERRORS IN GAUSSIAN ELIMINATION

Errors in the Constant Vector

The elements of the coefficient matrix **A** and the constant vector **b** in the system of linear equations $\mathbf{Ax} = \mathbf{b}$ will generally come from measured quantities, which are subject to error. Furthermore, when these quantities are input into a computer, representation error is introduced. Because of the errors affecting the elements of **b,** the constant vector actually used in the computation is $\mathbf{b} + \mathbf{h}$, where **h** includes all the above errors, and the solution vector that is actually obtained will be $\mathbf{x} + \mathbf{e}$. Subtracting the true equation from that which includes the errors gives

$$A(x + e) = b + h \quad \text{(Problem that was solved)}$$
$$\underline{A\,x \qquad = b} \quad \text{(True problem)}$$
$$Ae \qquad = h$$

and the error is $e = A^{-1}h$. In principle, if we knew the errors in **b**, we could correct for the error in the solution. However, this is almost never the case, and we can only estimate an upper bound for the error propagated into the solution.

Norms

Measures of the magnitude of matrices and vectors are "norms" (written as $\|A\|$ and $\|b\|$, respectively). A familiar norm is the "Euclidean norm" of a vector, namely its length.

$$\|\mathbf{b}\| = \left[\sum_{i=1}^{n} v_i^2 \right]^{1/2}$$

This norm is also called the "L_2 norm," $\|b\|_2$, and the corresponding matrix norm is $\|A\|_2 = [\lambda_{max}(A^TA)]^{1/2}$, where λ_{max} is the maximum eigenvalue of the indicated matrix. This norm is frequently approximated by $\|(A)\|_{max}$, which is exactly true only if **A** is symmetric. Other matrix and vector norms are the "L_1 norm" and the "L_∞ norm," which are defined as

L_1 norm maximal column sum of absolute values (note that vectors have only one column)

$$\|\mathbf{A}\|_1 = \max_{j} \sum_{i=1}^{n} |a_{ij}|$$

L_∞ norm: maximal row sum of absolute values or maximal element magnitude for vectors

$$\|\mathbf{A}\|_\infty = \max_{i} \sum_{j=1}^{n} |a_{ij}|$$

Any of these norms can be used to estimate an upper bound for the error in the solution vector, provided that the same type of norm is used for the matrix and the vectors in the system of equations.

Condition Number

Replacing the arrays in the equation for the error by their norms gives

$$\|\mathbf{e}\| = \|\mathbf{A}^{-1}\mathbf{h}\| \leq \|\mathbf{A}^{-1}\| \cdot \|\mathbf{h}\|$$

Dividing by $\|\mathbf{x}\|$ to put this equation in terms of a relative error,

$$\frac{\|\mathbf{e}\|}{\|\mathbf{x}\|} \leq \frac{\|\mathbf{A}^{-1}\| \cdot \|\mathbf{h}\|}{\|\mathbf{x}\|} = \frac{\|\mathbf{A}^{-1}\| \cdot \|\mathbf{h}\|}{\|\mathbf{A}^{-1}\mathbf{b}\|}$$

As $\|\mathbf{b}\| \leq \|\mathbf{A}\| \cdot \|\mathbf{x}\|$, $\|\mathbf{x}\| \geq \|\mathbf{b}\| / \|\mathbf{A}\|$ and

$$\frac{\|\mathbf{h}\|}{\|\mathbf{b}\|} \cdot \frac{1}{\|\mathbf{A}^{-1}\| \cdot \|\mathbf{A}\|} \leq \frac{\|\mathbf{e}\|}{\|\mathbf{x}\|} \leq \|\mathbf{A}^{-1}\| \times \|\mathbf{A}\| \cdot \frac{\|\mathbf{h}\|}{\|\mathbf{b}\|}$$

The quantity $K = \|\mathbf{A}\| \cdot \|\mathbf{A}^{-1}\|$ is called the "amplification factor" because it tells how much the relative error in $\mathbf{b}$ is magnified in computing $\mathbf{x}$. In the case where the L_2 norm is used, $\|\mathbf{A}\|_2 = |\lambda(\mathbf{A})|_{max}$ and $\|\mathbf{A}^{-1}\|_2 = |\lambda(\mathbf{A}^{-1})|_{max} = 1/|\lambda(\mathbf{A})|_{min}$. The amplification factor is $|\lambda(\mathbf{A})|_{max}/|\lambda(\mathbf{A})|_{min}$; it is called the "condition number" of the matrix $\mathbf{A}$. The larger the condition number, the greater is the amplification of errors.

A matrix with a large value of K is said to be "ill conditioned," and considerable round-off error accumulates when solution of the corresponding simultaneous equations is attempted. For example, if $K = 100$,

$$\frac{\|\mathbf{h}\|}{\|\mathbf{b}\|} \cdot \frac{1}{100} \leq \frac{\|\mathbf{e}\|}{\|\mathbf{x}\|} \leq 100 \cdot \frac{\|\mathbf{h}\|}{\|\mathbf{b}\|}$$

The possible round-off error covers a range of four orders of magnitude. For a singular matrix $|\lambda|_{min} = 0$, yielding an infinite condition number.

Example 3.6:

In the case of the matrix that was inverted in the previous section,

$$\begin{matrix} \mathbf{A} \\ \begin{pmatrix} 2 & 3 & -1 \\ 4 & 4 & -3 \\ -2 & 3 & -1 \end{pmatrix} \end{matrix} \qquad \begin{matrix} \mathbf{A}^{-1} \\ \begin{pmatrix} 0.5 & -0.2 & 0.1 \\ 1.0 & -0.6 & -0.2 \\ 0.25 & 0 & 0.1 \end{pmatrix} \end{matrix}$$

$\|\mathbf{A}\|_\infty = 11$ and $\|\mathbf{A}^{-1}\|_\infty = 1.8$

$$\frac{\|\mathbf{h}\|}{\|\mathbf{b}\|} (11)(1.8) \geq \frac{\|\mathbf{e}\|}{\|\mathbf{x}\|} \geq \frac{1}{(11)(1.8)} \frac{\|\mathbf{h}\|}{\|\mathbf{b}\|}$$

The amplification factor is 19.8, giving a 400-fold range of possible error.

Errors in the Matrix Elements

If there are errors in the elements of the matrix $\mathbf{A}$, the matrix actually used in solving the problem is $\mathbf{A} + \mathbf{F}$ and solution vector is $\mathbf{x} + \mathbf{e}$. Subtracting the true problem from the one solve gives

$$(\mathbf{A} + \mathbf{F})(\mathbf{x} + \mathbf{e}) = \mathbf{b}$$
$$\underline{\mathbf{A}\,\mathbf{x} \qquad\qquad = \mathbf{b}}$$
$$\mathbf{Ae} + \mathbf{Fe} + \mathbf{Fx} = 0$$

which can be rewritten as

$$\mathbf{A}(\mathbf{I} + \mathbf{A}^{-1}\mathbf{F})^{-1}\mathbf{e} = -\mathbf{Fx}$$

Solving for the error gives

$$\mathbf{e} = -(\mathbf{I} + \mathbf{A}^{-1}\mathbf{F})^{-1}\mathbf{A}^{-1}\mathbf{Fx}$$

If the errors $\mathbf{F}$ in $\mathbf{A}$ are sufficiently small, the matrix in parentheses can be approximated by the series

$$(\mathbf{I} + \mathbf{A}^{-1}\mathbf{F}) = \mathbf{I} - \mathbf{A}^{-1}\mathbf{F} + (\mathbf{A}^{-1}\mathbf{F})^2 - (\mathbf{A}^{-1}\mathbf{F})^3 + (\mathbf{A}^{-1}\mathbf{F})^4 - \cdots$$

As $\|\mathbf{A}^{-1}\mathbf{F}\| < 1$, the expansion for the norm of the above matrix may be truncated after the linear term. The norm of the error is then given by

$$\|\mathbf{e}\| \le \|(\mathbf{I} + \mathbf{A}^{-1}\mathbf{F})^{-1}\| \cdot \|\mathbf{A}^{-1}\| \cdot \|\mathbf{F}\| \cdot \|\mathbf{x}\| \le \|\mathbf{A}^{-1}\| \cdot \|\mathbf{F}\| \cdot \|\mathbf{x}\|/(1 - \|\mathbf{A}^{-1}\mathbf{F}\|)$$

So the fractional error in the solution is bounded by

$$\frac{\|\mathbf{e}\|}{\|\mathbf{x}\|} \le \frac{\|\mathbf{F}\|}{\|\mathbf{A}\|} \cdot \underbrace{\frac{\|\mathbf{A}\| \cdot \|\mathbf{A}^{-1}\|}{1 - \|\mathbf{A}^{-1}\mathbf{F}\|}}_{\substack{\text{amplification} \\ \text{factor}}}$$

Because $\|\mathbf{A}^{-1}\mathbf{F}\|$ is small, the amplification factor is not much different from the condition number of $\mathbf{A}$.

Errors in the Matrix and the Constant Vector

Subtracting the equation for the true problem from the problem actually solved in this case gives

$$(\mathbf{A} + \mathbf{F})(\mathbf{x} + \mathbf{e}) = \mathbf{b} + \mathbf{h}$$
$$\mathbf{A}\,\mathbf{x} \qquad\qquad = \mathbf{b}$$
$$\mathbf{Ae} + \mathbf{Fe} + \mathbf{Fx} = \mathbf{h}$$

Solving for the error and taking the norm yields

$$\|\mathbf{e}\| \le \|(\mathbf{I} + \mathbf{A}^{-1}\mathbf{F})^{-1}\| \cdot \|\mathbf{A}^{-1}\| \cdot \|\mathbf{h} - \mathbf{Fx}\|$$
$$\le (\|\mathbf{A}^{-1}\| \cdot \|\mathbf{F}\| \cdot \|\mathbf{x}\| + \|\mathbf{h}\|)/(1 - \|\mathbf{A}^{-1}\mathbf{F}\|)$$

Dividing by $\|\mathbf{x}\|$ to obtain the relative error and using $\|\mathbf{x}\| \le \|\mathbf{A}^{-1}\| \cdot \|\mathbf{b}\|$,

$$\frac{\|\mathbf{e}\|}{\|\mathbf{x}\|} \le \left(\frac{\|\mathbf{F}\|}{\|\mathbf{A}\|} + \frac{\|\mathbf{h}\|}{\|\mathbf{b}\|}\right) \cdot \frac{\|\mathbf{A}\| \cdot \|\mathbf{A}^{-1}\|}{1 - \|\mathbf{A}^{-1}\mathbf{F}\|}$$

The relative error in the case of errors in both **A** and **b** is approximately the sum of the relative errors expected for errors in **A** and **b** individually.

3.5 GAUSS-SEIDEL METHOD

Iterative Refinement

Suppose we have calculated x_1, an approximate solution to $Ax = b$. If we calculate the error **e** from $Ae = h$, we can obtain an improved estimate of the solution $x_2 = x_1 + e$, recompute the error, and reiterate until the difference between two successive estimates of **x** is within a preset tolerance. This is very time-consuming because each solution of the set of linear equations requires $O(n^3)$ arithmetic operations, where n is the number of rows of the matrix **A**. A more efficient method is necessary in order to solve very large matrix equations.

In the previous chapter's discussion of solution of a nonlinear equation by iteration to a fixed point introduced the concept of an iteration function $g(x^{(k)}) = x^{(k+1)}$. The series of x values so defined was said to converge to the root $x = r$ if

$$|g(x^{(k+1)}) - g(r)| \leq K|x^{(k)} - r|$$

Such behavior occurs when

$$0 < K = |g'(x^{(k)})| < 1$$

over the entire interval spanned by the x values. A similar approach may be used to solve systems of simultaneous linear equations, that is, a matrix function of a vector variable.

$$x^{(k+1)} = G(x^{(k)}) = Cx^{(k)} + d$$

The solution vector is obtained by computing successive approximations to **x**, provided that

$$|G(x^{(k)}) - G(x)| \leq K|x^{(k)} - x|$$

and $0 < K < 1$ at each iteration.

The rule for matrix multiplication is

$$\sum_{j=1}^{n} a_{ij} x_j = b_i.$$

If the term containing the element a_{ii} is separated from the summation and the equation solved for x_i, we obtain the back substitution algorithm

$$x_i = \left(b_i - \sum_{j \neq i} a_{ij} x_j \right) \Big/ a_{ii}.$$

If the x_j values used in this computation are those from the previous iterate's estimate $\mathbf{x}^{(k)}$, the above function may be a good iteration function **G**. Then the arrays **C** and **d** are given by

$$c_{ij} = \begin{cases} -\dfrac{a_{ij}}{a_{ii}}, i \neq j & \quad 0, i = j \end{cases}$$

$$d_i = b_i/a_{ii}$$

Algorithm

Given the coefficients for the n simultaneous equations and a convergence tolerance ε:

compute the arrays **C** and **d**

select a starting estimate $\mathbf{x}^{(0)}$

for $m = 1,...$ until converges do

$$x_i^{(m)} = \sum_{j \neq i} c_{ij}\, x_j^{(m-1)} + d_i, \; i = 1,..., n$$

If $\max_i \left| \dfrac{x_i^{(m)} - x_i^{(m-1)}}{x_i^{(m-1)}} \right| \leq \varepsilon$ then stop

This technique is called the "Jacobi method." It can be shown that if the largest elements of the matrix **A** are on the diagonal (that is, **A** is "diagonally dominant"), the iterated estimates $\mathbf{x}^{(m)}$ will converge to the solution **x**.

Gauss-Seidel Method

A naive programmer attempting to implement the Jacobi iterative method in FORTRAN might write:

```
      DO 10 I = 1, N
        SUM = 0.0
        DO 11 J = 1, N
          SUM = SUM + C(I,J) * X(J)
11      CONTINUE
10    CONTINUE
```

However, in this program, once $X(I)$ has been updated it is used as $X(J)$ in computing the next value of SUM. This modified technique is called the "Gauss-Seidel" method and has a "continuous replacement" algorithm, as opposed to a "block replacement" algorithm for the Jacobi method.

Algorithm

for $m = 1,...,$ until converges do

$$x_i^{(m)} = \sum_{j=1}^{i-1} c_{ij} x_j^{(m)} + \sum_{j=i+1}^{n} c_{ij} x_j^{(m-1)} + d_i, \quad i = 1,...,n$$

where the first summation is over the subdiagonal elements of the C matrix and the second summation is over the superdiagonal elements.

Convergence is considerably faster with the Gauss-Seidel method than with the Jacobi method.

Example 3.7:

The matrix equation

$$\begin{pmatrix} 10 & 1 & 1 \\ 1 & 10 & 1 \\ 1 & 1 & 10 \end{pmatrix} x = \begin{pmatrix} 12 \\ 12 \\ 12 \end{pmatrix}$$

has a solution at $x = (1, 1, 1)$. Using the starting estimate $(0, 0, 0)$, the two methods give the following results.

Iteration number	Jacobi			Gauss-Seidel		
	x_1	x_2	x_3	x_1	x_2	x_3
0	0.0	0.0	0.0	0.0	0.0	0.0
1	1.2	1.2	1.2	1.2	1.08	0.972
2	0.96	0.96	0.96	0.9948	1.0033	1.00019
3	1.008	1.008	1.008	0.99965	1.000016	1.000033
4	0.9984	0.9984	0.9984			
5	1.0032	1.0032	1.0032			
6	0.999936	0.999936	0.999936			

The Gauss-Seidel method converges about twice as fast as the Jacobi method, and is therefore preferred.

It can be shown that the Gauss-Seidel method converges when the matrix A is "positive definite," a somewhat less restrictive requirement than diagonal dominance. For example, the equation

$$\begin{pmatrix} 2 & 5 & 5 \\ 5 & 2 & 5 \\ 5 & 5 & 2 \end{pmatrix} x = \begin{pmatrix} 12 \\ 12 \\ 12 \end{pmatrix}$$

also has a solution at $x = (1, 1, 1)$, but the Jacobi method will not converge for an arbitrary starting guess for x whereas the Gauss-Seidel method will converge. The matrix, being symmetric, is positive definite although it is not diagonally dominant. This is another reason for preferring the Gauss-Seidel method.

Gaussian elimination followed by back substitution for a system of three equations, as in the above example, requires operating on 14 array elements. The Gauss-Seidel algorithm required operating on 18 array elements (two for each x_i value, the subdiagonal and superdiagonal elements). In fact, Gauss-Seidel can never perform fewer operations than Gaussian elimination in the general case. However, if the coefficient matrix A is sparse, that is, many of its elements are zero, the corresponding terms $c_{ij} x_j^{(m)}$ in the expansion for x_i, $i \neq j$ will equal zero and need not be evaluated. For a sufficiently sparse matrix the Gauss-Seidel method may require fewer arithmetic operations than Gaussian elimination and would be the preferred method of solution. This is especially true for very large sparse matrices.

3.6 SUCCESSIVE OVERRELAXATION METHOD

The algorithm for the Gauss-Seidel method for solution of simultaneous linear equations $Ax = b$ may be written as

$$x_i^{(m+1)} = x_i^{(m)} + \omega \left[\left(b_i + \sum_{j<i} a_{ij} x_j^{(m+1)} - \sum_{j>i} a_{ij} x_j^{(m)} \right) \Big/ a_{ii} - x_i^{(m)} \right]$$

for the mth iteration. The constant ω tells how much of the increment in $x_i^{(m)}$ that is computed by the algorithm should be added to $x_i^{(m)}$ to yield the next iterate of that element of the solution vector. For Gauss-Seidel, $\omega = 1$. Experience has shown that it is generally better to overestimate the correction to the solution, and ω typically has values in the range 1.2 to 1.6. This is the method of "successive overrelaxation." Depending on the application, the overrelaxation parameter ω may be fixed or may vary from iteration to iteration.

Convergence Properties of Iterative Methods

The Jacobi, Gauss-Seidel, and successive overrelaxation methods form a family in which the matrix iteration function G is a different partitioning of the elements of the matrix A for each method. The coefficient matrix A may be written as the sum of subdiagonal, diagonal, and superdiagonal elements.

$A = L + D + U$

The Jacobi iteration may be written in matrix form as

$$\mathbf{x}^{(m+1)} = \mathbf{G}(\mathbf{x}^{(m)}) := \mathbf{D}^{-1}\mathbf{b} - \mathbf{D}^{-1}(\mathbf{L} + \mathbf{U})\mathbf{x}^{(m)}$$

Ignoring the constant term in this equation, the Jacobi method involves repeatedly applying the iteration matrix $\mathbf{D}^{-1}(\mathbf{L} + \mathbf{U})$ to the most recent estimate of $\mathbf{x}$. After $\mathbf{n}$ iterations the cumulative iteration matrix becomes $[\mathbf{D}^{-1}(\mathbf{L} + \mathbf{U})]^n$. The method converges only if the calculated increment to $\mathbf{x}$ approaches zero as n approaches infinity. This will occur if $\|\mathbf{D}^{-1}(\mathbf{L} + \mathbf{U})\| < 1$, which is the case when the diagonal elements $\mathbf{D}$ are the largest elements in $\mathbf{A}$. Hence the requirement for diagonal dominance for convergence of the Jacobi method.

The Gauss-Seidel method is

$$\mathbf{x}^{(m+1)} = \mathbf{D}^{-1}(\mathbf{b} - \mathbf{L}\mathbf{x}^{(m+1)} - \mathbf{U}\mathbf{x}^{(m)}) = (\mathbf{D} + \mathbf{L})^{-1}[\mathbf{b} - \mathbf{U}\mathbf{x}^{(m)}]$$

and the iteration matrix is $(\mathbf{D} + \mathbf{L})^{-1}\mathbf{U}$. This method converges when the norm $\|(\mathbf{D} + \mathbf{L})^{-1}\mathbf{U}\| < 1$, which can be shown to be the case when the matrix $\mathbf{A}$ is positive definite (all eigenvalues > 0).

The successive overrelaxation method is

$$\mathbf{x}^{(m+1)} = \mathbf{x}^{(m)} + \omega\mathbf{D}^{-1}(\mathbf{b} - (\mathbf{D} + \mathbf{U})\mathbf{x}^{(m)} - \mathbf{L}\mathbf{x}^{(m+1)})$$

which has an iteration matrix $(\mathbf{I} + \omega\mathbf{L})^{-1}[(1 - \omega)\mathbf{I} - \omega\mathbf{U}]$. It can be shown that the L_2 norm of this matrix (let's call it $\mathbf{G}$) is $|1 - \omega|$. The method converges when ω lies between zero and two, that is, when $\|\mathbf{G}\| < 1$. This occurs when the matrix $\mathbf{A}$ is positive semidefinite (all eigenvalues ≥ 0). Convergence is much faster than for Gauss-Seidel if ω has its optimal value.

Optimization of the Overrelaxation Parameter

Because $\|\mathbf{G}\| < 1$, the error in the approximation to the solution

$$\|\mathbf{e}^{(m+1)}\| \leq \|\mathbf{G}\| \cdot \|\mathbf{e}^{(m)}\| = \|\mathbf{G}^{m+1}\| \cdot \|\mathbf{e}^{(0)}\|$$

approaches zero with increasing m. The rate of convergence can be shown to be

$$R^{(m)} = -(1/m) \log\|\mathbf{G}^m\| \approx -\log\|\mathbf{G}\|$$

if ω is constant. Finding a value for ω that will maximize the rate of convergence is a very difficult problem, but a reasonably simple way to approximate it is available. Define the increment to the solution vector that is computed on the mth iteration as

$$\mathbf{\Delta}^{(m)} = |\mathbf{x}^{(m)} - \mathbf{x}^{(m-1)}| = (\mathbf{x}^{(m)} - \mathbf{x}^*) - (\mathbf{x}^{(m-1)} - \mathbf{x}^*)| = |\mathbf{e}^{(m)} - \mathbf{e}^{(m-1)}|$$

where $\mathbf{x}^*$ is the true solution. The local relative convergence rate is given by

$$R^{(m)} = \frac{\|\Delta^{(m)}\|}{\|\Delta^{(m-1)}\|}$$

Suppose the current value of ω is $\omega^{(m)}$. If there exists a positive number f less than one such that

$$(\omega^{(m)} - 1)^f \geq \|G(\omega^{(m)})\|_2 \geq R^{(m)}$$

then the current value of ω gives an acceptable convergence rate. The quantity f typically lies between 0.65 and 0.8. If the local convergence rate is too small for f to fall in this range, the new value of ω must be evaluated from

$$(\omega^{(m+1)} - 1)^f \geq \|G(\omega^{(m)})\|_2$$

(A simple algorithm for evaluating the required norm will be given in Section 3.8.) If $R^{(m)}$ exceeds one, the local convergence rate is so fast that no test need be made on the value of ω.

Testing for Convergence

It is conceivable that two successive iterates of $x^{(m)}$ may be within some preset tolerance ε simply because of slow convergence of the selected algorithm. The above discussion suggests another way of terminating the algorithm for any one of the three iterative methods for solution of simultaneous linear equations. It can be shown that the relative error at the mth iteration is given by

$$\frac{\|e^{(m)}\|}{\|x^*\|} = \frac{1}{1 - R^{(m)}} \times \frac{\|\Delta^{(m)}\|}{\|x^{(m)}\|}$$

Instead of testing if the maximal difference $\|\Delta^{(m)}\|$ between two successive iterates for the solution vector is within some preset tolerance, it is better to test if the relative error computed from the above equation is within a preset tolerance. This approach ensures that the algorithm does not terminate until the correct solution has been reached. If ω is dynamically optimized, the iterations will converge at the maximal rate possible.

3.7 TRIDIAGONAL MATRICES

There are many examples in science and engineering of systems of linear equations in which the ith equation depends only on the variables x_{i-1}, x_i, and x_{i+1}. Such a system has the form

$$b_1x_1 + c_1x_2 = d_1$$
$$a_2x_1 + b_2x_2\, c_2x_3 = d_2$$
$$\vdots$$

$$a_{n-1}x_{n-2} + b_{n-2}x_{n-1} + c_{n-1}x_n = d_{n-1}$$

$$a_n x_{n-1} + b_n x_n = d_n$$

The coefficients in these equations may be represented by a matrix with the a_i's on the first subdiagonal, the b_i's on the main diagonal, and the c_i's on the first superdiagonal.

$$\begin{pmatrix} b_1 & c_1 & & & & \\ a_2 & b_2 & c_2 & & \mathbf{0} & \\ & & & & & \\ & \mathbf{0} & & a_{n-1} & b_{n-1} & c_{n-1} \\ & & & & a_n & b_n \end{pmatrix} \times \begin{pmatrix} x_1 \\ \cdot \\ \cdot \\ \cdot \\ x_n \end{pmatrix} = \begin{pmatrix} d_1 \\ \cdot \\ \cdot \\ \cdot \\ d_n \end{pmatrix}$$

The simultaneous equations can be solved by Gaussian elimination and back substitution, but because of the special structure of the matrix a more efficient method is possible.

Recursive Algorithm

Any nonsingular matrix can be represented as a product of a lower triangular matrix **L** (one whose superdiagonal elements are all zero and whose diagonal elements are all unity) and an upper triangular matrix **U** (one whose subdiagonal elements are all zero). The system of simultaneous equations may be written as

$$\mathbf{Ax} = \mathbf{LUx} = \mathbf{d}$$

Solving the system of equations

$$\mathbf{L\delta} = \mathbf{d}$$

for the vector $\mathbf{\delta} = \mathbf{Ux}$ (the procedure is called "forward substitution") permits us to solve for **x** by back substitution. When this is done for a tridiagonal matrix, the superdiagonal of **U** is found to be the array **c**, the superdiagonal elements of **A**. However, we need to calculate the subdiagonal $\mathbf{\alpha}$ of **L** and the diagonal $\mathbf{\beta}$ of **U**.

The first equation (no a_1 term) gives

$$x_1 = d_1/b_1 - x_2 c_1/b_1$$

Comparison of this result with the algebraic form resulting from solution of the above matrix equations indicates that $\beta_1 = b_1$ and $\delta_1 = d_1$. Similarly, the last equation (no c_n term) gives

$$x_n = (d_n - a_n x_{n-1})/b_n = \delta_n/b_n$$

and

$$x_{n-1} = d_{n-1} - x_n c_{n-1}/b_{n-1}$$

implying that $\alpha_n = a_n/\beta_{n-1}$ and $\beta_n = b_n - c_{n-1}\alpha_n$. This can be generalized as the recursive relations

$$\alpha_k = a_k/\beta_{k-1}$$
$$\beta_k = b_k - \alpha_k c_{k-1}$$
$$\delta_k = d_k - \alpha_k d_{k-1}, \quad k = 2, 3,..., n$$

Starting from $\beta_1 = b_1$ and $\delta_1 = d_1$, all the coefficients α, β, and δ can be computed. The value of β_k must be checked at each iteration to be sure that it is nonzero, that is, that the matrix is nonsingular. Then the solution can be computed by back substitution.

$$x_n = \delta_n/b_n$$
$$x_k = (\delta_k - c_k x_{k+1})/\beta_k, \quad k = n - 1, n - 2,..., 1$$

Notice that once d_k is used to compute δ_k it is no longer needed, so δ can overwrite $\mathbf{d}$ to conserve computer memory. Similarly, α can overwrite $\mathbf{a}$ and β can overwrite $\mathbf{b}$. The solution vector $\mathbf{x}$ can be placed in any of these arrays, but if it is desirable to save the **LU** factorization of the tridiagonal matrix it is best to store $\mathbf{x}$ in $\mathbf{d}$.

Example 3.8.

Solve the tridiagonal system.

$$\begin{pmatrix} 2 & -1 & 0 \\ -1 & 1 & 2 \\ 0 & 2 & 1 \end{pmatrix} \mathbf{x} = \begin{pmatrix} 1 \\ 2 \\ 3 \end{pmatrix}$$

Initialize:

$$\beta_1 = 2 \qquad \delta_1 = 1$$

Operate on row 2:

$$\alpha_2 = -1/2$$
$$\beta_2 = 1 - (-0.5)(-1) = 0.5$$
$$\delta_2 = 2 - (-0.5)(-1) = 0.5$$

Operate on row 3:

$$\alpha_3 = 2/0.5 = 4$$
$$\beta_3 = 1 - 4(2) = -7$$
$$\delta_3 = 3 - 4(2.5) = -7$$

Back-substitute:

$$x_3 = (-7)/(-7) = 1$$

$$x_2 = (2.5 - 2(1))/0.5 = 1$$
$$x_1 = (1 - (1)(1))/2 = 1$$

3.8 Eigenvalues and Eigenvectors by the Power Method

Eigenvalue problems are ubiquitous in science and engineering. Frequently, the state of a physical system will be described by one of the eigenvectors of the matrix representing the linear equations of the system, and measurable quantities will correspond to its associated eigenvalue. If a unit vector $\mathbf{w}$ ($\|\mathbf{w}\| = 1$) satisfies the condition

$$\mathbf{Aw} = \lambda\mathbf{w}$$

for some matrix $\mathbf{A}$, $\mathbf{w}$ is called an "eigenvector" of the matrix and the scalar λ is its associated "eigenvalue." An $n \times n$ matrix has n distinct eigenvectors, which may or may not have distinct eigenvalues. It is possible to find the eigenvalues by solving the characteristic equation

$$\det(\mathbf{A} - \lambda\mathbf{I}) = 0$$

for all the roots I and substitute each value into the set of equations

$$(\mathbf{A} - \lambda\,\mathbf{I})\mathbf{w} = 0$$

to find the eigenvectors. This is often very time-consuming, especially for large matrices. Furthermore, only the eigenvalue with the largest magnitude is often needed, as when finding the spectral (L_2) norm of a matrix for the purpose of error analysis.

Iterative Estimation of Eigenvalues

Earlier we introduced the notion that the columns (or rows) of a nonsingular matrix define a set of linearly independent vectors. Similarly, the eigenvectors of the matrix form such a set if their eigenvalues are distinct, and any n-dimensional vector may be written as a linear combination of these eigenvectors.

$$\mathbf{v} = c_1\mathbf{w}_1 + c_2\mathbf{w}_2 + \cdots + c_n\mathbf{w}_n$$

Premultiplying each side of the above equation $\mathbf{A}$ and dividing by the normalization constant λ_1 gives

$$\mathbf{Av}/\lambda_1 = (\lambda_1 c_1\mathbf{w}_1 + \lambda_2 c_2\mathbf{w}_2 + \cdots + \lambda_n c_n\mathbf{w}_n)/\lambda_1$$

If v were an eigenvector of $\mathbf{A}$, say $\mathbf{w}_1$, then

$$\mathbf{Av} = \lambda_1 c_1\mathbf{w}_1$$

and the constant c_1 is unity. If, however, $\mathbf{v}$ is not an eigenvector, the other

c_i's are nonzero, causing $\mathbf{A}\mathbf{v}/\lambda_1$ to be different from the original $\mathbf{v}$ (call it $\mathbf{v}^{(0)}$). If $\mathbf{A}$ is symmetric we can repeat the process m times, yielding

$$\mathbf{A}\mathbf{v}^{(m)}/\lambda_1 = c_1\mathbf{w}_1 + (\lambda_2/\lambda_1)^m c_2\mathbf{w}_2 + \cdots + (\lambda_n/\lambda_1)^m c_n\mathbf{w}_n.$$

The mth iterate for $\mathbf{v}$ will approach $\mathbf{w}_1$ if λ_1 is the largest (in absolute value) eigenvalue. This procedure is called the "power method."

Algorithm

If $\mathbf{v}^{(0)}$ is normalized

$$\mathbf{A}\mathbf{v}^{(m)}/\|\mathbf{A}\mathbf{v}^{(m)}\| = \mathbf{v}^{(m+1)}$$

defines an iteration function for the eigenvector $\mathbf{w}_1$ corresponding to λ_1. That is, $\mathbf{v}^{(m)}$ approaches $\mathbf{w}_1$ and $\|\mathbf{A}\mathbf{v}^{(m)}\|$ approaches $|\lambda_1|$ as m approaches infinity. If the signs of the elements of $\mathbf{v}$ alternate on successive iterations, the eigenvalue λ is actually $-\|\mathbf{A}\mathbf{v}^{(m)}\|$. Any norm may be used; the algorithm will converge to the same eigenvalue, but the elements of the eigenvectors will be different in magnitude for different normalizations.

Example 3.9:

Find the eigenvalue largest in absolute value and its corresponding eigenvector for the matrix $\mathbf{A}$.

$$\begin{pmatrix} 1 & 2 & 0 \\ 2 & 1 & 0 \\ 0 & 0 & -1 \end{pmatrix}$$

First solve the characteristic equation $\det(\mathbf{B} - \lambda\mathbf{I}) = 0$.

$$\det\begin{pmatrix} 1-\lambda & 2 & 0 \\ 2 & 1-\lambda & 0 \\ 0 & 0 & -1-\lambda \end{pmatrix} = 0 = -(1 + \lambda)[(1 - \lambda)^2 - 4]$$

which factors into $-(1 + \lambda)(1 + \lambda)(-3 + \lambda) = 0$. The solutions for the eigenvalues are $\lambda = -1, -1$, and 3. Substituting $\lambda = 3$ into $(\mathbf{A} - \lambda\mathbf{I})\mathbf{x} = 0$ gives

$$-2x_1 + 2x_2 + 0 = 0$$
$$2x_1 - 2x_2 + 0 = 0$$
$$0 + 0 - 4x_3 = 0$$

which is satisfied by $\mathbf{x} = (1, 1, 0)$. This is the eigenvector corresponding to $\lambda = 3$.

Next, solve the problem, using the power method. Start with an initial guess of $\mathbf{v}^{(0)} = (1, 2, 3)$ for the eigenvector, and use the L_∞ norm

(element with maximal magnitude) for normalizing the eigenvector.
Iteration 1:

$$
\overset{\mathbf{A}}{\begin{pmatrix} 1 & 2 & 0 \\ 2 & 1 & 0 \\ 0 & 0 & -1 \end{pmatrix}} \times \overset{\mathbf{v}^{(0)}}{\begin{pmatrix} 1 \\ 2 \\ 3 \end{pmatrix}} = \begin{pmatrix} 5 \\ 4 \\ -3 \end{pmatrix} \xrightarrow[\div 5 = \|\mathbf{v}\|]{\text{normalize}} \overset{\mathbf{v}^{(1)}}{\begin{pmatrix} 1.0 \\ 0.8 \\ -0.6 \end{pmatrix}}
$$

Iteration 2:

$$
\mathbf{A} \begin{pmatrix} 1.0 \\ 0.8 \\ -0.6 \end{pmatrix} = \begin{pmatrix} 2.6 \\ 2.8 \\ 0.6 \end{pmatrix} \xrightarrow[\div 2.8]{} \begin{pmatrix} 0.093 \\ 1.0 \\ 0.21 \end{pmatrix}
$$

Iteration 3:

$$
\mathbf{A} \begin{pmatrix} 0.093 \\ 1.0 \\ 0.21 \end{pmatrix} = \begin{pmatrix} 2.93 \\ 2.86 \\ -0.21 \end{pmatrix} \xrightarrow[\div 2.93]{} \begin{pmatrix} 1.0 \\ 0.98 \\ -0.07 \end{pmatrix}
$$

Iteration 4:

$$
\mathbf{A} \begin{pmatrix} 1.0 \\ 0.98 \\ -0.07 \end{pmatrix} = \begin{pmatrix} 2.96 \\ 2.98 \\ 0.07 \end{pmatrix} \xrightarrow[\div 2.98]{} \begin{pmatrix} 0.99 \\ 1.0 \\ 0.02 \end{pmatrix}
$$

Iteration 5:

$$
\mathbf{A} \begin{pmatrix} 0.99 \\ 1.0 \\ 0.02 \end{pmatrix} = \begin{pmatrix} 2.99 \\ 2.98 \\ -0.02 \end{pmatrix} \xrightarrow[\div 2.99]{} \begin{pmatrix} 1.00 \\ 1.00 \\ -0.01 \end{pmatrix}
$$

We see that $\lambda = \|\mathbf{v}^{(m)}\|$ approaches 3 and $\mathbf{v}^{(m)}/\lambda$ approaches $(1, 1, 0)$ rapidly.

Errors in Eigenvalues

Representation error produces uncertainties $\delta\mathbf{A}$ in the values for the elements of the $n \times n$ matrix $\mathbf{A}$. If the computer used for the calculations has d binary digits of precision, the uncertainties are given approximately by

$$\|\delta\mathbf{A}\| \leqslant n^2 2^{-d}\|\mathbf{A}\|$$

What errors in the eigenvalues and eigenvectors result? Let the kth (normalized) eigenvector of $\mathbf{A}$ be $\mathbf{v}_k$ and the kth eigenvector of $\mathbf{A}^T$ be $\mathbf{u}_k$. The error in the eigenvalue λ_k is given by

$$|e(\lambda_k)| \leqslant \|\delta\mathbf{A}\|_2/|\mathbf{u}_k{}^T\mathbf{v}_k| = \|\delta\mathbf{A}\|_2/\cos \theta_k.$$

where θ_k is the angle between the two eigenvectors. In the case of a symmetric matrix, $\mathbf{u}_k = \mathbf{v}_k$ and the denominator is 1. In the nonsymmetric

case the denominator is not 1 and some eigenvalues may be more sensitive to representation error than are others.

The error in the eigenvector $\mathbf{v}_k$ is given by

$$\|\mathbf{e}_k\| \leqslant \sum_{i \neq k} \frac{(\mathbf{u}_i^T \delta \mathbf{A} \mathbf{v}_k) \mathbf{v}}{(\lambda_k - \lambda_i) \cos \theta_i}.$$

In the symmetric case $\cos \theta_i$ is 1, and the sensitivities of the eigenvectors
depend only on the closeness of the eigenvalues.

3.9   METHOD OF JACOBI ROTATIONS

It is often necessary to find all the eigenvalues and eigenvectors of a matrix, but the power method only gives the eigenvalue which is largest in
absolute value and its associated eigenvector. A general solution to the
eigenvalue problem is an undertaking of considerable proportions; it is
beyond the scope of this book. However, for the case of symmetric matrices there is a conceptually simple method. Consider the $n \times n$ matrix
U whose columns $\mathbf{v}_i$ are the eigenvectors of a symmetric $n \times n$ matrix **A**.

$$\mathbf{U} = \begin{pmatrix} \mathbf{v}_1 & \mathbf{v}_2 & \cdots & \mathbf{v}_n \\ \downarrow & \downarrow & & \downarrow \end{pmatrix}$$

Premultiplying both sides of the above equation by **A** gives

$$\mathbf{AU} = \begin{pmatrix} \mathbf{Av}_1 & \mathbf{Av}_2 & \cdots & \mathbf{Av}_n \\ \downarrow & \downarrow & & \downarrow \end{pmatrix} = \begin{pmatrix} \lambda_1\mathbf{v}_1 & \lambda_2\mathbf{v}_2 & \cdots & \lambda_n\mathbf{v}_n \\ \downarrow & \downarrow & & \downarrow \end{pmatrix}$$

$$= \begin{pmatrix} \mathbf{v}_1 & \mathbf{v}_2 & \cdots & \mathbf{v}_n \\ \downarrow & \downarrow & & \downarrow \end{pmatrix} \cdot \begin{pmatrix} \lambda_1 & & 0 \\ & \lambda_2 & \\ 0 & & \cdots & \lambda_n \end{pmatrix} = \mathbf{U}\Lambda$$

where Λ is a diagonal matrix whose nonzero elements are the eigenvalues
of **A**. Premultiplying both sides of the equation by $\mathbf{U}^{-1}$ yields

$$\mathbf{U}^{-1}\mathbf{AU} = \mathbf{U}^{-1}\mathbf{U}\Lambda = \Lambda$$

The matrix **U** is an orthogonal matrix. It has the property that $\mathbf{U}^{-1} = \mathbf{U}^T$,
and it represents an orthogonal transformation (that is, rigid motion) in
the space defined by the eigenvectors.

Method of Jacobi Rotations

As rigid motion preserves both length and angles, the matrix **U** can be
viewed as describing a rotation of some arbitrary vector in the n-dimen-

sional space. The Jacobi strategy is to find a sequence of plane rotations, represented by matrices $\mathbf{Q}_k$, such that

$$\lim_{k \to \infty} \mathbf{Q}_1 \mathbf{Q}_2 \cdots \mathbf{Q}_k = \lim_{k \to \infty} \mathbf{T}_k = \mathbf{U}$$

The matrix $\mathbf{Q}_k$ has ones on the diagonal and zeroes everywhere else except for the pth and qth diagonal elements and the off-diagonal elements a_{pq} and a_{qp}.

$$\begin{pmatrix} 1 & \cdots & & & 0 \\ & \cos \theta & & \sin \theta & \\ & -\sin \theta & & \cos \theta & \\ 0 & & & & 1 \end{pmatrix} \begin{matrix} \\ \leftarrow p^{\text{th}} \text{ row} \\ \leftarrow q^{\text{th}} \text{ row} \\ \\ \end{matrix}$$

$$\begin{matrix} \uparrow & \uparrow \\ p^{\text{th}} & q^{\text{th}} \\ \text{column} & \text{column} \end{matrix}$$

The subscripts p and q denote the element of the matrix

$$\mathbf{B}_{k-1} = \mathbf{T}_{k-1}{}^T \mathbf{A} \mathbf{T}_{k-1}$$

with the largest absolute value. In other words, the strategy is to find a rotation in the plane defined by the pth and qth directions in the n-dimensional space such that the largest off-diagonal element b_{pq} is annihilated. The matrix $\mathbf{T}_k$ is built up by successive premultiplications by $\mathbf{Q}_k$, starting with the identity matrix. When the largest remaining off-diagonal element is within some tolerance ε_1, $\mathbf{T}_k$ is sufficiently close to $\mathbf{U}$ to consider the matrix $\mathbf{B}_k$ to be a good approximation to $\mathbf{L}$.

Finding the Rotation Angle

It can be shown by matrix multiplication that, after one rotation,

$$b_{pq} = [(a_{pp} - a_{qq})/2] \sin 2j + a_{pq}\cos 2j = 0$$

and

$$\tan 2\theta = 2a_{pq}/(a_{qq} - a_{pp})$$

where $-\pi/4 < \theta < \pi/4$. The rotation angle can be found by using this formula. If $b_{pp} = b_{qq}$ at any iteration, $\theta = \pi/4$, so it is important to guard against round-off error by checking if $b_{pp} - b_{qq} \le \varepsilon_2$. If the difference is less than this tolerance and $\tan 2\theta < 0$, $\theta = -\pi/4$; if the difference is less than this tolerance and $\tan 2\theta \ge 0$, $\theta = \pi/4$.

In practice, θ itself is not calculated but $\cos \theta$ and $\sin \theta$ are computed by

$$c = \cot 2\theta = (a_{qq} - a_{pp})/2a_{pq}$$
$$d = \text{sign}(c) \, [|c| + \sqrt{1 + c^2}]^{-1}$$
$$\cos \theta = [\sqrt{1 + d^2}]^{-1}; \quad \sin \theta = d \cos \theta$$

If $|a_{qq} - a_{pp}| \leq \varepsilon_2$, $\sin \theta = d \cos \theta = 1/\sqrt{2}$.

Once $\sin \theta$ and $\cos \theta$ have been calculated, the matrices $\mathbf{Q}_k$, $\mathbf{T}_k = \mathbf{T}_{k-1}\mathbf{Q}_k$, and $\mathbf{B}_k = \mathbf{Q}_k^T\mathbf{B}_{k-1}\mathbf{Q}_k$ can be computed. Note that only the pth and qth row and column of each matrix need to be recomputed, so a full matrix multiplication is not necessary. Furthermore, because the matrix $\mathbf{A}$ is symmetric, all iterates of $\mathbf{B}_k$ are symmetric and some more computation can be avoided by operating on only one triangle of the matrix. It is possible that an element b_{pq} set to zero in one iteration may become nonzero on a subsequent iteration, but by annihilating the largest off-diagonal element at each iteration, convergence is guaranteed.

Another method of checking for convergence is to compute the sum of the squares of the diagonal elements of $\mathbf{B}$ at each iteration.

$$S_k = \sum_{i=1}^{n} b_{ii}^2$$

This sum increases as the off-diagonal elements are annihilated, and when they become sufficiently small S_k is not significantly different from S_{k-1}. If ε_3 is the maximum tolerable relative error, the procedure may be stopped when

$$1 - S_{k-1}/S_k \leq \varepsilon_3$$

Convergence of the Jacobi rotations method can be shown by the following argument. Let τ be the sum of the squares of all the off-diagonal elements.

$$\tau = \sum_{\substack{i=1 \\ i \neq j}}^{n} b_{ij}^2$$

After k iterations,

$$\tau_k = \tau_{k-1} - 2b_{pq}^2$$

where b_{pq} is the element annihilated on the kth iteration. Because

$$\tau_k = \sum_{p \neq q} b_{pq}^2 \leq (n^2 - n) \, (\max b_{pq})^2$$
$$(\max b_{pq})^2 = \tau_{k-1}/(n^2 - n)$$

and

$$\tau_k \leq \tau_{k-1} [1 - 2/(n^2 - n)].$$

After m iterations,

$$\tau_k \approx \tau_0 [1 - 2/(n^2 - n)]^m$$

which approaches zero as m approaches infinity.

3.10 JACOBI ROTATIONS ALGORITHM

Algorithm for Jacobi Rotations

Calculating the eigenvalues and eigenvectors of a symmetric $n \times n$ matrix **A** by the Jacobi method involves computation of a sequence of matrices $\mathbf{B}_k$ (where $\mathbf{B}_0 = \mathbf{A}$) by rotation of the column vectors of $\mathbf{B}_{k-1}$, which define the n-dimensional space. To save computer memory we can place the kth iterate of the matrix in the same space as the original matrix **A**. Similarly, the product of the rotation matrices, $\mathbf{T}_k$, can be stored in $\mathbf{T}_{k-1}$ (where $\mathbf{T}_0 = \mathbf{I}$). On convergence of the algorithm, $\mathbf{B}_k$ is the diagonal matrix of eigenvalues and $\mathbf{T}_k$ is the matrix of eigenvectors. Set a maximum number of iterations allowable (called "maxiter" in the algorithm below) to guard against slow convergence.

$\mathbf{T}_0 = \mathbf{I}$

$S_0 = \sum\limits_{i=1}^{n} a_{ii}^2$

    for $k = 1, 2,...$, until satisfied or $k = $ maxiter do

        find p and q such that $a_{pq} > \varepsilon_1$ is largest off-diagonal element

        if no $a_{pq} > \varepsilon_1$, output results and stop

            else if $|a_{pp} - a_{qq}| \leq \varepsilon_2$, $\sin \theta = \cos \theta = 1/\sqrt{2}$

                else $c = (a_{qq} - a_{pp})/2a_{pq}$

                    $d = \text{sign}(c) [|c| + \sqrt{1 + c^2}]^{-1}$

                    $\cos \theta = 1/\sqrt{1 + d^2}$; $\sin \theta = d \cos \theta$

            set up the four elements of $\mathbf{Q}_k$ that are different from **I**

            update rows and columns p and q to compute $\mathbf{T}_k = \mathbf{T}_{k-1}\mathbf{Q}_k$

               and $\mathbf{A}_k = \mathbf{Q}_k^T\mathbf{A}_{k-1}\mathbf{Q}_k$

        $S_1 = \sum\limits_{i=1}^{n} a_{ii}^2$

        if $1 - S_0 /S_1 \leq \varepsilon_3$, output results and stop

            else set $S_0 = S_1$ and continue

Example 3.10:

Using $\varepsilon_1 = \varepsilon_2 = \varepsilon_3 = 10^{-4}$, find all the eigenvalues and eigenvectors of the matrix

$$\mathbf{A}_0 = \begin{pmatrix} 1 & 1 & 0.5 \\ 1 & 1 & 0.25 \\ 0.5 & 0.25 & 2 \end{pmatrix}$$

Initialize:

$$T_0 = I$$
$$S_0 = 1 + 1 + 4 = 6$$

Iteration 1:

$$a_{pq} = a_{1,2} = 1$$
$$a_{1,1} = a_{2,2} = 1, \text{ so } \cos\theta = \sin\theta = 1/\sqrt{2}$$

$$\mathbf{Q} = \begin{pmatrix} 1\sqrt{2} & 1/\sqrt{2} & 0 \\ -1/\sqrt{2} & 1/\sqrt{2} & 0 \\ 0 & 0 & 1 \end{pmatrix}$$

It is not necessary to calculate the new $a_{1,2}$ value, because it is known to be zero.

$$\mathbf{T}_1 = \mathbf{T}_0\,\mathbf{Q} = \mathbf{IQ} = \mathbf{Q} = \begin{pmatrix} 1/\sqrt{2} & 1/\sqrt{2} & 0 \\ -1/\sqrt{2} & 1/\sqrt{2} & 0 \\ 0 & 0 & 1 \end{pmatrix}$$

Perform arithmetic only on the upper triangle because the matrix $\mathbf{A}$ is symmetric.

$$\mathbf{A}_1 = Q^T A_0 Q = \begin{pmatrix} 1/\sqrt{2} & -1/\sqrt{2} & 0 \\ 1/\sqrt{2} & 1/\sqrt{2} & 0 \\ 0 & 0 & 1 \end{pmatrix}\begin{pmatrix} 1 & & .5 \\ 1 & & .25 \\ .5 & .25 & .2 \end{pmatrix}\begin{pmatrix} 1/\sqrt{2} & 1/\sqrt{2} & 0 \\ -1/\sqrt{2} & 1/\sqrt{2} & 0 \\ 0 & 0 & 1 \end{pmatrix}$$

$$= \begin{pmatrix} 0 & 0 & .25/\sqrt{2} \\ 0 & 2 & .75/\sqrt{2} \\ .25/\sqrt{2} & .75/\sqrt{2} & 2 \end{pmatrix}$$

Note that the diagonal elements of $\mathbf{A}$ have increased and the off-diagonal elements that were not annihilated have been reduced.

$S_1 = 8$; the change exceeds 10^{-4}, so there is no convergence. Set S_0 to 8. Repeat the process of finding $\mathbf{Q}$ and updating $\mathbf{T}$ and $\mathbf{A}$.

Iteration 2:

$$a_{pq} = a_{2,3} = 0.75/\sqrt{2}$$
$$a_{2,2} = a_{3,3} = 2, \text{ so } \cos\theta = \sin\theta = 1/\sqrt{2}$$

$$\mathbf{Q} = \begin{pmatrix} 1 & 0 & 0 \\ 0 & 1/\sqrt{2} & 1/\sqrt{2} \\ 0 & -1/\sqrt{2} & 1/\sqrt{2} \end{pmatrix}$$

$$\mathbf{T}_3 = \mathbf{T}_1\mathbf{Q} = \begin{pmatrix} 1/\sqrt{2} & 0.5 & 0.5 \\ -1/\sqrt{2} & 0.5 & 0.5 \\ 0 & -1/\sqrt{2} & 1/\sqrt{2} \end{pmatrix}$$

$$\mathbf{A}_3 = \mathbf{Q}^T\mathbf{A}_1\mathbf{Q} = \begin{pmatrix} 0.0 & -0.125 & 0.125 \\ -0.125 & 1.470 & 0.0 \\ 0.125 & 0.0 & 2.530 \end{pmatrix}$$

$S_1 = 8.562$, so convergence has not yet been achieved.

Note that $a_{1,2}$ is no longer zero, but it is still small. Continuing this process produces

$$\mathbf{T}_k = \begin{pmatrix} -0.721 & -0.444 & 0.531 \\ 0.686 & -0.562 & 0.461 \\ 0.094 & 0.698 & 0.710 \end{pmatrix}$$

$$\mathbf{A}_k = \begin{pmatrix} -0.166 & 0.0 & 0.0 \\ 0.0 & 1.480 & 0.0 \\ 0.0 & 0.0 & 2.537 \end{pmatrix}$$

Practical Limitations

The utility of the Jacobi rotations method is often limited by the time required to scan the upper triangle of the matrix for the element with the largest magnitude. Two techniques have been devised to improve the efficiency of the method. This first is to sweep through the upper triangle systematically, annihilating each element $a_{ij} > \varepsilon_1$. Repeat the procedure until $1 - S_0/S_1 < \varepsilon_3$. The time required to perform the extra iterations is apt to be less than the time required to search for the largest off-diagonal element.

The second method is to set up the following arrays:

$$u_i = \text{largest element in row } i$$

$$v_i = \text{column index of } u_i$$

Let a^* be the largest off-diagonal element (the maximal u_i) and i^* and j^* be its indices. At each iteration it is easy to find a^*, i^*, and j^*, so $\mathbf{Q}_k$ is determined. After calculating $\mathbf{T}_k$ and $\mathbf{A}_k$, scan the new row i^* and column j^* in $\mathbf{A}_k$ to see if the u_is or v_is need to be changed. Find new values for a^*, i^*, and j^* and repeat. This process requires examining $O(n)$ matrix elements at each iteration, instead of $O(n^2)$ elements, for scanning the full upper triangle.

3.11 COMPUTER PROGRAMS

```
                    SUBROUTINE GAUSS(N, M, A, B, EPS)
C**********************************************************************
C* Solves a system of simultaneous linear equations by Gaussian     *
C* elimination with partial pivoting. N is the number of linear     *
C* equations (maximum of 50). M is the number of constant vectors*
C* (maximum of 50). A is the matrix of coefficients; B is the       *
C* matrix whose M columns are the constant vectors. Matrix A is     *
C* destroyed in this process, and the columns of matrix B           *
C* contain the solution vectors in permuted order on return to      *
C* the calling program. If a pivot element < EPS, the matrix is     *
C* considered to be singular or ill-conditioned.                    *
C**********************************************************************
        DIMENSION A(50,50), B(50,50)
        INTEGER P(50)
C
C -- Initialize permutation vector
C
        DO 10 I = 1,N
10      P(I) = I
C
C -- Triangularize matrix A. Loop over all rows but the last
C
        DO 40 I = 1,N-1
C
C -- Find pivot row
C
        IPIVOT = P(I)
        ISAVE = I
        DO 50 K = I+1,N
          IF (ABS(A(P(K),I)).LE.A(IPIVOT,I)) GO TO 50
            IPIVOT = P(K)
            ISAVE = K
50          CONTINUE
        IF (ISAVE.EQ.I) GO TO 2
C
C -- Else swap entries in permutation vector
C
        P(ISAVE) = P(I)
        P(I) = IPIVOT
        DENOM = A(IPIVOT,I)
        IF (DENOM.GE.EPS) GO TO 1
C
C -- Else an underflow will result when dividing
C
          GO TO 2
C
C -- Operate on all lower rows
C
1       DO 30 J = I+1,N
          DO 20 K = I+1,N
20          A(J,K) = A(J,K) - A(J,I)*A(IPIVOT,K)/DENOM
```

```
           DO 25 K = 1,M
25            B(J,K) = B(J,K) - A(J,I)*B(IPIVOT,K)/DENOM
40      CONTINUE
C
C -- Perform back substitution
C
        DO 60 I = N,1,-1
          DO 70 K = 1,M
            IPIVOT = P(I)
            IF (I.EQ.N) GO TO 70
            DO 80 J = I+1,N
80            B(IPIVOT,K) = B(IPIVOT,K) - A(IPIVOT,J)*B(J,K)
70          B(IPIVOT,K) = B(IPIVOT,K)/A(IPIVOT,I)
60        CONTINUE
        GO TO 3
C
C -- Error Section
C
2       WRITE 1000
1000    FORMAT(' ***Error***Matrix is singular or ill-conditioned')
3       RETURN
        END

procedure Gauss (n, m: integer; var A: nxn; B: nxm; epsilon:
real);
{
**********************************************************************
* Solves a system of simultaneous linear equations by Gaussian      *
* elimination with partial pivoting. N is the number of linear      *
* equations. M is the number of constant vectors. A is the          *
* matrix of coefficients; B is the matrix whose m columns are       *
* the constant vectors. The two data types nxn and nxm must be      *
* defined in the calling program as array[1..n] of real (that is,*
* real arrays of the appropriate dimension). Matrix A is            *
* destroyed in this process, and the columns of matrix B contain *
* the solution vectors in permuted order on return to the           *
* calling program. If a pivot element < epsilon, the matrix is      *
* considered to be singular or ill-conditioned.                     *
**********************************************************************
}
type
  flag = (continue, singular);
var
  permut: array [1..n] of integer;
  i, j, k, ipivot, isave: integer;
  denom: real;
  status: flag;

begin

  {Initialize permutation vector and status}

  for i := 1 to n do
```

```
   permut [i] := i;
status := continue;

{Triangularize coefficient matrix}

for i := 1 to n-1 do   {Do not have to pivot on last row}
  begin

  {Find pivot element}

    ipivot = permut[i];
    isave := i;
    for k := i+1 to n do
      if (abs(A[permut[k],i]) > ipivot)
        then begin
          ipivot := permut [k];
          isave := k
        end;

    (If pivot row not i, swap entries in permutation vector}

    if ( isave <> i)
      then begin
        permut [isave] := permut [i];
        permut [i] := ipivot
      end;
    denom := A[ipivot, i];
    if (denom < epsilon) then status := singular;

    {operate on all lower rows}

    while (status = continue) do
      begin
        for j := i+1 to n do
          begin
            for k := i+1 to n do
              A[j,k] := A[j,k] - A[j,i]*A[ipivot,k]/denom;
            for k := 1,m do
              B[j,k] := B[j,k] - A[j,i]*B[ipivot,k]/denom
          end
      end
  end;

{Perform back substitution}

while (status = continue) do
  for i := n downto 1 do
    begin
      ipivot := permut [i];
      for k := 1 to m do
        begin
          for j := i+1 to n do
            B[ipivot,k]:=
              B[ipivot,k] - A[ipivot,j]*B[j,k];
```

```
             B[ipivot,k] := B[ipivot,k]/A[ipivot,i]
          end
      end;
  if (status = singular) then
     writeln ('***Error***Matrix is singular or ill-conditioned')
end;
```

```
SUBROUTINE SEIDEL(N, A, B, X, EPS1, EPS2, MAXITER)
C****************************************************************
C* Solution of simultaneous linear equations by the Gauss-Seidel *
C* method.  N is the number of equations (maximum of 50).  A is  *
C* the matrix of coefficients.  B is the constant vector.  If a  *
C* diagonal element < EPS1, the matrix is considered to be singu-*
C* lar or ill-conditioned.  X initially contains an initial esti-*
C* mate of the solution and the converged solution appears in X  *
C* on return to the calling program.  MAXITER is the maximum     *
C* number of iterations.  EPS2 is the convergence tolerance.     *
C****************************************************************

      DIMENSION A(50,50), B(50), X(50, XOLD(50)
C
C -- Initialize arrays A and B
C
      DO 10 I = 1,
         DENOM = A(I,I)
         IF (DENOM.LT.EPS1) GO TO 1
         B(I) = DENOM
         DO 10 J = 1,N
           IF (I.EQ.J GO TO 10
           A(I,J) = -A(I,J)/DENOM
10         CONTINUE

      ITER = 0
C
C -- Gauss-Seidel iteration
C
2     DO 20 I = 1,N
         XOLD(I) = X(I)
         SUM = 0.0
         DO 30 J = 1,N
30         IF (J.NE.I) SUM = SUM + A(I,J)*X(J)
20       X(I) = SUM + B(I)
C
C -- Check for convergence
C
      DEVMAX = ABS(XOLD(1) - X(1))/X(1)
      DO 40 J = 2,N
         DEV = ABS(XOLD(J) - X(J))/X(J)
40       IF (DEV.GT.DEVMAX) DEVMAX = DEV
      IF (DEVMAX.LE.EPS2) GO TO 3
C
C -- Else perform another iteration if maximum iterations not
C    exceeded
C
```

```
           ITER = ITER + 1
           IF (ITER.LT.MAXITER) GO TO 2
             GO TO 4
C
C -- Error section
C
1      WRITE 1000
1000   FORMAT(' ***Error***Matrix is singular or ill-conditioned')
       GO TO 5
4      WRITE 2000, MAXITER
2000   FORMAT(' ***Error***No convergence in ',I3,' iterations')
       GO TO 5
C
C -- Convergence achieved
C
3      WRITE 3000, ITER
3000   FORMAT(' Convergence achieved after ',I3,' iterations')
5      RETURN
       END
```

```
procedure Gauss_Seidel (n,maxit: integer; A:nxn; b:vector;
  var x: vector; epsilon1,epsilon2: real);
{
**********************************************************************
* Solution of simultaneous linear equations by the Gauss-Seidel   *
* method.  N is the number of equations.  A is the matrix of       *
* coefficients.  The data types nxn and vector must be defined     *
* as array[1..n,1..n] of real and array[1..n] of real,            *
* respectively, in the calling program.  B is the constant         *
* vector. If a diagonal element < epsilon1, the matrix is          *
* considered to be singular or ill-conditioned.  X initially       *
* contains an initial estimate of the solution and the converged   *
* solution appears in X on return to the calling program. Mmaxit   *
* is the maximum number of iterations.  Epsilon2 is the            *
* convergence criterion.                                           *
**********************************************************************
}
type
  flag = (continue, converge, singular, error);

var
  xold: array[1..n] of real;
  denom, sum, dev, dev_max: real;
  i, j, iter: integer;
  status: flag;

begin

  {Initialize arrays A and B}

  status := continue;
  for i := 1 to n do
    begin
```

```
          denom := A[i,i];
          if (denom < epsilon1)
            then status := singular
          b[i] := b[i]/denom;
          for j := 1 to n do
            if (j <> i) then A[i,j] := -A[i,j]/denom
       end;
    iter := 0;

  {Gauss-Seidel iteration}

  while (status = continue) do
     begin
       for i := 1,n do
         begin
           xold[i] := x[i];
           sum := 0,0;
           for j := 1 to n do
             if (j<> i) then sum := sum + A[i,j]*x[j];
           x[i] := sum + b[i]
         end;

       {Check for convergence}

       dev_max := abs(xold[i] - x[i])/x[1];
       for j := 2 to n do
         begin
           dev := abs (xold[i] - x[i])/x[i];
           if (dev > dev_max) then dev_max := dev
         end;
       if (dev <= epsilon2) then status := converge
         else begin
           iter := iter + 1;
           if (iter > maxiter) then status := error
         end
     end;

  {Error section}

  case status of
    singular: writeln('***Error***Matrix is singular or ',
      'ill-conditioned');
    error: writeln('***Error***No convergence in ',maxit:3,
      ' iterations');
    converge: writeln('Convergence achieved after',iter:3,
      ' iterations');
  end {of case}
end;
              SUBROUTINE TRIDIA(N, A, B, C, D, EPS)
C***************************************************************
C* Solution of simultaneous linear equations with tridiagonal   *
C* coefficient matrix. N is the number of equations (no maximum  *
C* needed). A, B, and C are the arrays of subdiagonal, diagonal, *
```

```
C* and superdiagonal elements, respectively.  D is the constant  *
C* vector on input and the solution vector on output. The matrix *
C* is singular or ill-conditioned if a diagonal element becomes   *
C* < EPS. Note that A(1) and C(N) are not used in this algorithm.*
C****************************************************************
      DIMENSION A(1), B(1), C(1), D(1)
C
C -- Perform LU factorization of tridiagonal matrix
C    Check that no diagonal element is too small
C
      IF (B(1).LT.EPS) GO TO 1
      DO 10 K = 2,N
        A(K) = A(K)/B(K-1)
        B(K) = B(K) - A(K)*C(K-1)
        IF (B(K).LT.EPS) GO TO 1
10      D(K) = D(K) - A(K)*D(K-1)
C
C -- Perform forward and backward substitution
C
      D(N) = D(N)/B(N)
      DO 20 K = N-1,1,-1
20      D(K) = (D(K) - C(K)*D(K+1))/B(K)
      GO TO 2
C
C -- Error Section
C
1     WRITE 1000
1000  FORMAT('***Error***Matrix is singular or ill-conditioned')
2     RETURN
      END

procedure tridiagonal(n: integer; a, b, c: vector; var d: vector
   epsilon: real);
{
****************************************************************
* Solution of simultanous linear equations with tridiagonal   *
* coefficient matrix.  N is the number of linear equations.  A, *
* b, and c are the arrays of the subdiagonal, diagonal, and    *
* superdiagonal elements, respectively.  D is the constant     *
* vector on input and the solution vector on output.  The matrix *
* is singular or ill-conditioned if a diagonal element becomes   *
* < epsilon.  Note that a(1) and c(n) are not used in this       *
* algorithm.  Define data type vector as array[1..n] of real in  *
* the calling program.                                          *
****************************************************************
}
type
   flag = (continue, singular);

var
   k: integer;
   status: flag;
```

```
begin
  if (b[1] < epsilon) then status := singular
    else status := continue;

  {Perform LU factorization}

  for k := 2 to n do
    while (status = continue) do
      begin
        a[k] := a[k]/b[k-1];
        b[k] := b[k] - a[k]*c[k-1];

        {Check that diagonal element doesn't become too small}

        if (b[k] < epsilon) then status := singular;
        d[k] := d[k] - a[k]*d[k-1]
      end;

  case status of
    continue: {Perform backward and forward substitution}
      begin
        d[n] := d[n]/b[n];
        for k := n-1 downto 1 do
          d[k] := (d[k] - c[k]*d[k+1])/b[k]
        end;

      singular: {Error section}
        writeln('***Error***Matrix is singular or ',
          'ill-conditioned')
  end {of case}
end;
              SUBROUTINE POWER(N, A, E, V, EPS, MAXIT)
C*******************************************************************
C* Find the eigenvalue with the largest magnitude and its corres-*
C* ponding eigenvector using the power method.  A is a symmetric *
C* N X N (maximum dimension of 50) matrix. E is the eigenvalue.  *
C* The eigenvector is returned in V.  EPS is the relative con-   *
C* vergence criterion, and MAXIT is the maximum number of        *
C* iterations permitted.                                         *
C*******************************************************************
      DIMENSION A(50,50), V(50)
C
C -- Initialize
C
      DO 10 I = 1,N
10       V(I) = 1.0
      ITER = 0
      E = 0.0
C
C -- Calculate A*V and its L2 norm
C
1     EOLD = E
```

```
         E = 0.0
         DO 20 I = 1,N
           SUM = 0.0
           DO 30 J = 1,N
30           SUM = SUM + A(I,J)*V(J)
           V(I) = SUM
20         E = E + SUM**2
           E = SQRT(E)
C
C -- Normalize eigenvector.  Note that E is zero only if A is
C    the zero matrix
C
         DO 40 I = 1,N
40       V(I) = V(I)/E
C
C -- Check for convergence
C
         IF (ABS(E - EOLD)/E.LT.EPS) GO TO 2
C
C -- Else check for maximum iterations
C
           ITER = ITER + 1
           IF (ITER.GT.MAXIT) GO TO 3
             GO TO 1
C
C -- Convergence achieved
C
2        WRITE 1000, E,V
1000     FORMAT (' Convergence achieved after ',I3,' iterations'/
     1     5X,'Eigenvalue =',1PE11.4/5X,'Eigenvector =',1PE11.4/
     2     (18X,1PE11.4/))
         RETURN
C
C -- Error Section
C
3        WRITE 2000, ITER
2000     FORMAT('***Error***No convergence in',I3,' iterations')
         RETURN
         END

procedure power(n, maxiter: integer; A: nxn; var v: vector;
  var e: real; epsilon: real);
{
********************************************************************
* Find the eigenvalue with the largest magnitude and its corres- *
* ponding eigenvector using the power method.  A is a symmetric   *
* matrix, typed as nxn = array[1..n,1..n] of real in the calling  *
* program.  E is the eigenvalue.  The eigenvector is returned in  *
* v, typed as vector = array[1..n] of real in the calling         *
* program.  Epsilon is the relative convergence criterion, and    *
* maxiter is the maximum iterations permitted.                    *
********************************************************************
}
```

```
type
  flag = (continue, converged, error);

var
  iter,i, j: integer;
  sum, e_old: real;
  status: flag;

begin

  {Initialize}

  for i := 1 to n do
    v[i] := 1.0;
  e := 0.0;
  iter := 0;
  status := continue;

  while (status = continue) do
    begin

      {Calculate A*v and its L2 norm}

      for i := 1 to n do
        begin
          e_old := e;
          e := 0.0;
          sum := 0.0;
          for j := 1 to n do
            sum := sum + A[i,j]*v[j];
          v[i] := sum;
          e = e + sqr(sum)
        end;
      e = sqrt(e);

      {Normalize eigenvector.  Note that e = 0 only if A is the
       zero matrix}

      for j := 1 to n do
        v[i] := v[i]/e;

      {Check for convergence}

      if (abs(e - e_old/e < epsilon)
        then status := converged
        else begin
          iter := iter + 1;
          if (iter > maxiter) then status := error
        end
    end {of while};

  case status of
    converged: {Output results}
```

```
      begin
        writeln('Convergence achieved after',iter:3,
          ' iterations');
        writeln('    Eigenvalue ='e:11);
        writeln('    Eigenvector ='e[1]:11);
        for i := 2 to n do
          writeln(e[i]:29)
      end;
    error: {Error Section}
      writeln('***Error***No convergence in',maxiter:3,
        ' iterations')
  end {of case}
end;
      SUBROUTINE JACOBI(N, A, T, EPS1, EPS2, EPS3, MAXIT)
C*****************************************************************
C* Eigenvalues and eigenvectors of symmetric matrices by the   *
C* method of Jacobi rotations. N is the dimension of the matrix A*
C* (maximum is 50).  On return, A contains the eigenvalues on the*
C* diagonal, and T contains the eigenvectors in its columns in  *
C* the same order as the eigenvalues.  EPS1, EPS2, and EPS3 are  *
C* tolerances for off-diagonal element = 0, two equal diagonal  *
C* elements, and equality of the sum of squares of the diagonal  *
C* elements (for convergence).  MAXIT is the maximum number of  *
C* iterations.                                                  *
C*****************************************************************
      DIMENSION A(50,50), T(50,50), U(50), V(50)
      INTEGER P, Q
C
C -- Initialize T, S1, U, and V
C
      DO 10 I = 1,N
        DO 10 J = 1,N
          IF (I.NE.J) GO TO 1
            T(I,I) = 1.0
            GO TO 10
1         T(I,J) = 0.0
10      CONTINUE
      S1 = 0.0
      DO 20 I = 1,N
        V(I) = 1
        U(I) = A(I,1)
        DO 30 J = 2,N
          IF (A(I,J).LE.U(I)) GO TO 30
            V(I) = J
            U(I) = A(I,J)
30      CONTINUE
20      CONTINUE
      ITER = 0
C
C -- Find largest off-diagonal element.  Check that it's > EPS1
C
2     P = 1
      Q = V(1)
```

```
         APQ = U(1)
         APQMAX = APQ
         DO 40 I = 2,N
           IF (U(I).LE.APQ) GO TO 40
             P = I
             Q = V(I)
             APQ = U(I)
             IF (APQ.GT.APQMAX) APQMAX = APQ
40         CONTINUE
         IF (APQMAX.LT.EPS1) GO TO 3
C
C -- Else compute sine and cosine of rotational angle
C
         IF ((A(Q,Q) - A(P,P)).LT.EPS2) GO TO 4
           C = (A(Q,Q) - A(P,P))/2.*APQ
           D = 1./(ABS(C) + SQRT(1. + C**2))
           IF (C.LT.0.0) D = -D
           COSTH = 1./SQRT(1.0 + D**2)
           SINTH = D*COSTH
           GO TO 5
4        COSTH = 0.70714285714
         SINTH = 0.70714285714
C
C -- Update columns p and q of T.  Note that the rotation matrix
C    need not be computed nor stored in full
C
5        DO 50 I = 1,N
           STORE1 = T(I,P)
           T(I,P) = STORE1*COSTH + T(I,Q)*SINTH
50         T(I,Q) = STORE1*SINTH - T(I,Q)*COSTH
C
C -- Compute new rows p and q of A
C
         A(P,P) = A(P,P)*COSTH**2 + 2.*APQ*COSTH*SINTH +
      1    A(Q,Q)*SINTH**2
         A(Q,Q) = A(P,P)*SINTH**2 - 2.*APQ*COSTH*SINTH +
      1    A(Q,Q)*COSTH**2
         A(P,Q) = 0.0
         DO 60 J = 1,N
           IF ((J.EQ.P).OR.(J.EQ.Q)) GO TO 60
             STORE1 = A(P,J)*COSTH + A(Q,J)*SINTH
             STORE2 = A(Q,J)*COSTH - A(P,J)*SINTH
             A(P,J) = STORE1
             A(J,P) = STORE1
             A(Q,J) = STORE2
             A(J,Q) = STORE2
60         CONTINUE
C
C -- Check for convergence
C
         S0 = S1
         S1 = 0.0
         DO 70 I = 1,N
```

```
70      S1 = S1 + A(I,I)**2
        IF ((1. - S0/S1).LT.EPS3) GO TO 3
C
C -- Else check that maximum iterations is not exceeded
C
        ITER = ITER + 1
IF (ITER.GT.MAXIT) GO TO 6
C
C -- Else see if largest element changed on rows p and q
C
        DO 80 J = 1,N
          IF (A(P,J).LE.U(P)) GO TO 7
          V(P) = J
          U(P) = A(P,J)
7         IF (A(Q,J).LE.U(Q)) GO TO 80
          V(Q) = J
          U(Q) = A(Q,J)
80        CONTINUE
        GO TO 2
C
C -- Convergence achieved
C
3     WRITE 1000, ITER
1000  FORMAT (' Convergence achieved in,'I3,' iterations')
      RETURN
C
C -- Error Section
C
6     WRITE 2000, MAXIT
2000  FORMAT('***Error***No convergence in',I3,' iterations')
      RETURN
      END

procedure Jacobi(n, maxiter: integer; var A, T: nxn;
  epsilon1, epsilon2, epsilon3: real);
{
*********************************************************************
* Eigenvalues and eigenvectors of symmetric matrices by the        *
* method of Jacobi rotations. n is the dimension of the matrix A,  *
* typed as array[1..n,1..n] of real in the calling program. On     *
* return, A contains the eigenvalues on the diagonal, and T         *
* contains the eigenvectors in its columns in the same order as    *
* the eigenvalues. epsilon1, epsilon2, and epsilon3 are the         *
* tolerances for off-diagonal element = 0, two equal diagonal      *
* elements, and equality of the sum of squares of the diagonal     *
* elements (for convergence). maxiter is the maximum number of      *
* iterations.                                                       *
*********************************************************************
}
type
  flag = (continue, converged, error);

var
```

```
   i, j, iter, p, q: integer;
   v: array[1..n] of integer;
   u: array [1..n] of real;
   c, d, apq, apq_max, store1, store2, cos_theta, sin_theta, s0,
     s1: real;
   status: flag;

begin

   {Initialize T, s1, u, and v}

   for i := 1 to n do
     for j := 1 to n do
       if (i = j) then T[i,i] := 1.0
         else T[i,j] := 0.0;
   s1 := 0.0;
   v[i] := 1;
   u[i] := A[i,1];
   for j := 2 to n do
     if (A[i,j] > u[i])
       then begin
         v[i] := j;
         u[i] := A[i,j]
       end;
   iter := 0;
   status := continue;

   while (status = continue) do
     begin

       {Find largest off-diagonal element.  Check that it's
        > epsilon1}

       p := 1;
       p := v[i];
       apq := u[1];
       apq_max := apq;
       for i := 2 to n do
         if (u[i] > apq)
           then begin
             p := i;
             q := v[i];
             apq := u[i];
             if (apq > apq_max) then apq_max := apq
           end;
       if (apq_max < epsilon1) then status := converged

         else {Compute sine and cosine of rotational angle}

           if ((A[q,q] - A[p,p]) > epsilon2)
             then begin
               c := (A[q,q] - A[p,p])/2.*apq;
               d=1./(abs(c) + sqrt(1. + sqr(c)));
```

```
      if (c < 0.0) d := -d;
      cos_theta := 1./sqrt(1.0 + sqr(d));
      sin_theta := d*cos_theta
   end
      else begin
        cos_theta := 0.70714285714;
        sin_theta := 0.70714285714
      end;
```

{Update columns p and q of T. Note that the rotation matrix need not be computed nor stored in full}

```
for i := 1 to n do
  begin
    storel := T[i,p];
    T[i,p] := storel*cos_theta + T[i,q]*sin_theta;
    T[i,q] := storel*sin_theta - T[i,q]*cos_theta
  end;
```

{Compute new rows p and q of A}

```
A[p,p] := A[p,p]*sqr(cos_theta) +
  2.*apq*cos_theta*sin_theta + A[q,q]*sqr(sin_theta);
A[q,q] := A[p,p]*sqr(sin_theta) -
  2.*apq*cos_theta*sin_theta + A[q,q]*sqr(cos_theta);
A[p,q] := 0.0;
for j := 1 to n do
  if (not j in [p,q])
    then begin
      storel := A[p,j]*cos_theta + A[q,j]*sin_theta;
      store2 := A[q,j]*cos_theta - A[p,j]*sin_theta;
      A[p,j] := storel;
      A[j,p] := storel;
      A[q,j] := store2;
      A[j,q] := store2;
    end;
```

{Check for convergence}

```
s0 := s1;
s1 := 0.0;
for i := i to n do
  s1 := s1 + sqr(A[i,i]);
if (abs(1. - s0/s1) < epsilon3)
  then status := converged
  else begin
    {check that maximum iterations is not exceeded}
    iter := iter + 1
    if (iter > maxiter) then status := error;
      else begin
      {Has largest element changed on rows p and q?}
      for j := 1 to n do
        begin
```

```
                  if (A[p,j] > u[p])
                    then begin
                    v[p] := j;
                    u[p] := A[p,j]
                    end;
                    if (A[q,j] > u[q])
                    then begin
                    v[q] := j;
                    u[q] := A[q,j]
                    end
              end
            end
          end {of convergence test}
    end; {of while}

  case status of
    converged: writeln('Convergence achieved after',iter:3,
                 ' iterations');
    error: writeln('***Error***No convergence in',maxiter:3,
                 ' iterations');
  end {of case}
end;
```

3.12 EXAMPLE PROBLEMS

Example 3.11: Deformation of a Beam

A steel beam is subjected to a tension (horizontal load) *t* of 1000 lb and supports against gravity a vertical load *w* of 1000 lb. The resulting torsional moment is *m* = 1500 lb·in. From the length and cross sectional area of the beam, its second moment, and Young's modulus for steel an engineer produced the following equations for the horizontal extension *h* of the beam, the vertical deflection *v*, and the angle ϕ of the sag in radians.

$$1.521 \times 10^6 \, h = t$$
$$2.204 \times 10^4 \, v - 7.714 \times 10^5 \, \phi = w$$
$$-7.714 \times 10^5 \, v + 3.600 \times 10^7 \, \phi = m$$

The coefficients of these equations form the "flexibility" matrix **F**, whose inverse is the "stiffness" matrix. Find *h*, *v*, ϕ, det **F** and $\mathbf{F}^{-1}$.

Solution

The matrix equation for this problem is

$$\begin{pmatrix} 1.521 \times 10^6 & 0 & 0 \\ 0 & 2.204 \times 10^4 & -7.714 \times 10^5 \\ 0 & -7.714 \times 10^5 & 3.600 \times 10^7 \end{pmatrix} \begin{pmatrix} h \\ v \\ \phi \end{pmatrix} = \begin{pmatrix} 1000 \\ 1000 \\ 1500 \end{pmatrix}$$

Because the inverse is to be calculated, the most efficient method is Gauss-Jordan elimination. For convenience, append the constant vector and the identity matrix I to F. When the elimination is completed, the constant vector will have been transformed into the solution, F into I, and I into F^{-1}. Set det F to 1.

$$\begin{pmatrix} 1.521 \times 10^6 & 0 & 0 \\ 0 & 2.204 \times 10^4 & -7.714 \times 10^5 \\ 0 & -7.714 \times 10^5 & 3.600 \times 10^7 \end{pmatrix} \begin{array}{|c} \mathbf{b} \\ \hline 1000 \\ 1000 \\ 1500 \end{array} \begin{array}{|ccc} \mathbf{I} \\ \hline 1 & 0 & 0 \\ 0 & 1 & 0 \\ 0 & 0 & 1 \end{array} \begin{array}{c} \mathbf{p} \\ 1 \\ 2 \\ 3 \end{array}$$

Step 1: Row 1 has the pivot in column 1, so no interchanges between positions in the permutation vector are necessary. Normalize row 1 and set det $F = -$ det $F \times 1.521 \times 10^6 = 1.521 \times 10^6$; the minus sign is needed because of the row interchange. Note that there is no need to perform row reduction of the other rows because column 1 for those rows already is all zeroes.

$$\begin{pmatrix} 1 & 0 & 0 \\ 0 & 2.204 \times 10^4 & -7.714 \times 10^5 \\ 0 & 7.714 \times 10^5 & 3.600 \times 10^7 \end{pmatrix} \begin{array}{|c} \mathbf{b} \\ \hline 6.573 \times 10^{-4} \\ 1000 \\ 1500 \end{array} \begin{array}{|ccc} \mathbf{I} \\ \hline 6.573 \times 10^{-7} & 0 & 0 \\ 0 & 1 & 0 \\ 0 & 0 & 1 \end{array} \begin{array}{c} \mathbf{p} \\ 1 \\ 2 \\ 3 \end{array}$$

Step 2: Pivot on row 3. Interchange p_2 and p_3. Normalize and set det $F = $ det $F \times (-7.714 \times 10^5) = -1.173 \times 10^{12}$. Perform row reductions on rows 1 and 2.

$$\begin{pmatrix} 1 & 0 & 0 \\ 0 & 0 & 2.572 \times 10^5 \\ 0 & 1 & -4.667 \times 10^7 \end{pmatrix} \begin{array}{|c} \mathbf{b} \\ \hline 6.573 \times 10^{-4} \\ 1.043 \times 10^3 \\ -1.945 \times 10^{-3} \end{array} \begin{array}{|ccc} \mathbf{I} \\ \hline 6.573 \times 10^{-7} & 0 & 0 \\ 0 & 1 & 2.856 \times 10^{-2} \\ 0 & 0 & -1.296 \times 10^{-6} \end{array} \begin{array}{c} \mathbf{p} \\ 1 \\ 2 \\ 3 \end{array}$$

Step 3: Pivot on row 2, the last row in $\mathbf{p}$. Normalize and set det $F = $ det $F \times (2.572 \times 10^5) = -1.173 \times 10^{12}$. Perform row reductions on rows 1 and 3.

$$\begin{pmatrix} 1 & 0 & 0 \\ 0 & 0 & 1 \\ 0 & 1 & 0 \end{pmatrix} \begin{array}{|c} \mathbf{x} \\ \hline 6.573 \times 10^{-4} \\ 4.055 \times 10^{-3} \\ 1.873 \times 10^{-1} \end{array} \begin{array}{|ccc} \mathbf{F^{-1}} \\ \hline 6.573 \times 10^{-7} & 0 & 0 \\ 0 & 3.888 \times 10 & 1.111 \times 10^{-7} \\ 0 & 1.815 \times 10 & 3.887 \times 10^{-6} \end{array} \begin{array}{c} \mathbf{p} \\ 1 \\ 3 \\ 2 \end{array}$$

Note that the rows of the arrays are in permuted order: row 2 is in the third position and row 3 is in the second position. Swapping the rows in x gives the solution $h = 6.573 \times 10^{-4}$, $v = 1.873 \times 10^{-1}$, and $\phi = 4.055 \times 10^{-3}$.

Error Analysis

If there were a relative error of 0.5 percent in the estimation of forces on the beam, what are the limits of error in the solution?

$$0.005/K \leqslant e \leqslant 0.005 \ K$$

The condition number K may be estimated by the L_∞ norms (maximum row sum of absolute values) of $\mathbf{F}$ and $\mathbf{F}^{-1}$.

$$K = \|\mathbf{F}\|_\infty \|\mathbf{F}^{-1}\|_\infty = 3.677 \times 10^7 \times 1.854 \times 10^{-4} = 6.817 \times 10^3,$$

and the limits of error are

$$7.335 \times 10^{-7} \leqslant e \leqslant 3.409 \times 10^1.$$

The large range of possible error arises from the large condition number; this illustrates the need for very close tolerances in such engineering applications.

Example 3.12: Why Jacobi rotation method works only for symmetrical matrices

A physics student measured the electronic spectrum of a gas and wished to relate the three absorption bands he found to transitions between energy levels in the gas molecules. Choosing convenient units, he set up the following Hamiltonian matrix, whose eigenvalues are the energy levels of the material.

$$\mathcal{H}_0 = \begin{pmatrix} 4 & 1 & 1 \\ 0 & -1 & 0 \\ 3 & 1 & 2 \end{pmatrix}$$

The student attempted to find the eigenvalues by the method of Jacobi rotations. On the first iteration, the matrix element to be annihilated was $h_{pq} = h_{3,1} = 3$.

$$c = (h_{1,1} - h_{3,3})/h_{3,1} = (4 - 2)/3 = 0.6667$$

yielding $\sin \theta = -0.5847$ and $\cos \theta = 0.8112$. Performing the orthogonal transformation $\mathbf{Q}^T \mathbf{A} \mathbf{Q}$ gave

$$\mathcal{H}_1 = \begin{matrix} \mathbf{Q}^T \\ \begin{pmatrix} .8112 & 0 & .5847 \\ 0 & 1 & 0 \\ -.5847 & 0 & .8112 \end{pmatrix} \end{matrix} \begin{matrix} \mathcal{H}_0 \\ \begin{pmatrix} 4 & 1 & 1 \\ 0 & -1 & 0 \\ 3 & 1 & 2 \end{pmatrix} \end{matrix} \begin{matrix} \mathbf{Q} \\ \begin{pmatrix} .8112 & 0 & -.5847 \\ 0 & 1 & 0 \\ .5847 & 0 & .8112 \end{pmatrix} \end{matrix}$$

$$= \begin{pmatrix} 5.2132 & 1 & -1.3162 \\ 0 & -1 & 0 \\ 0 & .2265 & 0.7863 \end{pmatrix}$$

The matrix element $h_{1,3}$ was not annihilated and actually increased in magnitude, illustrating the inapplicability of the method to nonsymmetric matrices.

chapter *4*

Approximation and Interpolation

4.1 CRITERIA FOR APPROXIMATING FUNCTIONS

There are several reasons why it may be desirable to approximate the value of a function rather than compute the value directly.

1. It may be difficult or impossible to evaluate the function analytically. Examples are transcendental functions such as sine, logarithm, and erf (the integral of the normal error function).
2. We may only have a table of values for the function and must interpolate between pairs of entries.
3. It may be much faster to compute the value of an approximating function than of the original function. In the extreme, the original function may be an infinite series expansion.
4. The function may be defined implicitly, that is, by an indirect rule rather than by an algebraic equation.

Types of Approximating Functions

Usually the approximating function is a linear combination of simpler functions

$$g(x) = \Sigma \, a_i \, f_i(x)$$

Several examples of this approach are:

1. Polynomial: $p(x) = \Sigma a_i x^i$
2. Piecewise polynomial, distinct polynomials approximating the function on adjacent intervals
3. Fourier series: $\Sigma [a_i \sin(ix) + b_i \cos(ix)]$
4. Rational function, a ratio of two polynomials $p_n(x)/p_m(x)$
5. Exponential functions: $\Sigma a_i \exp(b_i x^i)$

Criteria for "Best Fit"

For a scientific or engineering calculation to be credible, the coefficients in the linear combination of such simple functions must result in an approximation that is sufficiently accurate for that application. Therefore, the coefficients in approximating functions are determined such that some measure of the approximation error is minimized. Of course, the actual error is unknown because the original function cannot be computed readily. In such cases we must settle for an upper bound for the error. Often the value of the function is known at discrete points. In those cases the approximating function is chosen such that it equals (or nearly equals) the actual function values at those points.

Criterion Is a Particular Value of the Approximating Function Itself

Let $f(x)$ be the function to be approximated along an interval $[x_0, x_n]$. The Lagrange interpolating polynomial (Fig. 4.1) is the polynomial $p_m(x)$ of degree m where m is the smallest number such that $p_m(x_i)$ $f(x_j)$, $i = 0,..., n$ for $n + 1$ reference points on the interval. By this criterion $m = n$.

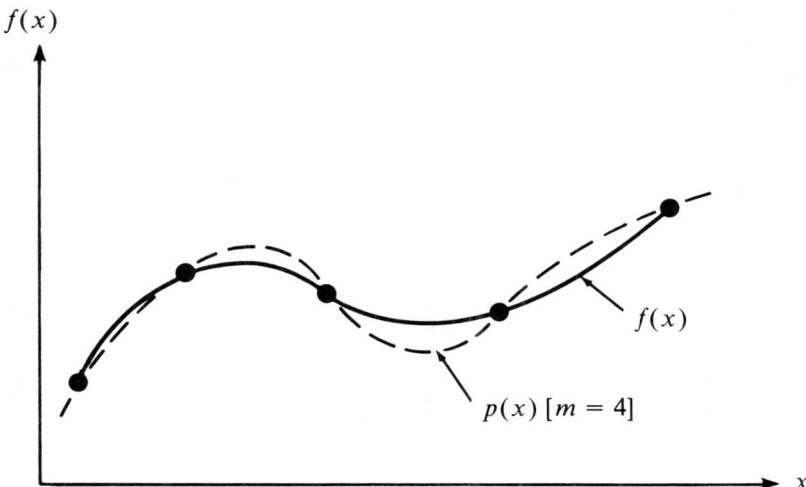

Fig. 4.1. Lagrange interpolating polynomial of degree 4 which approximates $f(x)$.

Criterion Is a Minimal Distance Between a Set of Reference Points and the Approximating Function

Suppose the function values $f(x_i)$ for the $n + 1$ reference points are not known exactly. For example, they may be measured values and include experimental error. If a polynomial approximation is desired, the best fit would be obtained with $p_m(x)$ of order $m < n$ such that the vector norm L_q given by

$$e = \left\{ \sum_{i=0}^{n} |p_m(x_i) - f(x_i)|^q \right\}^{1/q}$$

is minimized.

When $q = 2$, the result is the well-known least-squares approximation (Fig. 4.2). The polynomial order must be less than n because if $m = n$ the polynomial is the same as the Lagrange interpolating polynomial and the least-squares error is zero. That result implies that the function values $f(x_i)$ are known exactly, which is not the case. The deviations $p_m(x_i) - f(x_i)$ may be weighted to reflect the relative reliability of the function values at the reference points.

$$e = \left\{ \sum_{i=0}^{n} w_i[p_m(x_i) - f(x_i)]^2 \right\}^{1/2}$$

Often the weight is inversely proportional to the variance of the measured value of $f(x_i)$.

If $q = \infty$, the measure of the error is

$$e = \max_i |p_m(x_i) - f(x_i)|$$

which minimizes the maximal deviation from the reference points. This is called the "minimax," "Chebyshev," or "optimal polynomial approxi-

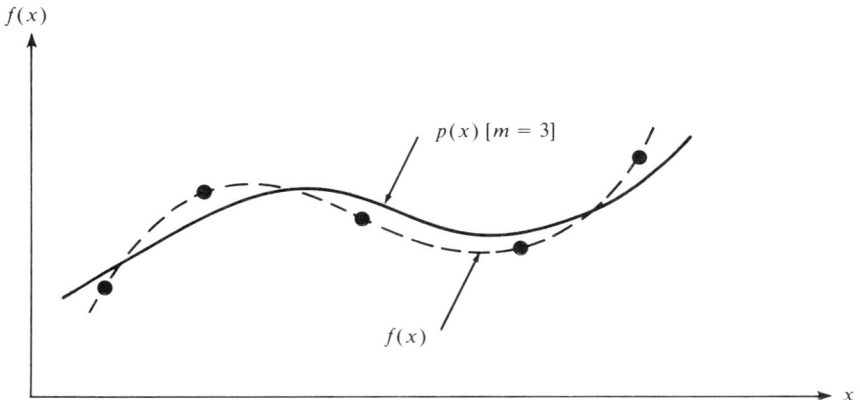

Fig. 4.2. Least-squares approximation of $f(x)$ by a cubic polynomial.

mation." A least-squares approximation may give a good fit to the reference points at all but, say, one point for which there may be a large deviation. The minimax approximation prevents the polynomial from being too far away from any reference point.

Criterion Is an Integral Function

When both the function $f(x)$ to be approximated and the approximating function $p(x)$ are continuous on an interval $[a, b]$ and their values are known at every point on the interval, a convenient criterion for goodness of fit is the integral of the square of the difference between the two functions.

$$e^2 = \int_a^b w(x)[p_m(x) - f(x)]^2 \, dx$$

where $w(x)$ is a weighting function, continuous on $[a, b]$. This kind of approximation is called "continuous least squares."

Criterion Is Truncation Error of a Series or a Maximal Tolerance

There are many functions which are equivalent to infinite series. A well known example is the Taylor series:

$$f(x) = f(x_0) + \sum_{i=1}^{\infty} \frac{(x - x_0)^i}{i!} f^{(i)}(x_0)$$

If the summation is truncated after m terms, the resulting approximating function $p_m(x)$ is defined by

$$f(x) = f(x_0) + p_m(x) + R_m(x)$$

where $R_m(x)$ is the remainder of the infinite series. If x is close to x_0 the remainder will be dominated by the $i + 1$st term of the series.

$$R_m(x) = \frac{(x - x_0)^{m+1}}{(m + 1)!} f^{(m+1)}(x_0)$$

Assuming that we know $f(x_0)$ and wish to approximate the function value in a region surrounding x_0, the problem is to find m such that the remainder is within some preset tolerance ε.

Interpolation

If the value of an arbitrary function is known at two or more distinct points in its domain, an approximating function can be passed through those points and evaluated for some intermediate point.

Example 4.1:

From a table of common logarithms we abstract the following numbers:

x	log x
3.150	0.4983
3.155	0.4990
3.160	0.4997

To find the value of log 3.157 we use the following familiar technique: As 3.157 is located 2/5 of the distance from 3.155 to 3.160, log 3.157 is estimated as 2/5 of the way from log 3.155 to 3.160.

$$\log 3.157 = 0.4990 + 2/5(0.4997 - 0.4990) = 0.4993,$$

which does equal log 3.157 to four decimal places. This is linear interpolation. The approximating function is a straight line between the points (3.155, 0.4990) and (3.160, 0.4997). Alternatively, log 3.157 could be approximated by a quadratic which passes through all three points.

4.2   LEAST SQUARES APPROXIMATION

Suppose that for each value x_i, $i = 1,\dots, n$, of some variable in the equations representing a physical system a measurement y_i of another property of the physical system were made. The y_i's would invariably contain experimental errors; a common problem in numerical analysis is to estimate the true values of the y_i's. This involves finding a mathematical model that explains the correlation between x_i and y_i.

$$f_i = f(x_i, \boldsymbol{\alpha}) + \varepsilon_i$$

where f_i is an approximation to y_i, $\boldsymbol{\alpha}$ is a set of constant parameters, and ε_i is an approximation to the experimental error.

In the special case of linear dependence of the f_i's on the α_i's,

$$f_i = \sum_{j=1}^{m} \alpha_j \phi_j(x_i) + \varepsilon_i$$

where ϕ_j is some function of x and m is the number of functions in the linear combination. We seek those values of α_j that will minimize $\|\varepsilon\|_2$, which is given by

$$\|\varepsilon\|_2^2 = \sum_{i=1}^{n} (y_i - f_i)^2$$

where $(y_i - f_i)$ is called the residual at x_i. An example of a least squares fit is given by Fig. 4.3.

The minimal value of $\|\varepsilon\|_2$ is obtained when the derivative of $(\|\varepsilon\|_2)^2$ with respect to α vanishes.

$$\sum_{i=1}^{n} \frac{\partial}{\partial \alpha_j} (y_i - f_i)^2 = -2 \sum_{i=1}^{n} \phi_j (x_i)(y_i - f_i) = 0, \quad j = 1,\ldots, m.$$

Substituting the definition of f_i and rearranging gives

$$\sum_{k=1}^{m} \sum_{i=1}^{n} \phi_j(x_i)\phi_k(x_i)\alpha_k = \sum_{i=1}^{n} \phi_j(x_i)y_i, \quad j = 1,\ldots, m.$$

The summation over i (the index of the experimental measurement) defines the elements of an $m \times m$ matrix $\mathbf{A} = [a_{jk}]$ of constant coefficients; α is an m-vector of parameters. The final summation defines a constant m-vector $\mathbf{b}$. The equation.

$$\mathbf{A}\alpha = \mathbf{b}$$

can be solved by Gaussian elimination.

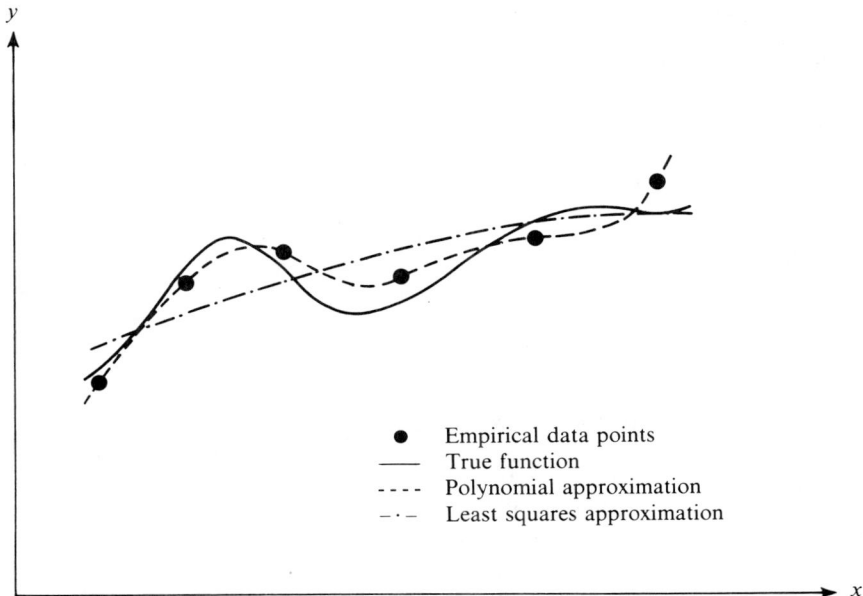

Fig. 4.3. Comparison of polynomial and least-squares fits to empirical data. The dots are the experimental data, the dashed line is the polynomial fit, and the chain-dotted line is the least-squares approximation.

Example 4.2:

For $n = 3$ measurements

x_i	y_i
1.0	2.000
2.0	6.079
3.0	9.296

$$f_i = \alpha_1\phi_1 + \alpha_2\phi_2 = \alpha_1 x_i + \alpha_2\ln(x_i) \qquad m = 2$$

Step 1: Set up **A** matrix.

$$A_{1,1} = \sum_{i=1}^{3} x_i^2 = 14.000$$

$$A_{1,2} = \sum_{i=1}^{3} x_i\ln(x_i) = 4.682$$

$$A_{2,1} = \sum_{i=1}^{3} \ln(x_i)x_i = 4.682$$

$$A_{2,2} = \sum_{i=1}^{3} [\ln(x_i)]^2 = 1.687$$

Note that the **A** matrix is symmetrical.

Step 2: Set up **b** vector.

$$b_1 = \sum_{i=1}^{3} x_i y_i = 42.046$$

$$b_2 = \sum_{i=1}^{3} \ln(x_i)y_i = 14.426$$

$$\begin{pmatrix} 14 & 4.682 \\ 4.682 & 1.678 \end{pmatrix} \begin{pmatrix} \alpha_1 \\ \alpha_2 \end{pmatrix} = \begin{pmatrix} 42.046 \\ 14.426 \end{pmatrix}$$

Step 3: Gaussian elimination.

$$\begin{pmatrix} 1 & 0.334 & | & 3.003 \\ 0 & 0.123 & | & 0.366 \end{pmatrix}$$

$$\alpha_2 = 0.366/0.123 = 2.975$$

$$\alpha_1 = 3.003 - 0.334 \times 2.975 = 2.009$$

The true values are $\alpha = (2.0, 3.0)$; the discrepancies are attributable to round-off due to carrying only three decimal places.

Polynomial Least-Squares Fit

For the special case where the approximating function $f(x_i, \alpha)$ is a linear combination of polynomials

$$f_i = \sum_{j=1}^{m} \phi_j(x_i)\, \alpha_j = \sum_{j=1}^{m} \alpha_j (x_i)^{\,j},$$

$$a_{jk} = \sum_{i=1}^{n} x_i^{\,j} x_i^{\,k} = \sum_{i=1}^{n} x_i^{\,j+k}$$

$$b_j = \sum_{i=1}^{n} y_i x_i^{\,j}$$

which can be solved for the coefficients of $(x_i)^{\,j}$ in the usual way. This approach works well for $m \leq 5$ or 6, but for higher values the method gives poor approximations. To see why, consider the case where the x_i's are fairly uniformly distributed on $[0, 1]$.

$$a_{jk} = \sum_{i=1}^{n} x_i^{\,j+k} \approx n \int_0^1 x^{j+k}\, dx = \frac{n}{j + k + 1}$$

$$A = \begin{pmatrix} 1 & \frac{1}{2} & \frac{1}{3} & \cdots & \frac{1}{m+1} \\ \frac{1}{2} & \frac{1}{3} & \frac{1}{4} & \cdots & \frac{1}{m+2} \\ \frac{1}{3} & \frac{1}{4} & \frac{1}{5} & \cdots & \frac{1}{m+3} \\ \vdots & & & & \vdots \\ \frac{1}{m+1} & & & \cdots & \frac{1}{2m+1} \end{pmatrix}$$

Such a matrix is called a "Hilbert" matrix. As its elements are all ≤ 1 in value, its inverse has large elements. For $m = 9$, $\|A^{-1}\|_\infty = 2 \times 10^{13}$. The amplification factor is approximately 5×10^{13}. As experimental errors in the y_i's produce errors in the b_i's, a large amplification factor will result in a large round-off error in the solution for α according to the equation derived in the discussion of errors in Gaussian elimination.

$$\frac{1}{\|A\| \cdot \|A^{-1}\|} \cdot \frac{\|r\|}{\|b\|} \leq \frac{\|e\|}{\|\alpha\|} \leq \|A\| \cdot \|A^{-1}\| \cdot \frac{\|r\|}{\|b\|}$$

That is, the least-squares fitting problem is very ill-conditioned for polynomial approximating functions of high order. Performing all the computations in double precision may improve the reliability of the solution in such cases.

4.3   LAGRANGE INTERPOLATING POLYNOMIAL

A frequent requirement when approximating the value of a (possibly un-known) function over some interval is to ensure that the approximating function matches data values at a set of discrete points on that interval. A common choice of approximating function is a polynomial that passes through the data points. Suppose there are $n + 1$ points, (x_0, y_0), $(x_1, y_1),\ldots, (x_n, y_n)$. The goal is to find a polynomial that interpolates the function $y = f(x)$ on the interval $[x_0, x_n]$. In fact, there is only one such polynomial, which is of degree n, that satisfies this requirement although there are many ways of constructing it.

Suppose there were two such polynomials, $p(x)$ and $q(x)$ of degrees $\leqslant n$. Then the polynomial

$$h(x) = p(x) - q(x)$$

must also be of degree $\leqslant n$. At any one of the base points (x_i, y_i)

$$h(x_i) = p(x_i) - q(x_i) = f(x_i) - f(x_i) = 0$$

because at the base points an interpolating polynomial must equal the value of the function to be approximated. Therefore, there are $n + 1$ zeros of $h(x)$. However, the order of $h(x)$ is by definition no greater than n, and $h(x)$ cannot have more zeros than its order unless $h(x) = 0$ for all values of x. Thus, $p(x) = q(x)$.

Definition of the Interpolating Polynomial

To identify the algebraic form of $p(x)$ examine the special case of a function $f(x_i) = 0$ except at $x_i = x_k$. The function

$$g_k(x) = \prod_{\substack{i=0 \\ i \neq k}}^{n} (x - x_i)$$

$$= (x - x_0)(x - x_1) \cdots (x - x_{k-1})(x - x_{k+1}) \cdots (x - x_n)$$

is such a polynomial. It equals zero at all base points except x_k, and

$$g_k(x_k) = \prod_{i \neq k} (x_k - x_i) \neq 0$$

because each base point is distinct from the others. Normalizing $g_k(x)$ by dividing by $g_k(x_k)$ yields

$$l_k(x) = \frac{g_k(x)}{g_k(x_k)} = \prod_{i \neq k} \frac{x - x_i}{x_k - x_i}$$

and by substitution of x_i for x

$$l_k(x_i) = \begin{cases} 1, & i = k \\ 0, & i \neq k \end{cases}$$

Any arbitrary function can be interpolated by a linear combination of the l_k's, the "Lagrangian multipliers."

$$p(x) = \sum_{k=0}^{n} f(x_k) \, l_k(x).$$

This is analogous to defining an arbitrary vector as a linear combination of basis vectors. The Lagrangian multipliers are the unit vectors in an $n + 1$-dimensional space. This manner of writing the interpolating polynomial is called the "Lagrange form."

Example 4.3:

Let $n + 1 = 2$ with base points (x_0, y_0) and (x_1, y_1).

$$l_0(x) = \frac{x - x_1}{x_0 - x_1}$$

$$l_1(x) = \frac{x - x_0}{x_1 - x_0}$$

and $p(x) = f(x_0) \, l_0(x) + f(x_1) \, l_1(x)$.

$$p(x) = f(x_0) \frac{x - x_1}{x_0 - x_1} + f(x_1) \frac{x - x_0}{x_1 - x_0}$$

$$= \frac{f(x_0)(x - x_1) - f(x_1)(x - x_0)}{x_0 - x_1}$$

Rearranging this equation gives

$$p(x) = f(x_0) + \underbrace{\frac{f(x_1) - f(x_0)}{x_1 - x_0}}(x - x_0)$$

slope of straight
line between x_0
and x_1

In this case the interpolating polynomial performs a linear interpolation between the base points to get an estimate of $f(x)$ at an intermediate value. If function values at three base points are available, quadratic interpolation would be performed.

Example 4.4:

$$y = \sin x.$$

Given the following base points, estimate the value of sin 23° to five decimal places.

i	x_i	y_i
0	20°	0.34202
1	22°	0.37461
2	24°	0.40674
3	26°	0.43837

$$l_0(x) = \prod_{i \neq 0} \frac{x - x_i}{x_0 - x_i} = \frac{x - x_1}{x_0 - x_1} \times \frac{x - x_2}{x_0 - x_2} \times \frac{x - x_3}{x_0 - x_3} = -0.0625$$

$$l_1(x) = \prod_{i \neq 1} \frac{x - x_i}{x_1 - x_i} = \frac{x - x_0}{x_1 - x_0} \times \frac{x - x_2}{x_1 - x_2} \times \frac{x - x_3}{x_1 - x_3} = 0.5625$$

$$l_2(x) = \prod_{i \neq 2} \frac{x - x_i}{x_2 - x_i} = \frac{x - x_0}{x_2 - x_0} \times \frac{x - x_i}{x_2 - x} \times \frac{x - x_3}{x_2 - x_3} = 0.5625$$

$$l_3(x) = \prod_{i \neq 3} \frac{x - x_i}{x_3 - x_i} = \frac{x - x_0}{x_3 - x_0} \times \frac{x - x_1}{x_3 - x_1} \times \frac{x - x_2}{x_3 - x_2} = -0.0625$$

From the formula

$$p(x) = \sum_{i=0}^{3} f(x_i) \, l_i(x)$$

$$p(x) = (0.34202)(-0.025) + (0.37461)(0.5625) + (0.40674)(0.5625)$$
$$+ (0.43837)(-0.0625)$$

$$= 0.39074$$

The true value of sin 23° to five decimal places is 0.39073. The discrepancy is due to the accumulation of round-off error.

Efficiency of the Lagrange Form

The above example with four base points required the evaluation of five polynomials, the four Lagrange multipliers and $p(x)$ itself. This seems inefficient, and it is a bad method to use if interpolated function values are desired only at a few points. However, the method is efficient if a large number of interpolations ($> n + 1$) must be performed using the same base points. By careful planning, the amount of computation can be reduced. The constant factors

$$\prod_{i \neq k} \frac{f(x_k)}{(x_k - x_i)}$$

can be computed only once and multiplied by the corresponding $\Pi(x - x_i)$, $i \neq k$, for each value of x at which an interpolation is desired. Furthermore, as the product of variable factors is equivalent to

$$\prod_{i=0}^{n} \frac{(x - x_i)}{(x - x_k)}$$

the extended product in the numerator need be calculated only once. A single division is then necessary instead of $n - 2$ multiplications.

4.4 NEWTON FORM OF THE INTERPOLATING POLYNOMIAL

Deficiencies of the Lagrange Form of the Interpolating Polynomial

It was stated in the last section that use of the Lagrange form of the interpolating polynomial is inefficient for a small number of interpolations using the same base points. After the constant denominators of the unit Lagrange multipliers have been calculated for $n + 1$ base points, it requires about $2(n + 1)$ multiplications (or divisions) and $2n + 1$ additions (or subtractions) to evaluate $p(x)$. In contrast, Horner's method only requires n multiplications and n additions to evaluate a polynomial of degree n. The extra work is required to calculate the coefficients of the interpolating polynomial.

If the optimal degree of the interpolating polynomial is unknown, all this work must be repeated should one trial degree turn out to be inadequate and a higher degree necessary. The Lagrange form does not make use of $l_i(x)$ to calculate $l_{i+1}(x)$, as all base points must be known to compute each multiplier. Because of the large investment in computing the coefficients of the interpolating polynomial, efficiency would be increased if all the computation performed for degree n could be used to reduce the computation necessary for degree $n + 1$.

Newton Form of the Interpolating Polynomial

It was shown for the case of two base points that the interpolating polynomial is given by

$$\sum_{k=0}^{n} l_i(x) f(x_i) = \sum_{i=0}^{n} f(x_i) \prod_{k \neq i} \frac{x - x_k}{x_i - x_k}$$

$$= \frac{f(x_1) - f(x_0)}{x_1 - x_0} (x - x_0)$$

The coefficient of $(x - x_0)$ is called a "divided difference"; it is a linear approximation to the derivative of $f(x)$ over the interval $[x_0, x_1]$. In fact, there must be at least one point x' on this interval where the derivative does equal this value as illustrated in Fig. 4.4. However, unless the value of x at which an approximation to $f(x)$ is desired is close to x', higher order terms (analogous to a Taylor series) are needed to obtain an accurate interpolation.

Assuming that x_0 and x_1 and the linear function $p_1(x)$ are known, how can a new base point x_2 be used to find the quadratic interpolating polynomial $p_2(x)$? More generally, if we have $p_k(x)$, how can we efficiently identify $p_{k+1}(x)$? Consider the function

$$h(x) = p_k(x) - p_{k-1}(x)$$

By definition of the interpolating polynomial, $h(x_i)$ is zero for all k base points of $p_k(x)$. Therefore $h(x)$ is of degree k and can be written as

$$h(x) = A_k(x - x_0)(x - x_1) \cdots (x - x_{k-1})$$

An expression for the coefficient A_k can be derived from the Lagrange polynomial formula.

$$p_k(x) = A_k x^k + \text{a polynomial of degree} < k$$

and the kth derivative with respect to x is

$$p_k^{(k)}(x) = k! \, A_k$$

The contribution to the kth derivative by lower order terms equals zero. A_k is called the "kth divided difference," a generalization of the linear

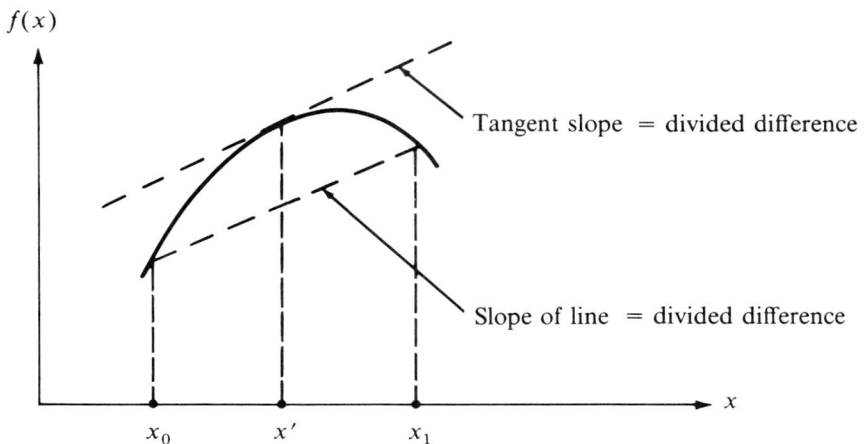

Fig. 4.4. Graphical comparison of the derivative (slope of the tangent) to the divided difference (slope of the secant).

case where the (first) divided difference is an approximation to the derivative $f'(x)$.

Substituting this definition into the Lagrange formula yields

$$p_k(x) = \sum_{i=0}^{k} f(x_i) \prod_{\substack{j=0 \\ j \neq i}}^{k} \frac{x - x_j}{x_i - x_j}$$

$$= \boxed{\frac{\displaystyle\sum_{i=0}^{k} f(x_i)}{\displaystyle\prod_{\substack{j=0 \\ j \neq i}}^{k} (x_i - x_j)}} \prod_{j=0}^{k-1} (x - x_j) + \text{a polynomial of degree} < k$$

The part of the equation in the box is A_k and is the coefficient of x^k as required by the equation for $h(x)$ above. Note that the indices of the sum and product go from zero to k whereas they go from zero to $k - 1$ for $p_{k-1}(x)$. Thus, to increase the degree of the interpolating polynomial by adding one base point, only one divided difference A_k need be calculated. The coefficients A_0 through A_{k-1} computed for $p_{k-1}(x)$ are still the coefficients of the lower order terms of $p_k(x)$. Furthermore, A_k can be computed from A_{k-1} by dividing each term by the appropriate $(x_i - x_j)$ and adding one more term in the above expansion.

Computing Divided Differences

The following notation is used to represent a divided difference. The base points needed to compute A_k are listed inside the square brackets.

$$A_k = f[x_0, x_1, \ldots, x_k] = \frac{\displaystyle\sum_{i=0}^{k} f(x_i)}{\displaystyle\prod_{\substack{j=0 \\ j \neq i}}^{k} (x_i - x_j)}$$

Note that there is a symmetry in this formula. It does not make any difference in what order the k base points are arranged, the result will always be the same.

Example 4.5:

For two base points, $k = 1$

$$f[x_0, x_1] = \frac{f(x_0)}{x_0 - x_1} + \frac{f(x_1)}{x_1 - x_0}$$

$$= \frac{f(x_0) - f(x_1)}{x_0 - x_1}$$

which, as was shown before, is the linear approximation to the derivative over $[x_0, x_1]$.

For three base points, $k = 2$:

$$f[x_0, x_1, x_3] = \frac{f(x_0)}{(x_0 - x_1)(x_0 - x_3)} + \frac{f(x_1)}{(x_1 - x_0)(x_1 - x_3)}$$

$$+ \frac{f(x_3)}{(x_3 - x_0)(x_3 - x_1)}$$

$$= \frac{f[x_0, x_1] - f[x_1, x_3]}{x_0 - x_3}$$

This is clearly a linear approximation to the derivative of the first derivative. In general, the kth divided difference is the first divided difference of any two $k - 1$st divided differences.

Define the zeroth divided difference as

$$f[x_0] = f(x_0)$$

and substitute into the expansion for $p(x)$.

$$p_n(x) = f[x_0] + f[x_0, x_1](x - x_0) + f[x_0, x_1, x_2](x - x_0)$$

$$(x - x_1) + \cdots + f[x_0, x_1, \ldots, x_n](x - x_0)(x - x_1)(x - x_k)$$

Written more compactly,

$$p_n(x) = \sum_{i=0}^{n} f[x_0, x_1, \ldots, x_i] \prod_{j=0}^{i-1} (x - x_j)$$

This is the Newton form of the interpolating polynomial. Once the divided differences A_k have been computed, Horner's method can be used to efficiently evaluate $p_k(x)$.

Algorithm

$$b_n = A_n$$
for $k = n-1, n-2, \ldots, 0$ do
$$b_k = A_k + (x - x_k)b_{k+1}$$
$$p(x) = b_0.$$

4.5 DIVIDED DIFFERENCE TABLE

The Newton form of the interpolating polynomial provides greater flexibility in the identification of the degree of polynomial that would serve best in a given application than does the Lagrange form. This is because the constant coefficients (the divided differences) in the Newton form can be computed from the coefficients obtained from a lower degree trial polynomial as described in the preceding chapter.

Example 4.6:

Find sin 23°

i	x_i	sin x_i
0	20°	0.34202
1	22°	0.37461
2	24°	0.40674
3	26°	0.43837

Step 1: find the divided differences.

$$A_0 = f[x_0] = f(x_0) = 0.34202$$

$$A_1 = f[x_0, x_1] = \frac{\sum_{i=0}^{1} f(x_i)}{\prod_{\substack{j=0 \\ j \neq i}}^{1} (x_i - x)} = \frac{f(x_0)}{x_0 - x_1} + \frac{f(x_1)}{x_1 - x_0}$$

$$= \frac{0.34202}{20 - 22} + \frac{0.37461}{22 - 20} = 0.016295$$

$$A_2 = f[x_0, x_1, x_2] = \frac{f(x_0)}{(x_0 - x_1)(x_0 - x_2)} + \frac{f(x_i)}{(x_1 - x_0)(x_1 - x_2)}$$

$$+ \frac{f(x_2)}{(x_2 - x_0)(x_2 - x_i)}$$

$$= \frac{-0.17101}{20 - 24} + \frac{0.18731}{22 - 24} + \frac{0.40674}{(24 - 20)(24 - 22)}$$

$$= 6.00 \times 10^{-5}$$

Notice how the values for the terms in the expansion for A_1 were used to minimize the calculation necessary to evaluate A_2. Using the three terms in the expansion for A_2 in a similar way yields

$$A_3 = \frac{4.2753 \times 10^{-2}}{20 - 26} - \frac{9.3655 \times 10^{-2}}{22 - 26} + \frac{5.0843 \times 10^{-2}}{24 - 26}$$

$$+ \frac{0.42837}{(26 - 20)(26 - 22)(26 - 24)}$$

$$= -5.4167 \times 10^{-7}$$

Step 2: Perform the nested multiplication (Horner's method) to evaluate the interpolating polynomial $p_3(x)$.

$b_3 = -5.4167 \times 10^{-7}$

$b_2 = -6.00 \times 10^{-5} - 5.4167 \times 10^{-7} (23 - 24) = -5.9458 \times 10^{-5}$

$b_1 = 0.016295 - 5.9458 \times 10^{-5} (23 - 22) = 0.016236$

$b_0 = 0.34202 + 0.016236 (23 - 20) = 0.39073$

This is the correct answer to five decimal places. The discrepancy between this result and that obtained with the Lagrange form of the interpolating polynomial is due to the greater accumulation of roundoff error with the latter method owing to its greater number of arithmetic operations.

Recursive Algorithm for Divided Differences

Even using the relationship between terms in the expansions for the divided differences, it required a great deal of computation to evaluate them. There is a still more efficient method for their evaluation. The definition of divided differences indicate that they can be written as polynomials, b_i, in $(x_n - x_i)$.

$$p(x) = b_0 + b_i (x - x_n) + b_2 (x - x_n)(x - x_0)$$

$$+ \cdots + b_n(x - x_n)(x - x_0) \cdots (x - x_{n-2})$$

This involves rearranging the base points in the order $x_n, x_0, x_1, \ldots, x_{n-1}$. Then apply Horner's method to evaluate these polynomials.

$$b_n = f[x_0, \ldots, x_n]$$
$$\text{For } i = n-1, n-2, \ldots, 0 \text{ do}$$
$$b_i = f[x_0, \ldots, x_i] + (x_n - x_i)b_{i+1}$$

Thus,

$$b_n = (b_{n-1} - f[x_0, \ldots, x_{n-1}])/(x_n - x_{n-1}).$$

The b_is are divided differences in the rearranged order of the base points.

$$b_i = f[x_n, x_0, \ldots, x_{i-1}]$$

Substituting this definition of b_i into the above recursive formula for b_L gives

$$f[x_0, \ldots, x_n] = (f[x_n, x_0, \ldots, x_{n-2}] - f[x_0, x_1, \ldots, x_{n-1}])/(x_n - x_{n-1}).$$

The divided difference on the left side of this equation spans $n + 1$ base points and that on the right side spans n base points. The x values in the denominator, x_n and x_{n-1} are the base points that the two divided differences in the numerator do not have in common. Thus, an nth divided difference is the divided difference between two $n - 1$st divided differences, as was shown previously for the second order case.

Divided Difference Table

This result can be used to generate a table of divided differences.

i	x_i	0th DD	1st DD	2nd DD	3rd DD
0	x_0 $f(x_0)$		$\dfrac{f[x_0] - f[x_1]}{x_0 - x_1}$	$\dfrac{f[x_0, x_1] - f[x_1, x_2]}{x_0 - x_2}$	$\dfrac{f[x_0, x_1, x_2] - f[x_1, x_2, x_3]}{x_0 - x_3}$
1	x_1 $f(x_1)$		$\dfrac{f[x_1] - f[x_2]}{x_1 - x_2}$	$\dfrac{f[x_1, x_2] - f[x_2, x_3]}{x_1 - x_3}$	
2	x_2 $f(x_2)$		$\dfrac{f[x_2] - f[x_3]}{x_2 - x_3}$		
3	x_3 $f(x_3)$				

The denominator of each entry has the x values for the range of base points spanned by the corresponding divided difference. Note that there is a unique nth divided difference for $n + 1$ base points. The function value for any base point can be used as $f[x_0]$ in the Newton expansion, and any path across the table reaches the same nth divided difference. The natural way to traverse the table is to start at x_0, add x_1 to obtain $f[x_0, x_1]$, and so on, following the top diagonal to the final divided difference.

Advantages of the Newton Form

As two $i - 1$st divided differences are required to compute an ith divided difference by the recursive method, the entire table must always be computed. However, at each step, only two subtractions and one division are required instead of computing an extended product. Furthermore, because of the recursive nature of the algorithm, to increase the degree of the interpolating polynomial a new top (or bottom) diagonal for the table is all that must be calculated; the rest of the table is unchanged.

Note that it is only necessary to store the top diagonal when computing the divided differences. As the jth divided differences are computed, they can overwrite the $j - 1$st divided differences from index j to index n.

Algorithm

For $i = 0,..., n$ do

$d_i = f(x_i)$ (Insert original function values)

For $i = 0,\ldots, n-1$ do

    For $j = i + 1,\ldots, n$ do

        $d_j = (d_{j-1} - d_j)/(x_{j-i} - x_j)$ (Compute jth divided differences)

The final values in the array d will be the top diagonal of the table; d_0 will contain $f[x_0]$, d_1 will contain $f[x_0, x_1]$, and so on.

4.6 AITKEN LINEAR INTERPOLATION METHOD

In order to perform polynomial interpolation $n + 1$ Lagrange multipliers or $n + 1$ Newton divided differences must be computed before calculating the expansion for $p_n(x)$ at the x value for which an approximation to $f(x)$ is desired. Although $p_n(x)$ itself may be computed efficiently, there is a high initial cost in calculating the above constant factors for a given set of base points. If many interpolations ($> n + 1$) are to be evaluated using the same base points, calculation of the Lagrange multipliers would be most efficient. If only a few interpolations are to be evaluated, calculation of the Newton divided differences would be most efficient. However, if exactly one interpolation is to be evaluated, a method which avoids the high initial computational investment is needed.

Iterated Linear Interpolation

Let $y_{0,1,\ldots,k} = p_k(x)$, where the subscripts of y are the subscripts of the base points used in evaluating $p_k(x)$, the interpolating polynomial of degree k, and x is the value at which some function $f(x)$ is to be interpolated. Further, define $y_i = f(x_i)$, the function value at base point i. Then the formula

$$y_{0,1,\ldots,k} = \frac{\begin{vmatrix} y_{0,1,\ldots,k-1} & x_{k-1} - x \\ y_{0,1,\ldots,k-3,k} & x_k - x \end{vmatrix}}{x_k - x_{k-1}}$$

gives the value of $p_k(x)$. Note that the first column of the determinant contains the interpolated value of $f(x)$ using $k - $ 1st-degree polynomials constructed with the base points $x_0, x_1,\ldots, x_k$. The value at the top of the column comes from eliminating x_k from the list of base points; the value at the bottom of the column comes from eliminating x_{k-1} from the list. The base points in the second column are arranged so that when the determinant is evaluated by cross multiplication, two polynomials of degree k result (all $k + 1$ base points are used). The difference between the values of these two polynomials is divided by the difference between the x values that the polynomials do not have in common (analogous to the procedure used to compute divided differences). The result is a polynomial of degree k which is a linear interpolation between two polynomials of degree $k - 1$.

Two interpolates of degree $n - 1$ are required to evaluate $p_n(x)$. To obtain each $p_{n-1}(x)$ requires two interpolates of degree $n - 2$, and so on until n interpolates of degree 1 are needed to evaluate $n + 1$ interpolates of degree zero. By definition, the zeroth degree interpolates are the function values at the base points. Using the above scheme, a triangular table of interpolations can be constructed. Starting with the y_i's, the n first order interpolates $y_{0,i}$, $i = 1,\ldots, n$, can be constructed. Then these values are used to compute the $n - 1$ second order interpolates $y_{0,1,i}$, and so on until the table is complete.

$$
\begin{array}{llll}
y_0 & & & \\
y_1 & y_{0,1} & & \\
y_2 & y_{0,2} & y_{0,1,2} & \\
\vdots & \vdots & \vdots & \cdots \ y_{0,1,\ldots,n-1} \\
y_n & y_{0,n} & y_{0,1,n} & \qquad y_{0,1,\ldots,n-2,n} \ \ y_{0,1,\ldots,n}
\end{array}
$$

Note that the indices for the elements of the ith column are obtained by adding the appropriate row index to the subscripts for the top element of the $i - 1$st column. The last entry on the last row of the table is the desired value of $p_n(x)$.

Example 4.7:

$$f(x) = \sin 23°$$

i	x_i	$\sin x_i$
0	20°	0.34202
1	22°	0.37461
2	24°	0.40674
3	26°	0.43837

The values for $\sin x_i$ constitute the first column of the triangular table.

Step 1: Calculate the $y_{0,1}$'s (second column of table).

$$
y_{0,1} = \frac{\begin{vmatrix} y_0 & x_0 - x \\ y_1 & x_1 - x \end{vmatrix}}{x_1 - x_0} = \frac{\begin{vmatrix} 0.34202 & 20 - 23 \\ 0.37461 & 22 - 23 \end{vmatrix}}{22 - 20}
$$

$$= 0.39091$$

$$
y_{0,2} = \frac{\begin{vmatrix} y_0 & x_0 - x \\ y_2 & x_2 - x \end{vmatrix}}{x_2 - x_0} = \frac{\begin{vmatrix} 0.34202 & 20 - 23 \\ 0.40674 & 24 - 23 \end{vmatrix}}{24 - 20}
$$

$$= 0.39056$$

$$y_{0.3} = \frac{\begin{vmatrix} y_0 & x_0 - x \\ y_3 & x_3 - x \end{vmatrix}}{x_3 - x_0} = \frac{\begin{vmatrix} 0.34202 & 20 - 23 \\ 0.43837 & 26 - 23 \end{vmatrix}}{26 - 20}$$

$$= 0.39020$$

Step 2: Calculate $y_{0.1.i}$'s (third column).

$$y_{0.1.2} = \frac{\begin{vmatrix} y_{0.1} & x_1 - x \\ y_{0.2} & x_2 - x \end{vmatrix}}{x_2 - x_1} = \frac{\begin{vmatrix} 0.39091 & 22 - 23 \\ 0.39056 & 24 - 23 \end{vmatrix}}{24 - 22}$$

$$= 0.39074$$

$$y_{0.1.3} = \frac{\begin{vmatrix} y_{0.1} & x_1 - x \\ y_{0.3} & x_3 - x \end{vmatrix}}{x_3 - x_1} = \frac{\begin{vmatrix} 0.39091 & 22 - 23 \\ 0.39020 & 26 - 23 \end{vmatrix}}{26 - 22}$$

$$= 0.39073$$

Step 3: Calculate $y_{0.1.2.3}$ (final value of table and value of $p_3(x)$).

$$y_{0.1.2.3} = \frac{\begin{vmatrix} y_{0.1.2} & x_2 - x \\ y_{0.1.3} & x_3 - x \end{vmatrix}}{x_3 - x_2} = \frac{\begin{vmatrix} 0.39074 & 24 - 23 \\ 0.39073 & 26 - 23 \end{vmatrix}}{26 - 24}$$

$$= 0.39074$$

The full triangular table is:

```
0.34202
0.37461   0.39091
0.40674   0.39056   0.39074
0.43837   0.39020   0.39073   0.39074
```

The interpolated value of 0.39074 is the same result as obtained with the Lagrange formula. The discrepancy between it and the true value of sin 23°, i.e., 0.39073, is due to round-off error. Although the numerical results may differ if a sufficient number of decimal places are not carried in the calculation, all three forms of the interpolating polynomial, Lagrange, Newton, and Aitken, represent the identical polynomial.

4.7 APPROXIMATION ERROR IN LAGRANGE INTERPOLATION

Because the function value obtained using the Lagrange interpolating polynomial $p_n(x)$ is only an estimate of the true function value, the calculated quantity includes approximation error. To be assured that the estimate is reliable we must have a measure of the upper limit of the approximation error. If the upper limit of the error is within an acceptable tolerance, the estimate may be considered reliable.

The error at x is given by

$$e_n(x) = f(x) - p_n(x) = R(x)$$

where $R(x)$ is called the "remainder." One way to estimate the value of the remainder is to add another base point to the set of points used to define $p_n(x)$ and calculate $p_{n+1}(x)$. The analogy between the Newton form of the interpolating polynomial and a Taylor series suggests that the error is dominated by the $n + 2$nd term of $p_{n+1}(x)$.

$$e_n(x) \approx R_n(x) = p_{n+1}(x) - p_n(x) = f[x_0, x_1,\ldots, x_n, x_{n+1}] \prod_{j=0}^{n} (x - x_j)$$

The implication is that a better approximation to $f(x)$ would be obtained if an interpolating polynomial of still higher degree were used but that for convenience the polynomial was truncated after the nth degree term. For this reason, the error is sometimes referred to as "truncation error." However, this is only an estimate of the error; what is needed is an upper bound.

Derivation of the Error Formula

Rolle's theorem from calculus states that if a function $f(x)$ is continuous on an interval $[a, b]$ and is differentiable on (a, b), and $f(a) = f(b)$, then $f'(\xi) = 0$ for at least one value ξ on (a, b). $R_n(x) = e_n(x) = 0$ at the base points, but the error is generally nonzero for points in between the base points. However, by Rolle's theorem there is at least one value ξ between two adjacent base points where the derivative $e_n'(x)$ is zero. For a polynomial of degree n there must be at least n points where $e_n'(x) = 0$. By a similar argument, there must be at least $n - 1$ points where $e_n''(x) = 0$, and so on, demonstrating that there must be at least one point on the interval (x_0, x_n) where $e_n^{(n)}(x) = 0$.

The function

$$g(x) = f(x) - p_n(x) - R_n(x)$$

is one degree higher than $p_n(x)$, so it has at least $n + 2$ zeroes. Then $g'(x)$ has at least $n + 1$ zeroes, $g''(x)$ has at least n zeroes, and so on, to obtain at least one zero for $g^{(n+1)}(x)$, say at $x = \xi$. As $p_n^{(n+1)}(x) = 0$,

$$g^{(n+1)}(\xi) = 0 = f^{(n+1)}(\xi) - (n + 1)! \, f[x_0, x_1,\ldots, x_n, x_{n+1}]$$

Recall that

$$f[x_0, x_1,\ldots, x_n, x_{n+1}] = f^{(n+1)}(\xi)/(n + 1)!$$

indicating that at the point $x = \xi$ the divided difference can be replaced by the derivative divided by $(n + 1)!$ if $f(x)$ is known analytically.

$$e_n(x) = R_n(x) = \frac{f^{(n+1)}(x)}{(n + 1)!} \prod_{j=0}^{n} (x - x_j)$$

At the base points, $e_n(x_j) = 0$. By the mean value theorem there must be at least one $x = \xi$ such that $e_n(x) = 0$ exactly.

$$e_n(x) = f(x) - p_n(x) = \frac{f^{(n+1)}(\xi)}{(n + 1)!} \prod_{j=0}^{n} (x - x_j)$$

We usually do not know ξ, but if $f(x)$ is analytically differentiable we can find a ξ for which $f^{(n+1)}(\xi)$, hence $R_n(x)$, is maximal.

$$e_n(x) = f(x) - p_n(x) = \frac{f^{(n+1)}(\xi)}{(n + 1)!} \prod_{j=0}^{n} (x - x_j)$$

This gives the desired upper bound for the approximation error.

Example 4.8:

What is the maximal truncation error in estimating sin 23° from the four base points 20°, 22°, 24°, and 26°?

$$e_3(x) = e_3(23) = \frac{f^{(4)}(\xi)}{4!} \prod_{j=0}^{3} (23 - x_j)$$

The fourth derivative of sin x equals sin x, which is maximal on this interval at $\xi = 26°$.

sin 26°/4! = 0.43837/24 = 0.018265

$e_3(23°) = 0.018265 (23 - 20)(23 - 22)(23 - 24)(23 - 26) = 0.16439$

This is an extremely large error, especially in view of the fact that the interpolation with $p_3(x)$ did produce the correct answer. The reason for this result is that the derivative of sin x is cos x and the derivative of cos x is $-(\sin x)$ only if x is in radians. Converting x to radians by multiplying by $\pi/180$ gives

$$e_3(23°) = 0.16439 (\pi/180)^4 = 1.5254 \times 10^{-8}$$

This result seems extremely small. In fact, the actual error was 10^{-5} when the Lagrange and Aitken methods were used. This illustrates the difference between approximation error (due to truncation of the interpolating polynomial after the cubic term) and round-off error (due to carrying only five decimal places in the calculation). Finally, note that, regardless of which interpolation formula is used, the truncation error is exactly the same because the three forms of $p(x)$ are representations of the same polynomial.

4.8 GREGORY-NEWTON INTERPOLATION

Equally Spaced Base Points

Before the advent of high-speed digital computers, scientists and engineers calculated the values of some functions, such as sine and logarithm, by linear interpolation between the tabulated values at the two base points nearest the desired value of the independent variable. The tabulated points were usually equally spaced. In such a situation computation of the interpolating polynomial for an arbitrary number of base points can be simplified.

The Forward Difference Operator

Equally spaced base points for a variable x on the interval $[a, b]$ can be represented as

$$x_0 = a$$

$$x_i = a + ih \qquad i = 0, 1,..., n \qquad h = (b - a)/n$$

$$x_n = b$$

where n is the number of base points on the interval and h is the difference between successive points. The forward difference operator Δ is defined by

$$\Delta f(x) = f(x + h) - f(x)$$

$$\Delta^2 f(x) = \Delta(\Delta f(x)) = \Delta f(x + h) - \Delta f(x)$$

$$.$$

$$.$$

$$.$$

$$\Delta^n f(x) = \Delta^{n-1} f(x + h) - \Delta^{n-1} f(x)$$

The nth forward difference is the first forward difference between two $n - 1$st forward differences. A forward difference is identical to the numerator of the corresponding divided difference; so it is not surprising that there is a relationship between the two.

$$f[x_1, x_0] = \frac{f(x_1) - f(x_0)}{x_1 - x_0} = \frac{\Delta f(x_0)}{h}$$

$$f[x_2, x_1, x_0] = \frac{\dfrac{f(x_2) - f(x_1)}{x_2 - x_1} - \dfrac{f(x_1) - f(x_0)}{x_1 - x_0}}{x_2 - x_0}$$

$$= \frac{\Delta^2 f(x_0)}{2h^2}$$

and so forth. In general,

$$f[x_n, x_{n-1}, \ldots, x_0] = \frac{\Delta^n f(x_0)}{n!\, h^n}$$

We can set up a table of forward differences that is analogous to the divided difference table. Because h is constant, the denominators of the corresponding divided differences can be inserted into the Newton formula later. The result is

$$p_n(x) = \sum_{i=0}^{n} \frac{\Delta^i f_0}{i!\, h^i} \prod_{j=0}^{i-1} (x - x_j)$$

which is called the "Gregory-Newton forward difference" formula.

A Simplified Notation

For convenience we introduce a change of variable. If x is the value at which an interpolation is desired,

$$f(x) = f(x_0 + sh) = f(a + sh) = f_s \qquad s = (x - a)/h$$

where s is the number of increments of length h required to get from a to x. Further, let the zeroth forward difference be

$$\Delta^0 f(x_k) = f[x_k] = f(x_k) = f_k$$

The deviation of x from each base point is given by

$$x - x_j = x_0 + sh - (x_0 + hj) = h(s - j)$$

and the interpolating polynomial becomes a polynomial in s.

$$p_n(x) = p_n(x_0 + sh) = \sum_{i=0}^{n} \frac{\Delta^i f_0}{i!\, h^i} \prod_{j=0}^{i-1} \frac{s - j}{j + 1}$$

$$\prod_{j=0}^{i-1} \frac{s - j}{j + 1} = \frac{s - 0}{j + 1} \times \frac{s - 1}{j + 1} \times \frac{s - 2}{j + 1} \cdots \frac{s - i + 1}{j + 1}$$

$$= \frac{s(s - 1)(s - 2) \cdots (s - i + 1)}{i!}$$

Suppose s is an integer. If the numerator of the above extended product had the additional factors $(s - i)!$, it would equal $s!$ and the product could be written as

$$\frac{s!}{(s - i)!\, i!} = \binom{s}{i}$$

(that is, as a binomial coefficient). The compact form of the Gregory-Newton formula becomes

$$p_n(x_0 + sh) = \sum_{i=0}^{n} \Delta^i f_0 \binom{s}{i}$$

Of course, s is not necessarily an integer, but we can still use the binomial coefficient symbol as an abbreviated representation of the extended product as long as we recognize that it is only a metaphor.

The Backward Difference Operator

Suppose there is a table of function values at equally spaced points from which $x_0, x, \ldots, x_n$ were selected in order to obtain an accurate interpolation of the function at some x value in the interval $[x_0, x_n]$. The next desired interpolation is for $x_0 - sh$, where s is a small number. Extrapolating $p_n(x)$ outside the interval may lead to great inaccuracy. Redefining the location of x_0 is clumsy. It would require remembering the changed numbering of the base points, an onerous chore if many interpolations are desired.

This problem is most conveniently solved by introducing backward differences, which form the same triangular table as forward differences. The only distinction is the order in which the base points are numbered. Forward differences begin with x_0 and end with x_n whereas backward differences begin with x_{-n} and end with x_0. The backward difference operator is defined as

$$\nabla f(x) = f(x) - f(x - h)$$
$$\nabla^2 f(x) = \nabla f(x)\, \nabla f(x - h)$$

.

.

.

$$\nabla^n f(x) = \nabla^{n-1} f(x) - \nabla^{n-1} f(x - h)$$
$$\text{Note: } \nabla^n f(x_i) = \Delta^{n-1} f(x_{i+1})$$

Substituting these definitions into the Newton formula for the interpolating polynomial yields

$$p_n(x) = \sum_{i=0}^{n} f\,[x_{-i}, x_{-i+1}, \ldots, x_0] \prod_{j=-i+1}^{0} (x - x_j)$$

$$= \sum_{i=0}^{n} \frac{\nabla^i f_{-i}}{i!\, h^i} \prod_{j=-i+1}^{0} (x - x_j)$$

Converting to s variables gives the backward difference Gregory-Newton formula

$$p_n(x_0 + sh) = \sum_{i=0}^{n} (-1)^i \nabla^i f_{-i} \binom{-s}{i}$$

Thus, instead of following the top diagonal of the forward difference table, the backward difference formula follows the bottom diagonal.

4.9 FORWARD DIFFERENCE TABLE

The coefficients of the Gregory-Newton form of the interpolating polynomial can be most efficiently computed by a triangular table of forward differences analogous to the divided difference table. The distinction is that forward differences are not divided by $x_i - x_j$, where i and j indicate the range of base points used in defining the difference. This denominator is not needed because it is known to be a multiple of h, the spacing between the base points.

x_{-3}	$f(x_{-3})$				
		Δf_{-3}			
x_{-2}	$f(x_{-2})$		$\Delta^2 f_{-3}$		
		Δf_{-2}		$\Delta^3 f_{-3}$	
x_{-1}	$f(x_{-1})$		$\Delta^2 f_{-2}$		$\Delta^3 f_{-2}$
		Δf_{-1}		$\Delta^3 f_{-2}$	... etc.
x_0	$f(x_0)$		$\Delta^2 f_{-1}$	$\Delta^3 f_{-1}$	
		Δf_0			
x_1	$f(x_1)$		$\Delta^2 f_0$	$\Delta^3 f_0$	
		Δf_1			
x_2	$f(x_2)$		$\Delta^2 f_1$	$\Delta^3 f_1$	
		Δf_2			
x_i	$f(x_3)$		$\Delta^2 f_2$		

Starting from x_0 and following a downward diagonal brings us to $\Delta^3 f_0$ after three applications of the forward difference formula. Following an upward diagonal from x_0 brings us to $\Delta^3 f_{-3}$ after three applications of the backward difference formula. Following the top diagonal of the table also brings us to $\Delta^3 f_{-3}$ after three applications of the forward difference formula. This property illustrates that

$$\Delta^2 f_{-3} = \nabla^3 f_0$$

and that forward and backward differences are numerically equivalent, differing only in the number of the base points.

Error Analysis for Gregory-Newton Interpolation

As the Newton form of an nth degree interpolating polynomial is analogous to a Taylor series, truncation of the series after the $n + 1$st degree term should yield a good value for the approximation error. The example given earlier to illustrate use of the Newton form of the interpolating polynomial indicated that the numerical values of the divided differences tend to decrease with increasing order of the divided difference. Therefore, the truncated terms should be small. If an $n + 2$nd base point were available, computation of the $n + 1$st forward (or backward) difference can be substituted into the Newton formula for the remainder to give

$$R_n(x_0 + hs) = \frac{\Delta^{n+1}f(x_0)}{(n + 1)!} \prod_{j=0}^{n} (s - j) = \Delta^{n+1}f_0 \binom{s}{n + 1}$$

using forward differences and

$$R_n(x_0 + hs) = \frac{\nabla^{n+1}f(x_{-n})}{(n + 1)!} \prod_{j=0}^{n} (s - j) = \nabla^{n+1}f_{-n} \binom{s}{n + 1}$$

for backward differences.

Example 4.9:

i	x_i	f_i	Δ	Δ^2	Δ^3
0	1	1.000			
			0.414		
1	2	1.414		−0.096	
			0.318		0.046
2	3	1.732		−0.050	
			0.268		
3	4	2.000			

Find the interpolated value of $f(2.5)$ to three decimal places. Using the forward difference formula yields:

$$p_3(2.5) = \sum_{i=0}^{3} \Delta^i f_0 \binom{s}{i}; \quad s = (2.5 - 1)/1 = 1.5$$

$$= 1.0 + 0.414 \frac{(1.5)}{1} - 0.096 \frac{(1/5)(0.5)}{(2)(1)} + 0.046 \frac{(1.5)(0.5)(-0.5)}{(3)(2)(1)}$$

$$= 1.582$$

To use the backward difference formula follow the bottom diagonal of the table.

Suppose a fifth base point $x = 5$, $f(x) = 2.236$ is given. A new bottom diagonal can be added to the forward difference table, and the interpolation error using the above four base points will be approximated by the fifth term of the Gregory-Newton formula.

i	x_i	f_i	Δ	Δ^2	Δ^3	Δ^4
0	1	1.000				
			0.414			
1	2	1.414		−0.096		
			0.318		0.046	
2	3	1.732		−0.050		−0.028
			0.268		0.018	
3	4	2.000		−0.032		
			0.236			
4	5	2.236				

$$e_3\,(x) \le \left| \Delta^4 f_0 \begin{pmatrix} 1.5 \\ 4 \end{pmatrix} \right| = \left| (-0.028)\,\frac{(1.5)(0.5)(-0.5)(-1.5)}{(4)(3)(2)(1)} \right|$$

$$e_3\,(x) \le 0.001$$

Suppose we are now told that $f(x) = \sqrt{x}$.

$$\sqrt{2.5} = 1.581$$

which does, in fact, differ from the interpolated value by $e_3(x)$. Note that this approach gives an estimate of the approximation error. To obtain an upper bound for the error, the $n + 1$st derivative of the analytical function $f(x)$ must be evaluated.

$$e_3\,(2.5) = \frac{f^{(4)}(\xi)}{4!} \prod_{j=0}^{3} (2.5 - x_j)$$

In the present case the fourth derivative is given by

$$f(x) = \sqrt{x}$$

$$f^{(4)}(x) = -\frac{15}{16}\sqrt{x^{-3}}$$

which is maximal on the interval $[1, 2]$ at $\xi = 1$. Then $e_3(2.5) \le 0.02197$.

4.10   CUBIC SPLINE INTERPOLATION

Avoiding High-Degree Interpolating Polynomials

In many engineering applications the values of a function to be approximated on a given interval $[a, b]$ are known at many base points $a = x_0$, $x_1, x_2, \ldots, x_n = b$. The corresponding interpolating polynomial is of high degree, and its value may oscillate violently between the base points although the actual function varies smoothly. A common tactic to avoid this problem is to divide the interval spanned by the base points into subintervals. The function over subinterval i can be approximated by an interpolating polynomial $p_i(x)$ of low degree.

Suppose each subinterval is delimited by successive base points x_i and x_{i+1}. The values of $f(x_i)$ and $f(x_{i+1})$ are sufficient to define a linear function between the points, but the piecewise linear function is not smooth (i.e., the derivative is discontinuous at the base points). If a quadratic were used as the approximating function, only one other item of information would be required, say, the slope at only one of the base points. But this lack of symmetry may make it impossible to achieve a smooth transition between the slopes of $p_i(x)$ in successive subintervals. One additional factor, normally the slope at the other end point, would define a cubic approximating function. If the polynomial on each of the subintervals is twice differentiable, the piecewise approximating function is called a "cubic spline" (Fig. 4.5).

Constraints for Smoothness

Piecewise interpolating polynomials of degree less than three were rejected because they do not produce a smooth fit to the base points. A spline function $p(x)$ may be called "smooth" if it has the following properties.

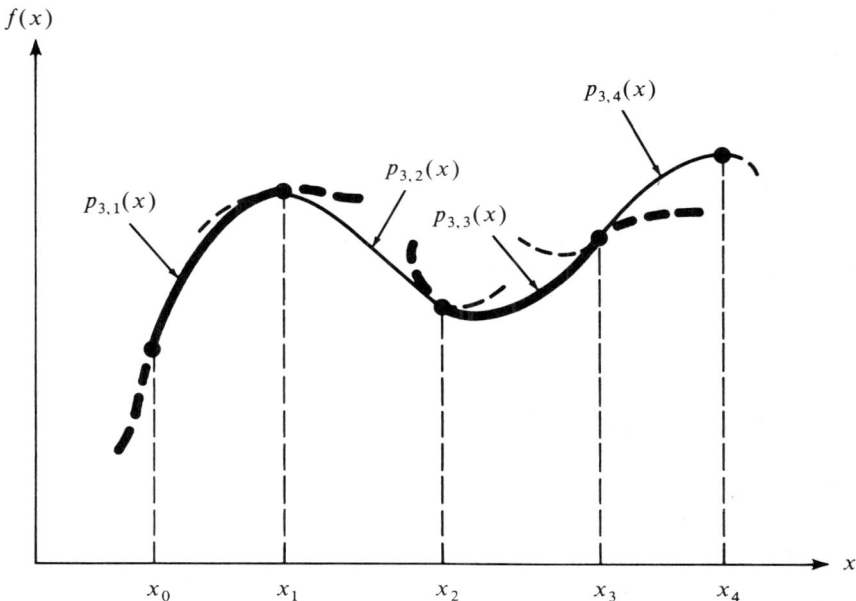

Fig. 4.5. Cubic spline interpolation. The piecewise cubic segments are indicated by alternating light and heavy lines. Portions of each cubic that extend beyond the base points delimiting its subinterval are indicated by broken lines.

1. The function is continuous at the base points; $p_{i-1}(x_i) = p_i(x_i)$ where the subscript of p is the index number of the subinterval.
2. The derivative of the function is continuous at the base points (the function has no "kinks"); $p'_{i-1}(x_i) = p'_i(x_i)$.
3. The curvature of the function is continuous at the base points; $p''_{i-1}(x_i) = p''_i(x_i)$.
4. The function has the minimal curvature (to avoid excessive oscillation of the function value) as given by

$$\sum_{i=0}^{n-1} \int_a^b [p''_i(x)]^2 \, dx.$$

Evaluation of the Cubic Functions

The slope $p'_3(x)$ of the spline is a piecewise quadratic; its derivative $p''(x)$ is a piecewise linear function. Let

$$h_i = x_i - x_{i-1}$$

Substituting into the Lagrange interpolation formula and forcing the second derivative to be continuous at the base points gives

$$p''_{3,i}(x) = \frac{x_{i+1} - x}{h_{i+1}} p''_{3,i}(x_i) + \frac{x - x_i}{h_{i+1}} p''_{3,i}(x_{i+1}),$$

$$i = 0,..., n - 1$$

Integrating this function twice and requiring that the result be continuous at the base points yields the following equation for the cubic spline.

$$p_{3+i}(x) = \frac{p''_{3,i}(x_i)}{6h_{i+1}} (x_{i+1} - x)^3 + \frac{p''_{3,i}(x_{i+1})}{6h_{i+1}} (x - x_i)^3$$

$$+ \left[\frac{f_{i+1}}{h_{i+1}} - \frac{h_{i+1}}{6} p''_{3,i}(x_{i+1}) \right] (x - x_i)$$

$$+ \left[\frac{f_i}{h_{i+1}} - \frac{h_{i+1}}{6} p''_{3,i}(x_i) \right] (x_{i+1} - x), i = 0,..., n - 1$$

Clearly, if the second derivative of the function to be approximated were known at the base points, those values could be substituted for the $p''_{3,i}(x_i)$'s in the above equation. However, these values are generally not known. Imposing the constraint that the slope of the spline must be continuous at the base points results in another equation.

$$\frac{h_{i+1}}{h_i} p''_{3,i-1}(x_{i-1}) + 2 \frac{(h_{i+1} - h_i)}{h_{i+1}} p''_{3,i}(x_i) + p''_{3,i}(x_{i+1})$$

$$= \frac{6}{h_{i+1}} \left[\frac{f_{i+1} - f_i}{h_{i+1}} - \frac{f_i - f_{i-1}}{h_i} \right], \quad i = 1, \dots, n-1$$

The result is a system of $n - 1$ equations in $n + 1$ unknowns, the second derivatives at the base points. Two additional equations are required in order to solve for the second derivatives.

Evaluating the Second Derivatives

To simplify the equations let

$$M_i = p''_{3,i}(x_i)$$
$$r_i = h_i/(h_i + h_{i+1})$$
$$q_i = 1 - r_i$$
$$\delta_i = (f_i - f_{i-1})/h_i$$
$$d_i = 6(\delta_{i+1} - \delta_i)/(h_i + h_{i+1})$$

Then the system of equations can be written as

$$q_i M_{i-1} + 2M_i + r_i M_{i+1} = d_i \qquad i = 1, \dots, n-1$$

At the point $x_0 = a$, q_0 is not defined, and at the point $x_n = b$, r_n is not defined. So there are two additional equations at the end points

$$2M_0 + r_0 M_1 = d_0$$
$$q_n M_{n-1} + 2M_n = d_n$$

Then the coefficients of the equations define a tridiagonal matrix, and the simultaneous equations for the second derivatives may be written as

$$\begin{pmatrix} 2 & r_0 & & & \\ q_1 & 2 & r_1 & & \mathbf{0} \\ & & \ddots & & \\ & \mathbf{0} & & q_{n-1} & 2 & r_{n-1} \\ & & & & q_n & 2 \end{pmatrix} \begin{pmatrix} M_0 \\ M_1 \\ \vdots \\ M_{n-1} \\ M_n \end{pmatrix} \begin{pmatrix} d_0 \\ d_1 \\ \vdots \\ d_{n-1} \\ d_n \end{pmatrix}$$

Because r_0, d_0, q_n, and d_n are undefined, they must be assigned values to permit solution of the equations. One choice for these values, resulting in what is termed a "natural" spline, is to set them all to zero, yielding zero for the second derivatives at the endpoints. A second choice is to set their values to those for the adjacent base points x_1 and x_{n-1}. Third, if the derivatives at the endpoints $p'(a)$ and $p'(b)$ are known or are estimated from a low-degree interpolating polynomial, $r_0 = q_n = 1$ and

$$d_0 = \frac{6}{h_1} \cdot \frac{f_1 - f_0}{h_1 - p'(a)}$$

$$d_n = \frac{6}{h_{n-1}} \left(p'(b) - \frac{f_n - f_{n-1}}{h_{n-1}} \right)$$

One attractive choice is to ignore the equations for the second derivatives at the endpoints, reducing the dimension of the tridiagonal system from $n + 1$ to $n - 1$. As all quantities are defined for x_1 and x_{n-1}, the reduced problem can be solved directly. However, interpolation between x_0 and x_1 and between x_{n-1} and x_n is no longer possible. Once the second derivatives have been calculated they may be substituted into the equation for the cubic on the subinterval containing the point at which an interpolation is desired.

Approximation Error in Spline Interpolation

Using the formula for the remainder of an interpolating polynomial, an upper bound for the approximation error can be shown to be

$$e_2 = \frac{\left(\max_i h_i \right)^3}{24} | f^{(4)}(\xi) |$$

where ξ is that value of x on $[a, b]$ which maximizes the fourth derivative of the function to be approximated. If the base points are equally spaced, the upper bound for the error is given by

$$e_3 = \frac{h^4}{60} | f^{(5)}(\xi) |$$

where ξ is chosen to maximize the fifth derivative of the function.

4.11   COMPUTER PROGRAMS

```
      SUBROUTINE LSTSQ(NEQNS, NPTS, X, Y, COEFF, ERROR, TOLER)
C*********************************************************************
C* Find the linear combination of NEQNS functions that yields    *
C* the least-squares fit to the NPTS data points (X, Y). The     *
C* optimal coefficients are returned in COEFF, and the least     *
C* squares error is returned in ERROR.  The maximum dimension is *
C* set to 50.  If any diagonal element of the least-squares      *
C* matrix computed in this routine becomes < TOLER in the        *
C* Gaussian elimination step, the matrix is considered to be     *
C* singular.  The user must supply a function subprogram         *
C* FUNC(I, X) which computes the value of the ith function in    *
C* the linear combination at a given x value.                    *
C*********************************************************************

      DIMENSION X(1), Y(1), A(50,50), B(50), COEFF(1)
```

```
C
C -- Evaluate the least squares matrix and constant vector
C
         DO 10 I = 1,NEQNS
           SUM1 = 0.0
           DO 20 K = 1,NPTS
             FI = FUNC(I,X(K))
             SUM1 = SUM1 + FI*Y(K)
             SUM2 = 0.0
             DO 30 J = 1,NEQNS
30             SUM2 = SUM2 + FI*FUNC(J,X(K))
             B(I) = SUM1
             A(I,J) = SUM2
20           A(J,I) = A(I,J)
10       CONTINUE
C
C -- Solve for coefficients
C
         CALL GAUSS(NEQNS, 1, A, B, TOLER)
C
C -- Compute least squares error
C
         ERROR = 0.0
         DO 40 I = 1,NPTS
           SUM1 = 0.0
           DO 50 K = 1,NEQNS
50           SUM1 = SUM1 + COEFF(K)*FUNC(K,X)I))
40         ERROR = ERROR + (SUM1 - Y(I))**2
C
C -- Output results
C
         WRITE 1000
1000     FORMAT(5X,'Curve fitting by linear least squares'/)
         WRITE 2000, (I,COEFF(I), I = 1,NEQNS)
2000     FORMAT('Coeff(',I2,') =',1PE11.4)
         WRITE 3000, ERROR
3000     FORMAT(/' Least squares error =',1PE11.4)

         RETURN
         END
```

```
procedure lstsq(neqns, npts: integer; x, y: datavector;
  var coeff: eqnvector; var error: real; toler: real);
{
************************************************************************
* Find the linear combination of neqns functions that yields the *
* least-squares fit to the npts data points (x, y). The optimal *
* coefficients are returned in coeff, and the least squares error*
* is returned in error. If any diagonal element of the least-   *
* squares matrix computed in this routine is or becomes < toler  *
* in the Gaussian elimination step, the matrix is considered to  *
* be singular. The user must supply a function subprogram        *
* func(i: integer; x: real): real which computes the value of    *
```

```
* the ith function in the linear combination at a given x value.  *
* The data types datavector and coeffvector must be defined as     *
* array[1..npts] of real and array[1..neqns] of real, respec-      *
* tively, in the calling program.                                  *
********************************************************************
}
type
  nxn = array[1..neqns,1..neqns] of real;
  nxm = array[1..neqns] of real;

var
  A: nxn;
  B: nxm;                    {m = 1}
  i,j,k: integer;
  sum1,sum2,fi: real;

begin

  {Evaluate the least squares matrix and constant vector}

  for i := 1 to neqns do
    begin
      sum1 := 0.0;
      for k := 1 to npts do
        begin
          fi := func(i, x[k]);
          sum1 := sum1 + fi*y[k];
          sum2 := 0.0;
          for j := 2 to neqns do
            sum2 := sum2 + fi*func(j,x[k])
        end
    end;
  {Solve for coefficients}

  Gauss(neqns, 1, A, B, toler);

  {Compute least squares error}

  error := 0.0;
  for k := 1 to npts do
    begin
      sum1 := 0.0;
      for i := 1 to neqns do
        sum1 := sum1 + coeff[i]*func(i,x[k]);
      error := error + sqr(sum1 - y[k])
    end;

  {Output results}

  writeln('    Curve fitting by linear least squares');
  writeln
  for i := 1 to neqns do
    writeln(' Coeff[',i:2,'] =',coeff[i]:11);
```

```
      writeln;
      writeln(' Least squares error =',error:12)

end;


                  SUBROUTINE MULTPL(NBASE, L, X, Y)
C******************************************************************
C* Computes the constant part of the Lagrange multipliers for the*
C* interpolating polynomial and multiplies them by the function  *
C* values at the NBASE base points, storing the result in L. The *
C* base points are (X, Y).  This routine should be called only   *
C* once prior to performing at least NBASE + 1 interpolations on  *
C* the interval spanned by the base points.                      *
C******************************************************************

      REAL L(1)
      DIMENSION X(1), Y(1)
C
C -- Compute the constant factors
C
      DO 10 I = 1,NBASE
         PRODUCT = 1.0
         DO 20 K = 1,NBASE
            IF (I.NE.K) PRODUCT = PRODUCT*(X(K) - X(I))
20       CONTINUE
10       L(I) = Y(K)/PRODUCT
      WRITE 1000
1000  FORMAT(5X,'Interpolation by Lagrange Multipliers'/)

      RETURN
      END


                  SUBROUTINE LAGRAN(NBASE, X, L, XINTER, YINTER)
C******************************************************************
C* Call this routine once for each interpolation on the interval *
C* spanned by the same base points.                              *
C******************************************************************

      REAL L(1)
      DIMENSION X(1)

      FACTOR = 1.0
      DO 30 I = 1,NBASE
30       FACTOR = FACTOR*(XINTER - X(I))
      YINTER = 0.0
      DO 40 I = 1,NBASE
40       YINTER = YINTER + L(I)*FACTOR/(XINTER - X(I))
C
C -- Output results
C
      WRITE 1000, XINTER, YINTER
1000  FORMAT(' Y (',1PE11.4,') =',1PE11.4)
```

```
      RETURN
      END

procedure multipliers(nbase: integer; var L: vector; x, y:
  vector);
{
*********************************************************************
* Computes the constant part of the Lagrange multipliers for the *
* interpolating polynomial and multiplies them by the function   *
* values at the nbase base points, storing the result in L.  The *
* base points are (x, y).  This routine should be called only    *
* once prior to performing at least nbase = 1 interpolations on   *
* the interval spanned by the base points.  The data type vector *
* must be defined as array[1..nbase] of real in the calling      *
* program.                                                       *
*********************************************************************
}
var
  i, k: integer;
  product: real;

begin

  {Compute the constant factors}

  for i := 1 to nbase do
    begin
      product := 1.0:
      for k := 1 to nbase do
        if (i <> k) product := product*(x[k] - x[i]);
      L[i] := y[k]/product
    end;

  writeln('     Interpolation by Lagrange multipliers');
  writeln

end;

procedure Lagrange(nbase: integer; x, L: vector; xinter: real;
  var yinter: real);
{
*********************************************************************
* Call this routine once for each interpolation on the interval  *
* spanned by the same base points.  The data type vector must be *
* defined as array[1..nbase] of real in the calling program.     *
*********************************************************************
}
var
  i: integer;
  factor: real;

begin

  factor := 1.0;
```

```
   for i := 1 to nbase do
     factor := factor*(xinter - x[i]);
   yinter := 0.0;
   for i := 1 to nbase do
     yinter := yinter + L[i]*factor/(xinter - x[i]);

   {Output results}

   writeln(' y[',xinter:11,'] =',yinter:12)

end;
```

```
               SUBROUTINE DIVDIF(NBASE, X, Y, TABLE)
C*******************************************************************
C* Sets up the divided difference table using the NBASE base      *
C* points (X, Y).  Only the top diagonal of the table is stored   *
C* in the array TABLE.  Call this routine once before performing  *
C* up to NBASE interpolations.                                    *
C*******************************************************************

      DIMENSION X(1), Y(1), TABLE(1)

      DO 10 I = 1,NBASE
10       TABLE(I) = Y(I)
      DO 20 I = 1,NBASE-1
        DO 30 J = I+1,NBASE
30         TABLE(J) = (TABLE(J-1) - TABLE(J))/(X(J-I) - X(J))

      WRITE 1000
1000  FORMAT(5X,'Interpolation by Newton divided differences'/)

      RETURN
      END
```

```
               SUBROUTINE INTERP(NBASE, X, TABLE, XINTER, YINTER)
C*******************************************************************
C* Call once for each interpolation.  Returns the approximated    *
C* function value at XINTER as YINTER.                            *
C*******************************************************************

      DIMENSION X(1), TABLE(1)
C
C -- Evaluate polynomial using Horner's method
C
      YINTER = TABLE(NBASE)
      DO 10 I = NBASE-1,1,-1
10       YINTER = TABLE(I) + (XINTER - X(I))*YINTER

      WRITE 1000, XINTER, YINTER
1000  FORMAT(' Y(',1PE11.4,') =',1PE11.4)

      RETURN
      END
```

```
procedure divdif(nbase: integer; x,y: vector; var table: vector);
{
************************************************************************
* Sets up the divided difference table using the nbase base         *
* points (x, y). Only the top diagonal of the table is stored       *
* in the array table. Call this routine once before performing      *
* up to nbase interpolations. The data type vector must be          *
* defined as array[1..nbase] of real in the calling program.        *
************************************************************************
}
var
  i,j: integer;

begin
  for i := 1 to nbase do
    table[i] := y[i];
  for i := 1 to nbase-1 do
    for j := i+1 to nbase do
      table[j] := (table[j-1] - table[j])/(x[j-i] - x[j];

  writeln('    Interpolation by Newton divided differences');
  writeln
end;

procedure interp(nbase: integer; x,table: vector; xinter: real;
  var yinter: real);
{
************************************************************************
* Call once for each interpolation. Returns the approximated        *
* function value at xinter as yinter. Define the data type          *
* vector as array[1..n] of real in the calling program.             *
************************************************************************
}
var
  i: integer;

begin

  {Evaluate polynomial using Horner's method}

  yinter := table[nbase];
  for i := nbase-1 downto 1 do
    yinter := table [i] + (xinter - x[i])*yinter;

  writeln(' y(',xinter:11,') =',yinter:11)
end;
```

```
                SUBROUTINE DERIVS(NBASE, X, Y, H, D, TOLER)
C************************************************************************
C* Compute the second derivatives needed to calculate the coeffi-*
C* cients of the piecewise cubic spline on NBASE (maximum of 50) *
C* base points (X, Y). The arrays H and D contain the spacings   *
```

```
C* of the base points and the second derivatives at the interior *
C* base points, respectively, on return to the calling program.  *
C* If a diagonal element of the tridiagonal matrix is < TOLER,    *
C* the matrix is considered to be singular.                       *
C*****************************************************************

      DIMENSION X(1), Y(1), A(50), B(50), C(50), H(1), D(1)
C
C -- Set up tridiagonal matrix and constant vector
C
      DO 10 I = 2,NBASE
        H(I) = X(I) - X(I-1)
10      D(I) = (Y(I) - Y(I-1))/H(I)
      DO 20 I = 2,NBASE-1
        B(I-1) = 2.0
        C(I-1) = H(I+1)/(H(I) + H(I+1))
        A(I-1) = 1.0 - C(I)
20      D(I-1) = 6.0*(D(I+1) - D(I))/(H(I) + H(I+1))
C
C -- Solve for second derivatives
C
      CALL TRIDIA(NBASE-2, A, B, C, D, TOLER)

      WRITE 1000
1000  FORMAT(5X,'Cubic spline interpolation'/)

      RETURN
      END


      SUBROUTINE SPLINE(NBASE, X, Y, H, D, XINTER, YINTER)
C*****************************************************************
C* Cubic spline interpolation.  Interpolation is not permitted   *
C* between the pairs of points at the ends of the interval. Call *
C* this routine once for each interpolation to be performed. The *
C* approximated function value at XINTER is returned as YINTER.  *
C*****************************************************************

      DIMENSION X(1), Y(1), H(1), D(1)
C
C -- Find subinterval containing XINTER
C
      DO 10 I = 2,NBASE-1
        IF ((XINTER.GE.X(I)).AND.(XINTER.LE.X(I+1))) GO TO 20
10      CONTINUE
      GO TO 40
C
C -- Compute value of cubic at XINTER
C
20    FACTOR = XINTER - X(I)
      FACTR1 = X(I+1) - XINTER
      YINTER = (D(I-1)*FACTR1**3)/(6.0*H(I+1)) +
     1         (D(I)*FACTOR**3)/(6.0*H(I+1) +
```

```
      2             (Y(I+1)/H(I+1) - D(I)*H(I+1)/6.0)*FACTOR +
      3             (Y(I)/H(I+1) - D(I-1)*H(I+1)/6.0)*FACTR1

      WRITE 1000, XINTER, YINTER
1000  FORMAT(' Y(',1PE11.4,') =',1PE11.4)
C
C -- Error section
C
40    WRITE 2000, XINTER, X(2), X(NBASE-1)
2000  FORMAT(' x =',1PE11.4,' is outside allowed range of [',
     1      E11.4,',',E11.4,']')
      RETURN
      END

procedure derivs(nbase: integer; x,y: vector; var h,d: vector;
  toler: real);
{
********************************************************************
* Compute the second derivatives needed to calculate the coeffi- *
* cients of the piecewise cubic spline on nbase (maximum of 50)  *
* base points (x, y).  The arrays h and d contain the spacings   *
* of the base points and the second derivatives at the interior  *
* base points, respectively, on return to the calling program.   *
* If a diagonal element of the tridiagonal matrix is < toler,     *
* the matrix is considered to be singular.  Define the data       *
* type vector as array[1..nbase] of real in the calling program. *
********************************************************************
}
var
  a,b,c: array[1..nbase] of real;

begin

  {Set up tridiagonal matrix and constant vector}

  for i := 2 to nbase do
    begin
      h[i] := x[i] - x[i-1];
      d[i] := (y[i] - y[i-1])/h[i]
    end;
  for i := 2 to nbase-1 do
    begin
      b[i-1] := 2.0;
      c[i-1] := h[i+1]/(h[i] + h[i+1]);
      a[i-1] := 1.0 - c[i-1];
      d[i-1] :=6.0*(d[i+1] - d[i])/h[i] + h[i+1])
    end;

  {Solve for second derivatives}

  tridiagonal(nbase-2, a, b, c, d, toler);

  writeln('    Cubic spline interpolation');
```

```
   writeln
end;

procedure spline(nbase: integer; x,y,h,d: vector; xinter: real;
   var yinter: real);
{
**********************************************************************
* Cubic spline interpolation.  Interpolation is not permitted      *
* between the pairs of points at the ends of the interval.  Call   *
* this routine once for each interpolation to be performed.  The   *
* approximated function value at xinter in returned as yinter.     *
* Define the data type vector as array[1..nbase] of real in the    *
* calling program.                                                 *
**********************************************************************
}
type
   flag = (inRange, outRange);

var
   status: flag;
   i: integer;
   factor,factor1: real;


begin

   {Find subinterval containing xinter}

   i := 1;
   repeat
     i := i + 1;
   until ((xinter >= x[i]) and (xinter <= x[i+1]))
     or (i = nbase-1);
   if (i = nbase-1) then status := outRange
     else status = inRange;

   case status of
     inRange:    {Compute value of cubic at xinter}
       begin
         factor := xinter - x[i];
         factor1 := x[i+1] - xinter;
         yinter := (d[i-1]*factor1*factor1*factor1)/(6.0*h[i+1])
                 + (d[i]*factor*factor*factor)/(6.0*h[i+1])
                 + (y[i+1]/h[i+1] - d[i]*h[i+1]/6.0)*factor
                 + (y[i]/h[i+1] - d[i-1]*h[i+1]/6.0)*factor1;

         writeln (' y(',xinter:11,') =',yinter:11)
       end;
     outRange:    {Error section}
       writeln(' x =',xinter:11,' is outside range of [',
         x[2]:11,',',x[nbase-1]:11,']')
   end {of case}
end;
```

4.12   EXAMPLE PROBLEMS

Example 4.10:

The molal heat capacity of nitrogen gas was determined at five temperatures; the values are listed in the following table.

T_i, °K	C_p, cal/mole·°K
300	6.8150
350	6.8947
400	6.9728
500	7.1238
550	7.1966

Estimate the heat capacity of nitrogen at 450°K, using the method of Lagrange polynomial interpolation. First compute the Lagrange multipliers.

$$l_0 = \prod_{i=1}^{4} (T - T_i)/(T_0 - T_i)$$

$$= \frac{(450 - 350)(450 - 400)(400 - 500)(450 - 550)}{(300 - 350)(300 - 400)(300 - 500)(300 - 550)}$$

$$= 0.1$$

$$l_1 = \prod_{\substack{i=0 \\ i \neq 1}}^{4} (T - T_i)/(T_1 - T_i)$$

$$= \frac{(450 - 300)(450 - 400)(450 - 500)(450 - 550)}{(350 - 300)(350 - 400)(350 - 500)(350 - 550)}$$

$$= -0.5$$

$$l_2 = \prod_{\substack{i=0 \\ i \neq 2}}^{4} (T - T_i)/(T_2 - T_i)$$

$$= \frac{(450 - 300)(450 - 350)(450 - 500)(450 - 550)}{(400 - 300)(400 - 350)(400 - 500)(400 - 550)}$$

$$= 1.0$$

$$l_3 = \prod_{\substack{i=0 \\ i \neq 3}}^{4} (T - T_i)/(T_3 - T_i)$$

$$= \frac{(450 - 300)(450 - 350)(450 - 400)(450 - 550)}{(500 - 300)(500 - 350)(500 - 400)(500 - 550)}$$

$$= 0.5$$

$$l_4 = \prod_{i=0}^{3} (T - T_i)/(T_4 - T_i)$$

$$= \frac{(450 - 300)(450 - 350)(450 - 400)(450 - 500)}{(550 - 300)(550 - 350)(550 - 400)(550 - 500)}$$

$$= -0.1$$

Next, compute the interpolated value of the heat capacity from the equation for the interpolating polynomial.

$$C_p = \sum_{i=0}^{4} C_p (T_i) l_i(T_i)$$

$$= 6.8150(-0.1) + 6.8947(-0.5) + 6.9728(1.0) + 7.1238(0.5)$$
$$+ 7.1966(-0.1)$$

$$= 7.14919 \text{ cal/mole·°K}$$

Example 4.11:

The compressibility of a gas is given by

$$C = PV/RT$$

where P is the pressure, V is the molal volume, R is the gas constant, and T is the absolute temperature. The compressibility of methane (natural gas) was determined at $-70°C$ for the following pressures.

P, atm	C
20	0.8683
40	0.7034
60	0.4515
80	0.3429

Estimate the compressibility of methane at $-70°C$ and 55 atmospheres pressure. As the base points are equally spaced, use the Gregory-Newton interpolation method.

Solution

First set up the forward difference table.

P	C	ΔC	Δ²C	Δ³C
20	0.8683			
		−0.1649		
40	0.7034		−0.0870	
		−0.2519		0.2303
60	0.4515		0.1433	
		−0.1086		
80	0.3429			

Next, calculate the interpolated value from the Gregory-Newton formula

$$C(s) = \sum_{i=0}^{3} \Delta^i C_0 \binom{s}{i}$$

$$s = (55 - 20)/20 = 1.75$$

$$\begin{aligned} C(55°) &= 0.8683 - 0.1649(1.75)/1 - 0.0870(1.75)(0.75)/(2)(1) \\ &\quad + 0.2303(1.75)(0.75)(-0.25)/(3)(2)(1) \\ &= 0.5100 \end{aligned}$$

Now, say that you are told that the compressibility of methane at −70°C and 100 atmospheres is 0.3767. Find an upper bound for the error in the interpolated value for the compressibility at 55 atmospheres. The upper bound is given by

$$e_3(55) = \left| \Delta^4 C_0 \binom{1.75}{4} \right|$$

To calculate $\Delta^4 C_0$, the forward difference table must be extended by adding a new bottom diagonal starting from the new base point at 100 atmospheres.

P	C	ΔC	Δ²C	Δ³C	Δ⁴C
20	0.8683				
		−0.1649			
40	0.7034		−0.0870		
		−0.2519		0.2303	
60	0.4515		0.1433		−0.2312
		−0.1086		−0.0009	
80	0.3429		0.1424		
		0.0338			
100	0.3767				

$$e_3(55) \leq |(-0.2312)(1.75)(0.75)(-0.25)(-1.25)/(4)(3)(2)(1)| = 0.00395$$

Example 4.12:

An electrical engineering student constructed an oscillator circuit consisting of a battery ($E = 12$ volts), a variable ($C = 0$ to 5 μfarads) capacitor, and an inductor ($L = 0.4$ mhenry).

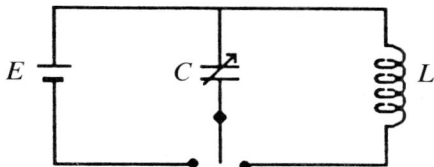

When the switch was closed to the left, the capacitor was charged to 12 volts. When the switch was subsequently closed to the right, the capacitor discharged through the inductor with a sustained oscillating current with amplitude i_{max}. This peak current was measured for several values of the capacitance as given in the following table.

C, μfarads	i_{max}, amperes
0.7	0.5020
1.0	0.6000
1.2	0.6573
1.4	0.7099
1.9	0.8270
2.5	0.9487

The student wishes to estimate the peak current at several other capacitances by cubic spline interpolation.

Solution

First, calculate the coefficients of the tridiagonal matrix.

$$r_1 = h_2/(h_1 + h_2) = 0.2/(0.3 + 0.2) = 0.2$$
$$r_2 = h_3/h_2 + h_3) = 0.2/(0.2 + 0.2) = 0.5$$
$$q_2 = 1 - r_2 = 0.5$$

and so on. Then calculate the constant vector **d**.

$$\delta_1 = (y_1 - y_0)/h_1 = (0.6 - 0.502)/0.3 = 0.3267$$
$$\delta_2 = (y_2 - y_1)/h_2 = (0.6573 - 0.6)/0.2 = 0.2865$$
$$d_1 = 6(\delta_2 - \delta_1)/(h_2 + h_1) = 6(0.2865 - 0.3267)/(0.2 + 0.3) = -0.4820$$

and so on.

The complete matrix equation for this problem is

$$\begin{pmatrix} 2 & 0.4 & 0 & 0 \\ 0.5 & 2 & 0.5 & 0 \\ 0 & 0.2857 & 2 & 0.7143 \\ 0 & 0 & 0.45455 & 2 \end{pmatrix} \mathbf{M} = \begin{pmatrix} -0.482 \\ -0.3525 \\ -0.2469 \\ -0.1711 \end{pmatrix}$$

Notice that this is a system of only four linear equations in four unknowns. Equations for the terminal base points are not being used. Solving the tridiagonal system with the program listed in Chapter 3 yields for the second derivatives at the interior base points

$$\mathbf{M}^T = (-0.22108, -0.09958, -0.08560, -0.06609)$$

The student requires an estimate of the peak current at 1.35 μfarads. This point falls in the third subinterval (between base points 2 and 3). Substituting the values for C, i_{max}, and M at the appropriate base points into the equation for the cubic on this subinterval gives

$$
\begin{aligned}
i_{max}(1.35) &= M_2\,(C_3 - 1.35)^3/(6 \cdot h_3) + M_3\,(1.35 - C_2)^3/(6 \cdot h_3) \\
&\quad + (i_{max3}/h_3 - M_3 \cdot h_3/6)\,(1.35 - C_2) \\
&\quad + (i_{max2}/h_3 - M_2 \cdot h_3/6)\,(C_3 - 1.35) \\
&= -0.09958(1.2 - 1.35)^3/(6 \cdot 0.2) \\
&\quad - 0.0856(1.35 - 1.4)^3/(6 \cdot 0.2) \\
&\quad + (1.4/0.2 + 0.0856 \cdot 0.2/6)\,(1.35 - 1.2) \\
&\quad + (1.2/0.2 + 0.09958 \cdot 0.2/6)\,(1.4 - 1.35) \\
&= 0.6971 \text{ amperes}
\end{aligned}
$$

Similarly, if an interpolation at $C = 1.5$ μfarad is desired, the cubic on the fourth subinterval (between base points 3 and 4) would be used. Substitution of the appropriate values in the formula for the cubic gives an interpolated value of 0.7349 ampere at this point. Only interpolation between interior base points is possible, unless some assumption is made regarding the second derivatives at the terminal base points. If they are assumed to be zero (the so-called "natural" spline), interpolation is possible over the interval spanned by all the base points. Using this approximation for M_5 gives an interpolated value of 0.8690 ampere for the peak current at 2.1 μfarads.

chapter 5

Numerical Differentiation and Integration

5.1 NUMERICAL DIFFERENTIATION

Derivatives appear frequently in scientific and engineering equations, but calculating the value of a deprivative analytically may be very difficult (e.g., for a matrix function) or even impossible (e.g., for a tabulated function). However, if the values of the function to be differentiated are known at several base points, the derivative of the interpolating polynomial which passes through those base points can be easily evaluated. The Newton divided difference form is most appropriate for this procedure.

Consider the more common case, where the base points are equally spaced. Differentiating the Gregory-Newton formula

$$p(s) = f(x_0 + sh) = f_0 + s\Delta f_0 + \frac{s(s-1)}{2} s\Delta^2 f_0$$

$$+ \frac{s(s-1)(s-2)}{6} \Delta^3 f_0 + \dots$$

term by term gives

$$p'(s) = f'(x_0 + sh) = \frac{\Delta f_0}{h} + \frac{2s-1}{2h} \Delta^2 f_0 + \frac{3s^2 - 6s + 2}{6h} \Delta^3 f_0 + \dots$$

for the derivative of the interpolating polynomial. Note that the first term is a forward difference divided by $x_1 - x_0$, the separation of the base points, also called the "step size." This term is the linear approximation to the derivative of the function $f(x)$. The other terms are analogous to higher order terms of a Taylor series. Repeated application of the above procedure yields the general formula

$$\frac{d^m f(x)}{dx^m} = \frac{1}{h^m} \cdot \frac{d^m f(s)}{ds^m} \Bigg|_{s\,=\,0}$$

$$= \frac{1}{h^m} \sum_{k=1}^{n} \frac{d^m}{ds^m} \left[\frac{s(s-1)(s-2)\cdots(s-k-1)}{k!} \right] \Delta^k f_0$$

for the mth derivative.

Example 5.1:

Estimate $f'(1.30)$ for the following tabulated function.

x_i	f_i	Δf_i	Δf_i
1.00	0.0000	0.0792	−0.0123
1.20	0.0792	0.0669	
1.40	0.1461		

Transform to s variables.

$$s = (x - x_0)/h = (1.3 - 1.0)/0.2 = 1.5$$

Substitute into the differentiation formula.

$$p'(1.5) = \frac{1}{h} \left[\Delta f_0 + \frac{2s-1}{2} \Delta^2 f_0 \right]$$

$$= \frac{1}{0.2} \left[0.0792 + \frac{2(1.5)-1}{2}(-0.0123) \right] = 0.3345$$

Note that $p'(x)$ is linear whereas $p(x)$ is quadratic.

The function $f(x)$ is actually log x, and $f'(x) = 1/2.3026x$. So $f'(1.3) = 0.3341$, to four decimal places. A more accurate estimate of the derivative could be obtained by using a smaller step size or a higher-order approximation, (i.e., more base points).

The most common application of numerical integration is when s is integral; that is, an estimate of the derivative at one of the base points is desired. If $s = 0, f'(x_0)$ is estimated by $p'(x_0)$. Substituting $s = 0$ into the formula for the derivative gives

$$f'(x_0) = \frac{1}{h} \left[\Delta f_0 + \frac{1}{2} \Delta^2 f_0 + \frac{2}{6} \Delta^3 f_0 + \cdots \right]$$

If $s = 1, f'(x_1)$ is estimated by $p'(x_1)$

$$f'(x_1) = \frac{1}{h}\left[\Delta f_0 + \frac{1}{2}\Delta^2 f_0 + \frac{1}{6}\Delta^3 f_0 + \ldots\right]$$

and so forth for other values of s. In practice, of course, the series is truncated after one to n terms, where n is the degree of the interpolating polynomial. The forward differences of order greater than n are all zero.

If only two base points are used, $n = 1$ and $s = 0$.

$$f'(x_0) = \frac{\Delta f}{h} = \frac{f(x_0 + h) - f(x_0)}{h}$$

This is the well-known "forward finite difference" approximation. If three base points are used and the derivative is desired at the middle base point, $n = 2$ and $s = 1$.

$$f'(x_1) = \frac{1}{h}\left[\Delta f_0 + \frac{1}{2}\Delta^2 f_0\right]$$

Substituting the definitions of the first and second forward differences yields

$$f'(x_1) = \frac{f(x_0 + 2h) - f(x_0)}{2h}$$

This is the well-known "central finite difference" approximation.

As indicated by Fig. 5.1, these formulas approximate the derivative at the desired x value by the slope of a secant line drawn through the terminal base points. Clearly, as the step size gets smaller, the secant line approaches a tangent to the curve at the desired x value. The forward differences, however, will be small differences between relatively large numbers, leading to round-off error and loss of precision in the calculation. The proper choice of stepsize is critically important to an accurate

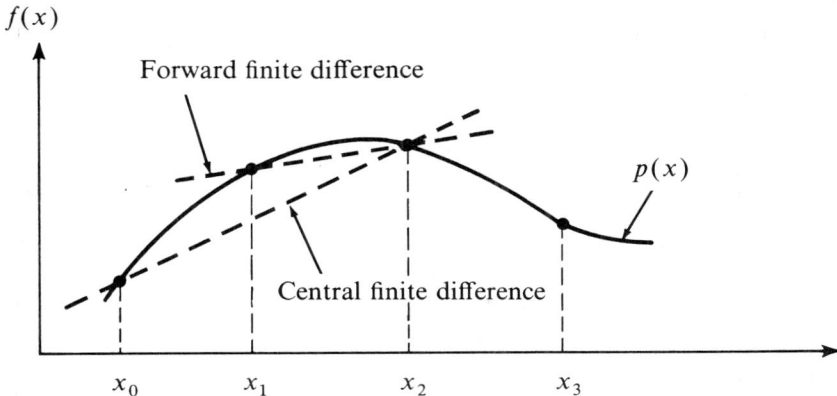

Fig. 5.1. Finite difference approximation to the derivative.

approximation of the derivative. A later section will discuss the identification of the optimal step size.

5.2   APPROXIMATION ERROR IN DIFFERENTIATION

Because the accuracy of numerical differentiation is so sensitive to the step size, it is important to have an upper bound for the error introduced by replacing the (perhaps unknown) function to be differentiated by an interpolating polynomial. From the Newton form of the polynomial

$$f(x) = p_n(x) + R_n(x) = p_n(x) + f[x_0, x_1,\ldots, x_n, x] \prod_{j=0}^{n} (x - x_j)$$

The point x has been added to the list of base points to supply the additional point needed to evaluate the $n + 1$st divided difference. The product in the above equation will be denoted by $\Psi_n(x)$. Note that

$$g'(x) = \lim_{h \to 0} g[x, x + h] = g[x, x]$$

Therefore,

$$\frac{d}{dx} f[x_0,\ldots, x_n, x] = f[x_0,\ldots, x_n, x, x]$$

From the rule for differentiating the product of two functions

$$f'(x) = p_n'(x) + f[x_0,\ldots, x_n, x_n, x, x]\Psi_n(x) + f[x_0,\ldots, x_n, x]\Psi_n'(x)$$

Substituting the nth derivative divided by $n!$ for the nth divided difference yields

$$e_n(f') \leq \frac{f^{(n+2)}(\xi)}{(n + 2)!} \Psi(x) + \frac{f^{(n+1)}(\xi')}{(n + 1)!} \Psi'(x)$$

where x is the point at which the derivative is desired. ξ and ξ' are the points on the interpolation interval where the indicated derivatives are maximal.

If the base points are equally spaced, the approximation error in terms of s variables is given by

$$e_n(f') \leq \frac{f^{(n+2)}(\xi)}{n + 2} \binom{s}{n + 1} + \frac{f^{(n+1)}(\xi')}{h} \frac{d}{ds} \binom{2}{n + 1}$$

If the number of base points $n + 1 = 2$,

$$\frac{d}{ds} \left(\frac{s(s - 1)}{2!} \right) = s - 1/2$$

For a three-point differentiation rule,

$$\frac{d}{ds} \left(\frac{s(s - 1)(s - 2)}{3!} \right) = \frac{s^2}{2} - s + 1/3$$

For a four-point rule,

$$\frac{d}{ds}\left(\frac{s(s-1)(s-2)(s-3)}{4!}\right) = \frac{s^3}{6} - \frac{3}{4}s^2 + \frac{11}{12}s + 1/4$$

and so on.

If x is one of the base points x_i, then $\Psi_n(x)$ has one factor $(x_i - x_i)$ $= 0$ and $\Psi_n(x) = 0$. As $\Psi_n'(x) = \Psi_n(x)/(x - x_i)$, the first term in the formula for the error vanishes and the approximation error is given only by the second term.

$$e_n(f') = \frac{f^{(n+1)}(\xi')}{(n+1)!} \prod_{\substack{j=0 \\ j\neq i}}^{n} (x_i - x_j)$$

Example 5.2:

$$f(x) = 5x^2 - x$$

x_i	$f(x_i)$
1.0	4.000
1.1	4.950
1.2	6.000

Estimate $f'(1.1)$ and an upper bound for the error in the numerical differentiation. Let $a = x_1 = 1.1$.

Forward Difference Approximation

$$f'(a) = f[a, a+h] = \frac{f(a+h) - f(a)}{h}$$

$$= \frac{6.00 - 4.95}{0.1} = 10.50$$

$$e(f') \leq \left|\frac{f''(\xi')}{2!}(x_0 - x_1)\right| = \left|-\frac{1}{2}hf''(\xi')\right|$$

The true value is $10x - 1 = 10$. As $f''(x) = 10$ over the entire interval,

$$e(f') \leq 0.5(0.1)(10) = 0.5$$

which is the actual error. This indicates that round-off error is negligible compared to the approximation error in this case.

Central Difference Approximation

$$f'(a) = \frac{f(a+h) - f(a-h)}{2h}$$

$$= \frac{6 - 4}{2(0.1)} = 10.00$$

$$e(f') \leq \left| \frac{f'''(\xi')}{3!} (a - a - h)(a - a + h) \right| = \left| -\frac{h^2}{6} f'''(\xi') \right|$$

As the true function is a quadratic, its third derivative is zero for all x and $e(f')$ is zero. That is, the central difference approximation is exact for this function. Note that as more base points are used, h is raised to a higher power in the error formula. Because the step size is usually quite small, the higher-order formulas will be more accurate than the low-order ones.

Suppose all three base points in the above problem are used but the derivative is desired at $a = x_0 = 1$.

$$f'(a) = \frac{1}{h} \left[\Delta f_0 - \frac{1}{2} \Delta^2 f_0 \right] = e(f')$$

$$f'(a) = \frac{-3f(a) + 4f(a + h) - f(a + 2h)}{2h}$$

$$= \frac{-3(4) + 4(4.95) - 6}{2(0.1)} = 9.0$$

The true solution is $f'(1.0) = 9.0$, the approximation error

$$e(f') \leq \left| \frac{f'''(\xi')}{3!} (a - x_1)(a - x_2) \right| = \left| \frac{2h^2}{3!} f'''(\xi') \right|$$

is again zero because the third derivative of $f(x)$ is zero. However, the error formula for this differentiation rule gives a result which is twice that for the central differences rule. This property reflects the fact that the secant line is more likely to be parallel to the tangent at a point within the interval spanned by the base points than at a terminal point of the interval.

Higher-Order Derivatives

Differentiating the above three point rule with $a = x_0$ gives a formula for the second derivative $f''(a)$.

$$f''(a) = 2f[a, x_1, x_2] + 2f[a, x_1, x_2, a, a](a - x_1)(a - x_2)$$
$$+ f[a, x_1, x_2, a]2(a - x_1 + a - x_2)$$
$$= \frac{f(a) - 2f(a + h) + f(a + 2h)}{h^2} = \frac{1}{h^2} \Delta^2 f_0$$

$$e(f'') = h^2 f^{(iv)}(\xi)/6 - hf'''(\xi)$$

If $a = x_1$, the midpoint of the interval,

$$f''(a) = \frac{f(a - h) - 2f(a) + f(a + h)}{h^2}$$

$$e(f'') = h^2 f^{(iv)}(\xi)/12$$

Note that for symmetrical placement of the base points about $x = a$ the odd-order derivative term vanishes and the error of the remaining term is halved.

5.3 ROUND-OFF ERROR AND THE OPTIMAL STEP SIZE

Because the approximation error that is associated with numerical differentiation is proportional to a power of the step size, one would think that the finite difference formulas should become increasingly more accurate approximations to the derivative as h approaches zero. However, only a finite number of significant digits are carried in such calculations, and loss of precision can occur when two nearly equal numbers are subtracted in the numerator of the differentiation rules. The resulting round-off error can be appreciable.

Example 5.3:

Find the first derivative of $\ln x$ at $x = 1$, using the central finite difference approximation. The true solution is, of course $1/x = 1$. We shall carry eight decimal places of precision in the calculations and use various step sizes.

h	$\ln(1 + h)$	$\ln(1 - h)$	$\dfrac{\ln(1 + h) - \ln(1 - h)}{2h}$
0.1	0.09531017	−0.10536051	1.00335340
0.01	0.00995033	−0.01005033	1.00003300
0.001	0.00099950	−0.00100050	1.00000000
0.0001	0.00009999	−0.00010000	0.99995000
0.00001	0.00000999	−0.00001000	0.99950000
0.000001	0.00000099	−0.00000100	0.99500000

At $h = 0.0001$ the approximation begins to get worse instead of better. At $h = 0.000001$ the error is in the third decimal place, a serious defect when eight-place precision is expected from the calculation. Eight-decimal-place precision is not sufficient to retain eight significant digits as h is reduced. Even at $h = 0.001$, where the correct answer is obtained, $\ln(1 + h)$ has only five significant digits of precision and the derivative is actually known to only five decimal places.

Suppose the central difference formula is used to approximate the derivative of some function $f(x)$ at $x = a$. Let the round-off error in calculating $f(a + h)$ be represented by e_+, and let the round-off error in calculating $f(a - h)$ be represented by e_-.

$$f'(a) \approx \frac{(f(a + h) + e_+) - (f(a - h) + e_-)}{2h}$$

$$= \frac{f(a + h) - f(a - h)}{2h} + \frac{e_+ - e_-}{2h}$$

Then the approximation to true derivative $f'(a)$ is given by

$$f'(a)_{\text{computed}} = f'(a) + \frac{h^2 f'''(\xi)}{6} + \frac{e_+ - e_-}{2h}$$

where the second term on the right-hand side is the approximation error and the third term is the round-off error. If k decimal places are carried in the computation, $e_+ = e_- = 10^{-k}$ for chopping or 0.5×10^{-k} for rounding. The upper bound for the round-off error is

$$R = \frac{2 \times 10^{-k}}{2h} = \frac{10^{-k}}{h}$$

The total error accompanying the calculation of a central difference estimate of the derivative is

$$g(h) = R + e(f') = \frac{10^{-k}}{h} + \frac{1}{6} h^2 f'''(\xi')$$

The error $g(h)$ is minimal where $g'(h)$ is zero. Suppose the central difference formula was evaluated to eight-decimal-place precision. Substituting $k = 8$ and differentiating $g(h)$ gives

$$g'(h) = -\frac{10^{-8}}{h^2} + \frac{h}{3} f'''(\xi')$$

Setting this expression equal to zero and solving for h yields the optimal step size.

Example 5.4:

$$f(x) = \ln x; x = 1; f'''(x) = 1/2x^3; f'''(1) = 1$$

$$g'(h) = -\frac{10^{-8}}{h^2} + \frac{h}{3} = 0$$

$$h = (3 \times 10^{-8})^{1/3} = 0.0031$$

This value is slightly larger than the value of 0.001, which fortuitously gave the correct answer for the derivative even though only five places of precision remained.

Numerical differentiation is, therefore, inherently unstable. The approximation does not necessarily improve as the step size becomes infinitesimal. It is essential to estimate the optimal step size in each application to obtain accurate results. The optimum is always a compromise between decreasing approximation error and increasing round-off error as h is reduced.

5.4   NEWTON-COTES CLOSED INTEGRATION RULES

Origin of the Newton-Cotes Formulas

Readers will be familiar with the following strategy of approximating the definite integral of a function $f(x)$ between the points $x = x_0$ and $x = x_1$. First a secant line is drawn between the points $(x_0, f(x_0))$ and $(x_1, f(x_1))$ as illustrated by the following figure. Then the integral is approximated by the area of the shaded trapezoid, hence the name "trapezoid rule" for this approximation. The accuracy of the approximation increases as the interval h narrows and the secant line approaches the curve for $f(x)$ between the integration limits.

Of course, a straight line is rarely a good approximation to an arbitrary function over a sizable interval $x_0 - x_1$. One way to improve the approximation is to select additional points within the interval and approximate the function $f(x)$ by an interpolating polynomial. Integrating the expression for the interpolating polynomial term by term yields a formula for the integral in terms of the base points. The family of such formulas

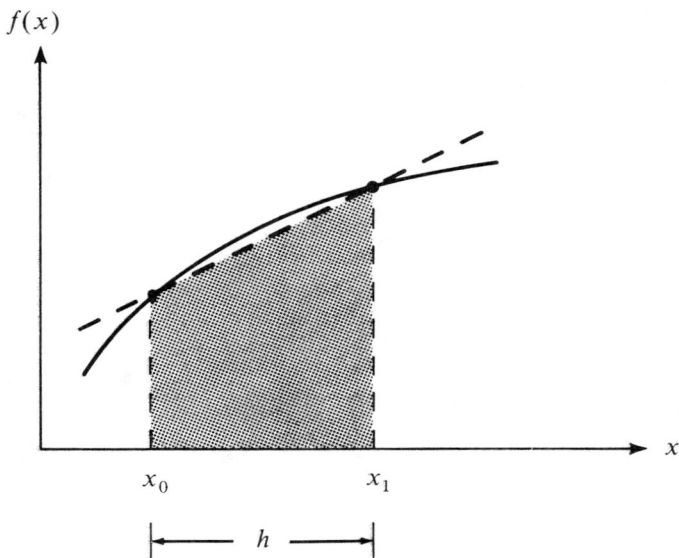

Fig. 5.2.   A simple form of numerical integration.

for various degrees of interpolating polynomial with equally spaced base points is called the "Newton-Cotes closed formulas."

Let a and b be the limits of integration and $x_0 = a, x_1,\ldots, x_n = b$ be the base points of the nth degree polynomial through those points.

$$F(x) = \int_a^b f(x)\, dx \approx \int_a^b p_n(x)\, dx$$

Converting to s variables gives

$$F(x) = \int_0^n p_n(x_0 + sh)\, ds = h \int_0^n \left[f_0 + s\Delta f_0 + \frac{s(s-1)}{2!}\Delta^2 f_0 \right.$$
$$\left. + \frac{s(s-1)(s-2)}{3!}\Delta^3 f_0 + \ldots + \binom{s}{n}\Delta^n f_0 \right] ds$$
$$= nh\left[f_0 + \frac{n}{2}\Delta f_0 + \frac{n(2n-3)}{12}\Delta^2 f_0 + \frac{n(n-2)^2}{24}\Delta^3 f_0 + \ldots \right]$$

The number of base points $n + 1$ may be selected to give as good an approximation to $f(x)$ as is necessary. Although this result is the normally used form of the Newton-Cotes formulas, it is not necessary that the limits of integration span all these points. The terms for the interpolating polynomial may be integrated from $s = q \geqslant 0$ to $s = r \leqslant n$.

Error of Integration

The error introduced by approximating the integral in the manner may be estimated from the remainder term of the polynomial.

$$e(F) = f(x) - \int_a^b p_n(x)\, dx \approx \int_a^b R_n(x)\, dx$$

Because

$$R_n(x) = \frac{f^{(n+1)}(\xi)}{(n+1)!}\prod_{j=0}^n (x - x_j) = \frac{f^{(n+1)}(\xi)}{(n+1)!}\Psi_n(x)$$

an upper bound for the error in the integral is

$$e(F) = \frac{f^{(n+1)}(\xi)}{(n+1)!}\int_a^b \Psi_n(x)\, dx$$

Specific Formulas

For two base points, $n = 1$, and the Newton-Cotes formula is the trapezoid rule.

$$F(x) = h\left(f_0 + \frac{1}{2}\Delta f_0 \right) + \frac{f''(\xi)}{2!}\int_a^b (x - a)(x - b)\, dx$$

$$= \frac{h}{2} [f(x_0) + f(x_1)] + \frac{f''(\xi)}{12} h^3$$

where ξ is that point on the interval where the second derivative is maximal. The first term in the above expression is the area of the trapezoid under the curve, as shown in Fig. 5.3. The second term is the upper limit of the approximation error.

For three base points, $n = 2$, and a parabola, rather than a straight line, is passed through the base points (Fig. 5.3).

$$F(x) = 2h \left(f_0 + \Delta f_0 + \frac{1}{6} \Delta^2 f_0 \right) + \frac{f'''(\xi)}{3!} \int_{x_0}^{x_2} \Psi_2(x) \, dx$$

The approximation to the integral

$$F(x) = \frac{h}{3} [f(x_0) + 4f(x_1) + f(x_2)]$$

is known as "Simpson's rule."

When the integration is performed on the remainder, a result of zero is obtained. This will always happen for even-order rules. The odd-order derivative terms vanish upon integration, as they do for symmetrically placed base points in numerical differentiation. Taking the next term in

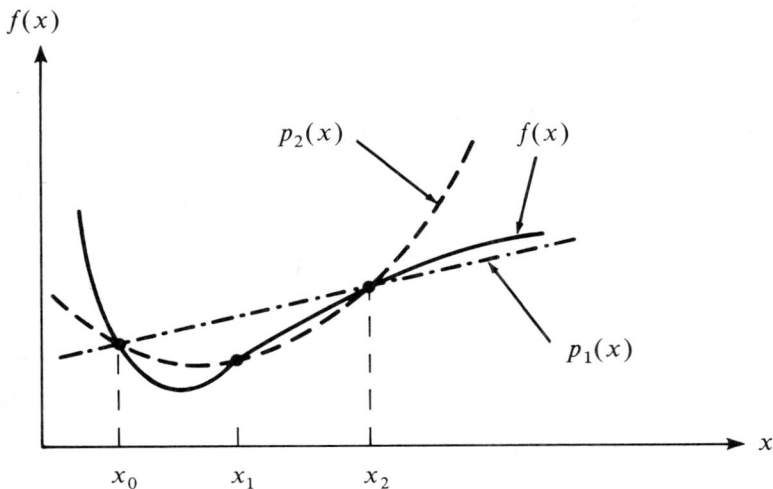

Fig. 5.3. Newton-Cotes closed integration formulas. Integration of the linear interpolating polynomial is the trapezoid rule; integration of the quadratic interpolating polynomial is Simpson's rule.

the Newton expansion for the interpolating polynomial and integrating gives

$$e(F) = \frac{f^{(iv)}(\xi)}{90} \left(\frac{b - a}{2}\right)^5 = \frac{f^{(iv)}(\xi)h^5}{90}$$

For the upper bound of the approximation error. If h is sufficiently small, Simpson's rule is much more accurate than the trapezoid rule because a parabola is likely to be a better approximation to $f(x)$ than is a straight line.

Example 5.5:

$$f(x) = \sin x; \ a = x_0 = \pi/4; \ b = x_2 = 3\pi/4.$$

Find $F = \int \sin x \, dx$ on the interval $[a, b]$.

x_i	$\sin x_i$
$\pi/4$	0.7071
$\pi/2$	1.0000
$3\pi/4$	0.7071

Using the trapezoid rule, $h = \pi/2$ radians.

$$F = \frac{h}{2} (f_0 + f_2) = \frac{\pi}{4} (2 \times 0.7071) = 1.1107$$

As $\sin x$ is maximal on this interval at $x = \pi/2$,

$$e(F) = \frac{f''(\xi)h^3}{12} = \frac{1}{12} \left(\frac{\pi}{2}\right)^3 \sin\frac{\pi}{2} = 0.3230$$

The integral of $\sin x$ is $-\cos x$, and the true value of the definite integral to four decimal places is

$$\cos a - \cos b = 1.4142$$

Although the calculated value deviates from the true value by less than the approximation error, it is not accurate because h is too large. Using Simpson's rule with $h = \pi/4$ gives

$$F = \frac{\pi/4}{3} (0.7071 + 4(1) + 0.7071) = 1.4174$$

$$e(F) = \frac{f^{(iv)}(\xi)h^5}{90} = \frac{1}{90} \left(\frac{\pi}{4}\right)^5 \sin\frac{\pi}{2} = 0.0033$$

which is much more accurate.

5.5 NEWTON-COTES OPEN INTEGRATION RULES

The limits of integration for the Newton-Cotes closed formulas are at base points of the interpolating polynomial defined by the base points. We may, however, want the value of a definite integral between limits that are not base points of the interpolating polynomial, as is illustrated in Fig. 5.4. Suppose the degree of the interpolating polynomial would be n if there were base points at $x = a$ and $x = b$. Because there are no base points at a and b, the interpolating polynomial is of degree $n - 2$. For equally spaced base points,

$$\int_a^b f(x)\,dx = \int_a^b p_{n-2}(x)\,dx = h \int_0^\beta p_{n-2}(a + sh)\,ds$$

where $s = (x - a)/h$ and $\beta = (b - a)/h$, the number of steps of length h in the entire interval of integration. Substituting the Gregory-Newton form of the interpolating polynomial yields

$$p_{n-2}(a + sh) = f(x_1) + (s - 1)\Delta f(x_1) + \frac{(s - 2)(s - 2)}{2!}\Delta^2 f(x_1)$$

$$+ \frac{(s - 2)(s - 2)(s - 3)}{3!}\Delta^3 f(x_1)$$

$$+ \ldots + \binom{s - 1}{n - 2}\Delta^{n-2} f(x_1)$$

Integrating term by term gives

$$F = \int_a^b f(x)\,dx = h[sf(x_1) + (s^2/2 = s)\Delta f(x_1)$$

$$+ (s^3/6 - 3s^2/4 + s)\Delta^2 f(x_1) + \ldots]_0^\beta$$

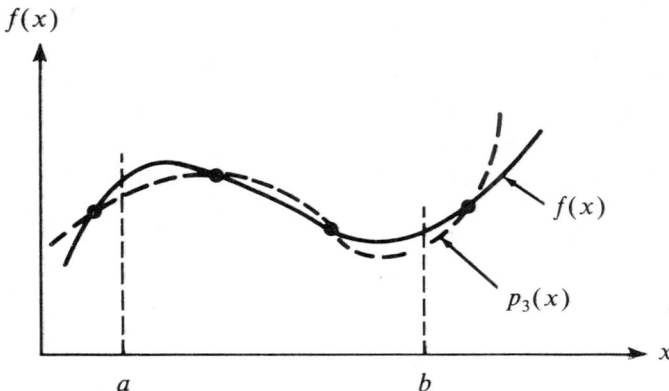

Fig. 5.4. Newton-Cotes open integration. Only the two points lying in the interval [a, b] are used to generate the interpolating polynomial from which the integration formula is derived.

As all terms vanish at $s = 0$,

$$F = h [\beta f(x_1) + (\beta^2/2 - \beta)\Delta f(x_1) + (\beta^3/6 - 3\beta^2/4 + \beta)\Delta^2 f(x_1) + \dots]$$

and the upper bound of the approximation error is

$$h \int_0^\beta R_{n-2} (a + sh) \, ds = h^n \int_0^\beta \binom{s-1}{n-1} \Delta^{n-1} f(\xi) ds$$

These are the "Newton-Cotes open integration formulas."

Specific Cases

The open formulas are especially useful when β is integral, that is, when $a = x_0$ and $b = x_n$ would be the terminal base points of the nth degree Gregory-Newton interpolating polynomial if $f(a)$ and $f(b)$ were known. Substitution into the above general formula gives a family of m-point integration rules. For $m = 2$ base points and $\beta = 3$,

$$\int_{x_0}^{x_3} f(x) \, dx = \frac{3h}{2} [f(x_1) + f(x_2)] + \frac{3h^3}{4} f''(\xi)$$

The last term in the above equation is the upper bound for the approximation error; ξ is that value of x on the interval spanned by the base points which maximizes $f''(x)$.

For $m = 3$ base points and $\beta = 4$,

$$\int_{x_0}^{x_4} f(x) \, dx = \frac{4h}{3} [2f(x_1) - f(x_2) + 2f(x_3)] + \frac{14h^5}{45} f^{(iv)}(\xi)$$

This formula is known as "Milne's rule."

Note that the fourth rather than the third derivative of $f(x)$ appears in the term for the approximation error. As occurs for the closed integration rules, the integral of the odd-order derivative terms are zero for even-order interpolating polynomials. Because formulas for an odd number of base points and even β have the same approximation error as the next higher odd order, even-order formulas are more frequently used.

Example 5.6:

Integrate the following tabulated function between the given limits:

$$\int_{0.1}^{0.5} f(x) \, dx$$

x_i	$f(x_i)$
0.1	?
0.2	5.0000
0.3	3.3333
0.4	2.5000
0.5	?

Use the three point formula with $h = 0.1$.

$$F = \frac{4 \times 0.1}{3} (2 \times 5 - 3.3333 + 2 \times 2.5) = 1.5556$$

Given the additional information that $f(x) = 1/x$,

$$\int_{0.1}^{0.5} dx/x = \ln 0.5 - \ln 0.1 = 1.6094$$

The upper bound of the approximation error is

$$e(F) = \frac{14(0.1)^5}{45} \times \frac{24}{\xi^5}$$

which will have its largest value on the interval [0.2, 0.4] at $\xi = 0.2$;

$$e(F) = \frac{14(0.1)^5}{45} \times \frac{24}{(0.2)^5} = 0.2333$$

Although the calculated value differs from the true value by less than this bound for the approximation error, the solution is inaccurate. The function $1/x$ is very steep at small values of x and extrapolation of the parabola defined by the base points is a poor approximation to the actual hyperbolic function (Fig. 5.5). Of course, if the value of h were sufficiently small, the extrapolation would not be so much in error. Furthermore, the approximation error for this three-point rule is 28 times larger than that for the closed three-point rule (Simpson's rule). Therefore, the closed formulas are preferred for numerical integration.

5.6   COMPOSITE INTEGRATION FORMULAS

Deficiencies of Newton-Cotes Rules

The Newton-Cotes integration rules have an upper bound of the approximation error given by $ch^k f^{(k-1)}(\xi)$ where c is a constant peculiar to each formula and k depends on the number of base points used. Open formulas for two or three points have slightly smaller errors than closed formulas with the same number of base points and the same integration limits. Closed formulas are considerably more accurate if there are greater than

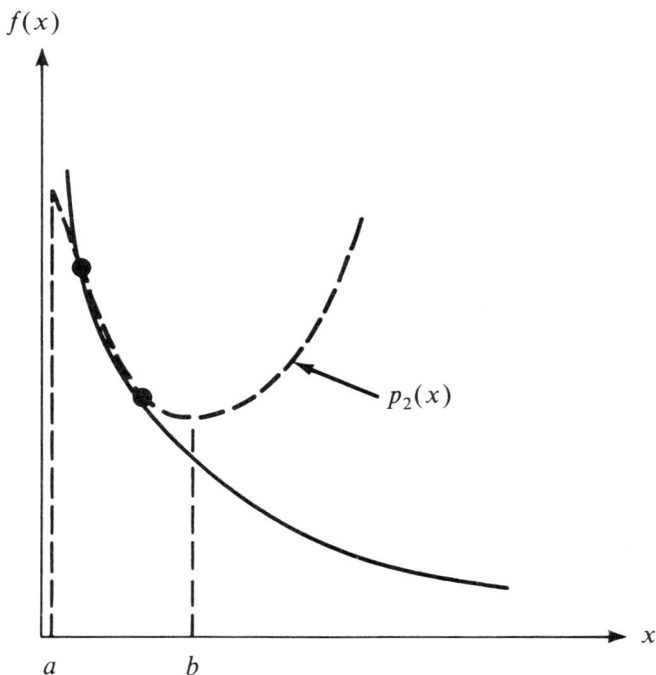

Fig. 5.5.   Integration from $x = a$ to $x = b$ will result in significant error.

three base points. It would seem, therefore, that closed formulas of high order should give the most accurate estimate of the integral because the step size h decreases and k increases as more base points are added between the integration limits. However, at very high order the accumulation of round-off error actually makes the calculated value less accurate.

One way to take advantage of the smaller step size attending an increase in the number of base points is to divide the entire interval of integration into N smaller subintervals and on each subinterval apply a simpler integration formula which produces less round-off error. That is, the elementary integration rule is applied N times.

$$\int_a^b f(x)\ dx = \sum_{i=1}^N \int_{x_{i-1}}^{x_i} f(x)\ dx;\ x_0 = a;\ x_N = b$$

The resulting formulas are called "composite integration rules." Substituting the interpolating polynomial of degree m obtained for the $m + 1$ base points on each subinterval

$$\int_{x_0}^{x_N} f(x)\ dx = \int_{x_0}^{x_1} P_m\ (x)\ dx + \int_{x_1}^{x_2} P_m\ (x)\ dx + \ldots + \int_{x_{N-1}}^{x_N} P_m\ (x)\ dx$$

If $p_m(x)$ is linear, that is, the trapezoid rule is used on each subinterval,

$$F = \frac{h}{2} [f(x_0) + f(x_1)] + \frac{h}{2} [f(x_1) + f(x_2)] + \ldots$$

$$+ \frac{h}{2} [f(x_{N-1}) + f(x_N)] + \frac{h^3}{12} \sum_{i=1}^{N} f''(\xi_i)$$

where $h = (b - a)/N$ and the last term is the sum of the approximation errors for each subinterval. Fig. 5.6 illustrates the method. The integral is approximated by the sum of the shaded trapezoidal areas.

Note that the function values at all base points except x_0 and x_N appear twice in the above equation. Collecting terms yields

$$F = \frac{h}{2} [f(x_0) + f(x_N)] + h \sum_{i=1}^{N-1} f(x_i) + \frac{h^3}{12} \sum_{i=1}^{N} f''(\xi_i)$$

In terms of a, b, and N the composite trapezoid rule is

$$F = \frac{b - a}{N} \left[\frac{1}{2} f(a) + \frac{1}{2} f(b) \right]$$

$$+ h \sum_{i=1}^{N-1} f\left(a + \left(\frac{b - a}{N} \right) i \right) - \frac{(b - a)^3}{12N^2} f''(\xi)$$

where ξ is in $[a, b]$. The error term simplifies because if $f''(x)$ is continuous on $[a, b]$, there must be some ξ on $[a, b]$ for which

$$Nf''(\xi) = \sum_{i=1}^{N} f''(\xi_i).$$

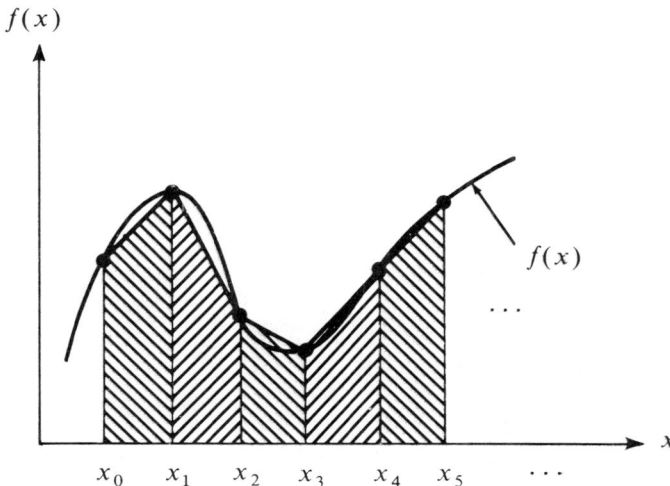

Fig. 5.6. Composite trapezoid rule. The integral is the sum of the areas of the trapezoidal regions.

So the upper bound of the approximation error is

$$e(F) = \frac{h^2(b - a)}{12} f''(\xi)$$

If each subinterval contains three base points, there are $2N + 1$ base points in all with $a = x_0$ and $b = x_{2N+1}$. The interpolating polynomial on each subinterval is quadratic and there are N applications of Simpson's rule. The integral is approximated by the sum of the shaded areas bounded above by the parabolic sections. Fig. 5.7 provides a graphical picture of the procedure. Note that an odd number of base points are required to use the composite Simpson's rule.

$$F = \int_a^b f(x)\ dx$$

$$= \frac{h}{3} \left[f(a) + f(b) + 2 \sum_{\substack{i=2 \\ \Delta=2}}^{2N-2} f(x_i) + 4 \sum_{\substack{i=1 \\ \Delta=2}}^{2N-1} f(x_i) \right] - \sum_{i=1}^{N} f^{(iv)}(\xi_i) \frac{h^5}{90}$$

The first summation is over the even-numbered points; the second summation is over the odd-numbered points. The even-numbered points are counted twice because they are on the borders between subintervals; the odd-numbered points are counted once because they are internal to the subintervals. Simplifying the above formula gives

$$F = \sum_{\substack{i=1 \\ \Delta=2}}^{2N-1} \frac{h}{3} [f(x_i) + 4f(x_{i+1}) + f(x_{i+2})]$$

$f(x)$

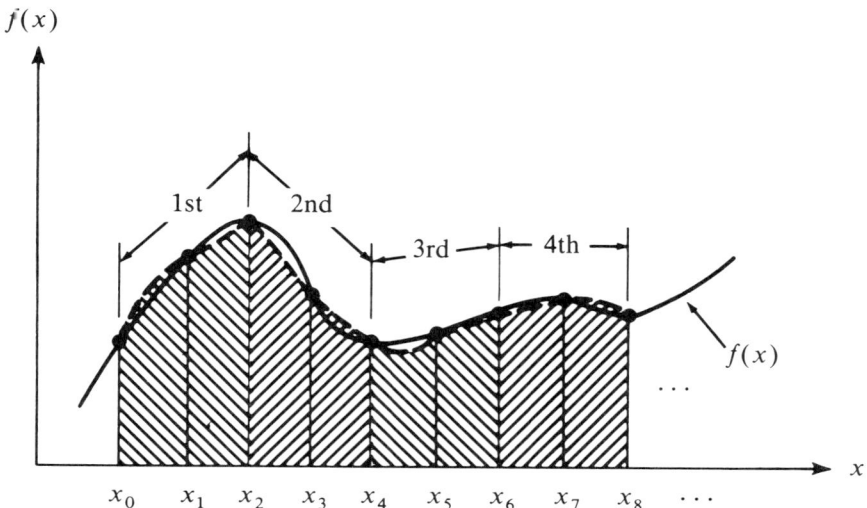

Fig. 5.7. Composite Simpson's rule. The integral is the sum of the integrals over the designated subintervals.

where $h = (b - a)/2N$. The upper bound for the approximation error can be simplified by the technique used for the composite trapezoid rule.

$$e(F) = \frac{h^4 (b - a)}{180} f^{(iv)}(\xi)$$

Example 5.7:

Find the integral of $\sin x$ from $\pi/4$ to $3\pi/4$.

In a previous section the elementary integration rules were found to be insufficiently accurate for this problem.

x_i	$\sin x_i$
$\pi/4$	0.7071
$\pi(1/4 + 1/12)$	0.8660
$\pi(1/4 + 1/6)$	0.9659
$\pi/2$	1.0000
$\pi(1/2 + 1/12)$	0.9659
$\pi(1/2 + 1/6)$	0.8660
$3\pi/4$	0.7071

Select every other base point and apply the trapezoid rule three times with $h = \pi/6$.

$$F = (\pi/6)[0.5 (0.7071 + 0.7071) + 0.9659 + 0.9659] = 1.3817$$

The fourth derivative of $\sin x$ is $\sin x$, which is maximal on the interval of integration at $\xi = \pi/2$. Thus, the upper bound for the approximation error is

$$e(F) = \frac{\sin(\xi)(\pi/6)^2(\pi/2)}{12} = \frac{\pi^3}{864} = 0.0359$$

Example 5.8:

This result is closer to the true solution of 1.4142 than was obtained with a single application of the trapezoid rule ($F = 1.1107$), but it is less accurate than even one application of Simpson's rule ($F = 1.4174$). If all seven base points are used and the trapezoid rule applied six times with $h = \pi/12$, a better result is obtained.

$$F = (\pi/12)[0.5 (0.7071 + 0.7071) + 2(0.8660) + 2(0.9659) + 1.0]$$
$$= 1.4061$$
$$e(F) = \frac{(\pi/12)^2(\pi/2)}{12} = 0.0090$$

Using the composite Simpson's rule with $h = \pi/12$

$$F = (\pi/36)[2\ (0.7071) + 2(0.9659 + 0.9659)$$
$$+ 4(0.866 + 1. + 0.866)] = 1.4142$$

$$e(F) = \frac{\sin(\pi/2)(\pi/12)^4(\pi/2)}{180} = \frac{\pi^5}{360 \times 12^5} = 4.099 \times 10^{-5}$$

So this formula is exact to within the four decimal places carried in the calculation.

5.7 ROMBERG QUADRATURE

Error Reduction for the Composite Trapezoid Rule

For a sufficiently small step size, composite integration rules are more accurate than Newton-Cotes formulas for the same number of base points. If the function to be integrated between given limits is known analytically, additional base points can be generated until the corresponding approximation error is within an acceptable tolerance. A systematic way to generate these additional base points is needed.

The composite trapezoid rule may be written as

$$F = \int_a^b f(x)\ dx = h\left\{0.5[(f(x_0) + f(x_N)] + \sum_{i=1}^{N-1} f(x_i)\right\} + \sum_{j=1}^{\infty} c_j h^{2j}$$

where N is the number of subintervals on $[a, b]$, the final summation is the approximation error $e(F)$, and c_j is a constant. Suppose two estimates $T_{1,r}$ and $T_{1,s}$ of the integral F were obtained with $N = r$ and $N = s$, respectively. Then there is a linear combination $T_{2,s}$ of $T_{1,r}$ and $T_{1,s}$ such that the first term in the series for the approximation error vanishes and $e(F) = O(h^4)$ instead of $O(h^2)$. A third estimate $T_{1,t}$ of F permits a linear combination $T_{2,t}$ of $T_{1,s}$ and $T_{1,t}$ with an approximation error $e(F) = O(h^4)$. A linear combination of $T_{2,s}$ and $T_{2,t}$ which has an approximation error of $O(h^6)$ can now be found. This strategy is sometimes called "acceleration" because the approximation error is reduced more rapidly than it is by merely adding new base points to the composite trapezoid rule.

Richardson Extrapolation

Let the quantity T_{jk} be an estimate of F with $k - 1$ halvings of $h = (b - a)/N$ and equal a linear combination of estimates based on j evaluations of the composite trapezoid rule. After the first halving of the step size

$$T_{1,1} - T_{1,2} = \frac{3}{48}(b - a)\ h^2 f''(\xi) = 3\ (T_{1,2} - F) + O(h^4)$$

and

$$F = \frac{4}{3} T_{1,2} - \frac{1}{3} T_{1,1} + O(h^4)$$

$$T_{2,2} = T_{1,2} + \frac{1}{3} (T_{1,2} - T_{1,1})$$

The approximation error has been reduced by a factor of 1/4 by halving the step size, $(h/2)^2 = h^2/4$. Eliminating the $O(h^2)$ term by computing the linear combination reduces the error by another factor of 1/4, $(h/2)^4 = h^4/16$.

If the step size is halved again and $T_{1,3}$ is computed by the composite trapezoid rule,

$$T_{2,3} = T_{1,3} + \frac{1}{3} (T_{1,3} - T_{1,2})$$

with $e(F) = O(h^4)$. This error term is eliminated by computing the linear combination

$$T_{3,3} = T_{2,3} + \frac{1}{7} (T_{2,3} - T_{2,2})$$

Halving the step size again and repeating this process gives

$$T_{4,4} = T_{3,4} + \frac{1}{15} (T_{3,4} - T_{3,3})$$

The general formula is

$$T_{j+1,k+1} = T_{j,k+1} + \frac{1}{4^j - 1} (T_{j,k+1} - T_{jk})$$

This technique is called "Richardson extrapolation" and is the basis of the "Romberg quadrature" algorithm.

Romberg Tableau

The quantities T_{jk} form a triangular table whose kth entry in column $j + 1$ is calculated from the kth and the $k - 1$st entries in column j.

$$
\begin{array}{llll}
T_{1,1} \\
T_{1,2} & T_{2,2} \\
T_{1,3} & T_{2,3} & T_{3,3} \\
T_{1,4} & T_{2,4} & T_{3,4} & T_{4,4} \\
\hline
\end{array}
$$

After the first halving of the step size, $T_{1,1}$ and $T_{1,2}$ are known. They are used to compute $T_{2,2}$. Note that once $T_{1,1}$ and $T_{1,2}$ have been used to calculate $T_{2,2}$ they are never again used. Therefore, the entire tableau does not have to be stored during the computation; only the most recently computed row is retained.

After m rows of the tableau have been calculated, T_{mm} is compared with $T_{m-1,m-1}$. If they differ by less than some preset tolerance, the algorithm has converged to the desired degree of precision. In the limit of infinitesimal step size, that is, as m approaches infinity, T_{mm} approaches F, the true value of the integral.

Algorithm

$h = b - a$

calculate $T_{1,1}$ by the elementary trapezoid rule

for $k = 2, 3,...$ until satisfied do

$h = h/2$

calculate $T_{1,k}$ by the composite trapezoid rule

for $m = 2,..., k$ do

$T_{mk} = T_{m-1,k} + (T_{m-1,k} - T_{m-1,k-1})/(4^{m-1} - 1)$

if $T_{mm} - T_{m-1,m-1} < \varepsilon$, output solution and stop

if $k =$ maxiter, stop

5.8   GAUSSIAN QUADRATURE

Unequally Spaced Base Points

The quadrature, or integration, formulas presented so far can be represented by a weighted sum of function values at equally spaced base points.

$$F = \int_a^b f(x)\,dx = \int_a^b p_n(x)\,dx + R_n(x) \approx \sum_{i=0}^n w_i\,f(x_i)$$

where the weights w_i depend on the spacing of the base points. These formulas are derived by integrating term by term the interpolating polynomial which passes through the $n + 1$ base points. That is, because

$$p_n(x) = \sum_{i=0}^n l_i(x)\,f(x_i)$$

the weights are given by

$$w_i = \int_a^b l_i(x)\,dx.$$

For a given set of abscissa values x_i, the $n + 1$ function values $f(x_i)$ are the $n + 1$ parameters in the formula. Therefore, the Lagrange interpolating polynomial is of degree n, making the rule exact for polynomial functions of degree $\leqslant n$. If the locations of the base points were allowed to vary as well, there would be another $n + 1$ parameters, the x_i's, and the resulting integration rule would be exact for polynomials of degree $\leqslant 2n + 1$. The locations of the base points and the weights which give this behavior can be found by solving the $2n + 2$ simultaneous equations

$$\int_a^b x^j \, dx = \sum_{i=0}^n w_i \, x_i^j \qquad j = 0, 1,..., 2n + 1$$

Gauss-Legendre Quadrature

Solution of the above $2n + 2$ nonlinear equations adds considerably to the cost of computing the integral. This problem may be overcome by a change of variable

$$z = \frac{2x - (a + b)}{b - a}$$

$$g(z) = f(x) = f\left(\frac{z(b - a) + a + b}{2}\right)$$

where z is defined on $[-1, 1]$. The interpolating polynomial on this interval which satisfies the $2n + 2$ equations is called the "Legendre polynomial" of degree n and is given the symbol $P_n(x)$. The first four of these polynomials are

$$P_0(x) = 1$$
$$P_1(x) = -x + 1$$
$$P_2(x) = (3x^2 - 1)/2$$
$$P_3(x) = (5x^3 - 3x)/2$$

The formula for the integral in terms of z is

$$F = \int_{-1}^1 g(z) \, dz = \int_{-1}^1 P_n(z) \, dz = \sum_{i=0}^n w_i g(z_i)$$

where the weights are the integrals of the terms of $P_n(x)$ and the z_i's are the zeros of $P_n(x)$. Because these values depend only on n, the degree of the polynomial, they are generally tabulated rather than computed anew for each application of the quadrature formula.

Transforming back from z to x gives the most useful form of the quadrature rule.

$$F = \int_a^b f(x) \, dx \approx 0.5(b - a) \sum_{i=0}^n w_i f(0.5(z_i(b - a) + b + a))$$

The zeros of the polynomial and the corresponding weights for two-, three-, and four-point formulas are:

z_i	w_i
($n = 1$)	
± 0.577350	1.000000
($n = 2$)	
0.000000	0.888889
± 0.774597	0.555556
($n = 3$)	
± 0.339981	0.652145
± 0.861136	0.347855

The upper bound for the approximation error is

$$e(F) = \frac{2^{2n+1}(n!)^4}{(2n+1)[(2n)!]^3} f^{(2n)}(\xi)$$

Example 5.9:

Find

$$\int_{\pi/4}^{3\pi/4} \sin x \, dx$$

to four decimal places using the three-point Gauss-Legendre rule.

$$F = \sum_{i=0}^{2} w_i f(0.5(z_i\pi/2 + \pi))$$

Using the tabulated values of the zeros of $P_2(x)$ and their corresponding weights,

$$F = (\pi/4)[0.5556 \sin(-0.7746\pi/4 + \pi/2) + 0.8889 \sin(\pi/2)$$
$$+ 0.5556 \sin (0.7746\pi/4 + \pi/2)]$$
$$= (\pi/4)[0.5556 \times 0.8205 + 0.8889 + 0.5556 \times 0.8205] = 1.4142$$

The upper bound of the approximation error is

$$e(F) = [2^3 \cdot (2!)^4 \sin (\pi/2)]/[5 \cdot (4!)^3] = 0.0296$$

This result is exact to the precision carried in the calculation and is more accurate than Simpson's rule, which produced an error of 0.0032 in the value of the integral. Use of the two-point Gauss-Legendre rule gives a value of

$$F = \sin(\pi/(-4\sqrt{3}) + \pi/2) + \sin(\pi/(4\sqrt{3}) + \pi/2) = 1.4121$$

with an approximate error of 0.3333 for the integral. Even this result is more accurate than that given by the three-point Newton-Cotes rule. In practical applications, the function to be integrated is generally more complicated or varies less smoothly than sin x, and a higher-order quadrature formula must be used. The same accuracy could be obtained using Romberg quadrature, but much more computation would be necessary. Romberg integration is most useful when extreme accuracy is required and the number of base points which would produce that degree of accuracy is not known in advance.

5.9 COMPUTER PROGRAMS

```
            SUBROUTINE DERIV(X, H, FUNC, DX)
C*****************************************************************
C* Derivatives by central finite differences.  X is the point at *
C* which the derivative is desired, H is the step size, and FUNC *
C* is the name of the function to be differentiated.  FUNC must  *
C* be supplied by the user and declared EXTERNAL in the calling  *
C* routine.  The value of the derivative is returned in DX.      *
C*****************************************************************

      YPLUS = FUNC(X + H)
      YMINUS = FUNC(X - H)
      DX = (YPLUS - YMINUS)/(2.0*H)
      RETURN
      END
```

```
procedure deriv(x, h: real; function func(arg: real): real;
var            dx: real);
{
 *****************************************************************
 * Derivatives by central finite differences.  x is the point at *
 * which the derivative is desired, h is the step size, and func  *
 * is the name of the user-supplied function to be differentiated.*
 * The value of the derivative is returned in dx.                *
 *****************************************************************
}
var
  yplus, yminus: real;

begin
  yplus := func(x + h);
  yminus := func(x - h);
  dx := (yplus - yminus)/2.*h)
end;
```

```
            SUBROUTINE COMSMP(NBASE, H, Y, INTGRL)
C*****************************************************************
C* Integration by the composite Simpson's rule with NBASE (must  *
```

```
C* be an odd number) base points. H is the step size, and Y is a  *
C* vector of function values at the base points.  The result is   *
C* returned in INTGRL.                                            *
C*****************************************************************

      REAL INTGRL
      DIMENSION Y(1)

      INTGRL = 0.0
      DO 10 I = 1, NBASE-2, 2
10       INTGRL = INTGRL + Y(I) + 4.*Y(I+1) + Y(I+2)
      INTGRL = INTGRL*H/3.0
C
C -- Output results
C
      WRITE 1000
1000  FORMAT(5x,'Integration by the Composite Simpson's Rule/')
      WRITE 2000, INTGRL
2000  FORMAT(5X,'Integral =',1PE12.5)

      RETURN
      END

procedure CompSimpson(nbase: integer; h: real; y: vector;
                      var integral: real);
{
*****************************************************************
* Integration by the composite Simpson's rule with nbase (must  *
* be an odd number) base points.  h is the step size, and y is a *
* vector of function values at the base points.  The data type   *
* vector must be defined as array[1..nbase] of real in the call- *
* ing routine.  The result is returned in integral.             *
*****************************************************************
}
var
  i: integer;

begin
  integral := 0.0;
  i := 1;
  repeat
    integral := integral + y[i] + 4.*y[i+1] + y[i+2];
    i := i + 2
  until i = nbase;
  integral := integral*h/3.0;

{Output results}

  writeln('     Integration by the Composite Simpson's Rule');
  writeln;
  writeln('     Integral =',integral:12)
end;
```

```
      SUBROUTINE ROMBRG(A, B, TOLER, MAXHLV, FUNC, INTGRL)
C**********************************************************************
C* Integration of the user-supplied function FUNC by Romberg      *
C* quadrature.  FUNC must be declared EXTERNAL in the calling     *
C* routine.  A and B are the limits of integration. TOLER is the  *
C* desired precision of the solution, which is returned in        *
C* INTGRL.  MAXHLV is the maximum number (up to 50) of interval   *
C* halvings permitted.                                            *
C**********************************************************************

      REAL INTGRL
      DIMENSION T(51), FVAL(49)

      WRITE 1000
1000  FORMAT(5X,'Integration by Romberg Quadrature'//
     1   12X, 'Composite', 2X, 'Extrapolated'/
     2   ' Iteration  Integral    Integral'/)
C
C -- First estimate of integral from elementary trapezoid rule
C
      NHALVE = 0
      NSTEPS = 1
      H = B - A
      FA = (FUNC(A) - FUNC(B))/2.0
      T(I) = H*FA
      INTGRL = T(1)
      WRITE 2000, NHALVE+1,INTGRL
2000  FORMAT(4X, I3, 3X, 1PE11.4, IX, 1PE11.4)
C
C -- Halve step size
C
1     NHALVE = NHALVE + 1
      H = H/2
      NSTEPS = 2*NSTEPS
      STORE1 = T(1)
C
C -- Get new estimate of integral by composite trapezoid rule.
C    Evaluate the function values only for the base points
C    newly created by interval halving
C
      J = 0
      DO 10 I = NSTEPS-1, 1, 2
        J = J + 1
        FVAL(I) = FUNC(A + I*H)
10      IF (I.GT.1) FVAL(I-1) = FVAL(NSTEPS/2 - J)
      T(1) = FA
      DO 20 I = 1, NSTEPS-1
20      T(1) = T(1) + FVAL(I)
      T(1) = H*T(1)
C
C -- Richardson extrapolation
C
```

```
          DO 30 I = 2, NHALVE+1
            STORE2 = T(I)
            T(I) = T(I-1) + (T(I-1) - STORE1)/(4.**(I-1) - 1.)
30          STORE1 = STORE2
            WRITE 2000, NHALVE+1,T(1),T(NHALVE+1)
C
C -- Check for convergence or maximum interval halvings
C
          IF (ABS(T(NHALVE+1) - INTGRL).LE.TOLER) GO TO 2
          IF (NHALVE.GE.MAXHLV) GO TO 3
C
C -- Else continue algorithm
C
            INTGRL = T(NHALVE+1)
            GO TO 1
C
C -- Output results
C
2         WRITE 3000, NHALVE, INTGRL
3000      FORMAT (' Convergence achieved after',I3,' interval
halvings'
      1   /'5x,'Integral =',1PE12.5)
C
C -- Maximum halvings exceeded
C
3         WRITE 4000, MAXHLV, INTGRL
4000      FORMAT(' No convergence achieved after',I3,
      1   ' interval halvings'/5x,'Integral =',1PE12.5)

          RETURN;
          END


procedure Romberg(a, b, toler: real; maxhlv: integer; function
        func(arg: real): real; var integral: real);
{
**********************************************************************
* Integration of the user-supplied function func by Romberg quad-*
* rature.  a and b are the limits of integration.  Toler is the  *
* desired precision of the solution, which is returned in the    *
* variable integral.  Maxhlv is the maximum number (up to 50) of *
* interval halvings permitted.                                   *
**********************************************************************
}
type
  flag = (continue, converge, maxiter);

var
  i, j, nhalve, nsteps: integer;
  fval: array[1..49] of real;
  T: array[1..51] of real;
  h, FA, store1, store2: real;
  status: flag;
```

```
function power(base: real; exponent: integer): real;

{Compute base to the exponent power}

var
  i: integer;

begin
  power := base;
  if (exponent > 1) for i := 2 to exponent
    power := power*base
end;

begin
  writeln('       Integration by Romberg quadrature');
  writeln;
  writeln('               Composite   Extrapolated');
  writeln(' Iteration  Integral     Integral');
  writeln;

  status := continue;

  {First estimate of integral from elementary trapezoid rule}

  nhalve := 0;
  nsteps := 1;
  h := b - a;
  FA := (func(a) + func(b))/2.0;
  T[1] := h*FA;
  integral := T[1];
  writeln('      ', nhalve+1:3, '    ', integral:11);

  while status = continue do
    begin

      {halve step size}

      nhalve := nhalve + 1;
      h := h/2.0;
      nsteps := 2*nsteps;
      store1 := T[1];

      {Get new estimate of integral by composite trapezoid rule.
       Evaluate the function values only for the base points
       newly created by interval halving}

      j := 0;
      i := nsteps - 1;
      repeat
        j := j + 1;
        fval[i] := func(a + i*h);
        if (i > 1) fval[i-1] := fval[nsteps/2 - j];
        i := i - 2
```

```
      until i = 1;
      T[1] := FA;
      for i := 1 to nsteps-1 do
        T[1] := T[1] + fval[i]:
      T[1] := h*T[1];

      {Richardson extrapolation}

      for i := 2 to nhalve+1 do
        begin
          store2 := T[i];
          T[i] := T[i-1] + (T[i-1] - store1)/
                  (power(4.0, i-1) - 1.0);
        end;
      writeln('       ', nhalve+1:3, '     ', T[1]:11, ' ',
              T[nhalve+1]:11);

      {Check for convergence or maximum interval halvings}

      if (abs(T[nhalve+1] - integral) <= toler)
        status := converge
        else if (nhalve >= maxhlv) status := maxiter;
      integral := T[nhalve+1]
    end; {of while}

  case status of

    converge:
      begin
        writeln('Convergence achieved after',nhalve:3,
                'interval halvings');
        writeln('       Integral =',integral:12)
      end;

    maxiter:
      begin
        writeln('No convergence achieved after',nhalve:3,
                'interval halvings');
        writeln('     Current estimate of integral =',
                integral:12)
      end
  end {of case}
end;

               SUBROUTINE LGENDR(A, B, INTGRL, FUNC)
C****************************************************************
C* Integration by 10-point Gauss-Legendre quadrature.  A and B  *
C* are the limits of integration, and FUNC is the user-supplied *
C* function to be integrated.  The result is returned in INTGRL. *
C****************************************************************

      REAL INTGRL
      DIMENSION Z(10), WEIGHT(10)
```

```
        DATA (Z(I),
I=1,10)/-.9739065285,-.8650633667,-.6794095683,
     1   -.4333953941,-.1488743390,.1488743390,.4333953941,
     2   .6794095683,.8650633667,.9739065285/
        DATA (WEIGHT(I),
I=1,10)/.0666713443,.1494513492,.2190863625,
     1   .2692667193,.2955242247,.2955242247,.2692667193,
     2   .2190863625,.1494513492,.0666713443/

        INTGRL = 0.0
        DO 10 I = 1, 10
          Y = (Z(I)*(B - A) + A + B)/2.0
10        INTGRL = INTGRL + WEIGHT(I)*FUNC(Y)
        INTGRL + INTGRL*(B - A)/2.0
C
C -- Output results
C
        WRITE 1000
1000    FORMAT(5X,'Integration by 10-point Gauss-Legendre',
     1   ' Quadrature'/)
2000    FORMAT(5X,'Integral =',1PE12.5)
        RETURN
        END
```

```
procedure Legendre(a, b,: real; var integral: real;
                 function func(arg: real): real);
{
**********************************************************************
* Integration by 10-point Gauss-Legendre quadrature.  a and b     *
* are the limits of integration, and func is the user-supplied    *
* function to be integrated.  The result is returned in integral. *
**********************************************************************
}
var
  z, weight: array[1..10] of real;
  i: integer;
  y: real;

begin

  {Set up z and weight arrays}

  z[1]  := -.9739065285;      weight[1]  := .0666713443;
  z[2]  := -.8650633677;      weight[2]  := .1494513492;
  z[3]  := -.6794095683;      weight[3]  := .2190863625;
  z[4]  := -.4333953941;      weight[4]  := .2692667193;
  z[5]  := -.1488743390;      weight[5]  := .2955242247;
  z[6]  :=  .1488743390;      weight[6]  := .2955242247;
  z[7]  :=  .4333953941;      weight[7]  := .2692667193;
  z[8]  :=  .6794095683;      weight[8]  := .2190863625;
  z[9]  :=  .8650633667;      weight[9]  := .1494513492;
  z[10] := .9739065285;       weight[10] := .0666713443;
```

```
integral := 0.0;
for i := 1 to 10 do
   begin
      y := (z[i]*(b - a) + a + b)/2.0;
      integral := integral + weight[i]*func(y)
   end;
integral := integral*(b - a)/2.0;

{Output results}

writeln('     Integration by 10-point Gauss-Legendre',
        'Quadrature');
writeln;
writeln('     integral =',integral:12)
end;
```

5.10 EXAMPLE PROBLEMS

Example 5.10:

Electrical power is defined as the time rate of change of current. An engineering student measured the current in an electrical circuit at four points in time and obtained the following results.

time, min	*i*, mA
0.40	5.595
1.00	9.633
1.60	11.275
2.20	11.943

The student was to estimate the power dissipation at 1.6 min to three decimal places with the most accurate formula applicable.

Solution

Because the approximation error decreases as $h^n/(n + 1)!$, where n is the degree of the Gregory-Newton interpolating polynomial which passes through the base points, using all four base points will result in the most accurate differentiation rule. The fourth-order formula in terms of s variables is

$$i'(s) = \frac{\Delta f_0}{h} + \frac{2s - 1}{2h}\, \Delta^2 f_0 + \frac{3s^2 - 6s + 2}{6h}\, \Delta^3 f_0$$

For this problem $s = 2$ and $h = 0.6$. The forward differences are

```
5.595
        4.038
9.633               -2.396
        1.642                   1.422
11.275              -0.974
        0.668
11.943
```

Substituting for the forward differences

$$i'(s) = i'(2) = 4.038/0.6 + (3/1.2)(-2.396) + (2/3.6)(1.422)$$
$$= 1.527 \text{ mA/min}$$

Example 5.11:

The rate of heat loss per unit length for a vapor passing through a tubular condenser is given by

$$q = -2\pi rk \frac{dT}{dx}$$

where r is the radius of the inner tube of the condenser, k is the heat conduction coefficient, and x is the distance from the vapor inlet. A chemical engineer measured the following temperatures of a vapor at several points within a condenser tube 4 centimeters in diameter and 36 centimeters long.

x, cm	T, °C
0	80
12	52
24	39
36	32

The engineer estimated the slope of the T vs. x curve at the above four points, using a curve-fitting procedure.

x, cm	dT/dx, °C/cm
0	-3.5000
12	-1.4983
24	-0.7619
36	-0.4910

The total rate of heat loss in the condenser is given by

$$Q = \int_0^{36} q \, dx = -2\pi r k \int_0^{36} (dT/dx) \, dx$$

The heat conduction coefficient of the cooling water in the condenser jacket is $k = 0.00145$ cal/sec $\cdot$ cm $\cdot$ °C. Find the total rate of heat loss.

Solution

Substituting $n = 3$ into the general Newton-Cotes closed formula gives

$$F = \int_a^b f(x) \, dx = h \left(3f_0 + \frac{9}{2} \Delta f_0 + \frac{9}{4} \Delta^2 f_0 + \frac{3}{8} \Delta^3 f_0 \right)$$

for the integral of the cubic which passes through the four base points. On expansion of the forward differences and simplification, the four-point integration rule becomes

$$F = \frac{3}{8} h \left(f_0 + 3f_1 + 3f_2 + f_3 \right)$$

In the present case

$$F = (-4\pi k) (3 \times 12/8) (-3.5000 - 3 \times 1.4983$$
$$- 3 \times 0.7619 - 0.4910) = 0.8832 \text{ cal/sec}$$

Example 5.12:

A physicist measured the energy flux $q(\lambda)$ at four wavelengths and obtained the following values

λ, cm	q, ergs/sec
0.5	0.4155
1.0	0.0260
1.5	0.0051
2.0	0.0016

The total radiant energy flux between wavelengths λ_1 and λ_2 is given by

$$Q = \int_{\lambda_1}^{\lambda_2} q(\lambda) \, d\lambda$$

The physicist requires the total radiant energy flux with four-decimal-place precision. He suspects that he does not have a sufficient number of base points on the interval of integration to obtain this precision with the four-point Newton-Cotes closed formula. This formula has the same approximation error as Simpson's rule

$$e(F) = h^5 f^{(iv)}(\xi)/90$$

but estimating the approximation error by evaluating the fourth derivative is onerous. Instead, the physicist, knowing the black-body radiation law, used Romberg integration with $a = 0.5$, $b = 2$, and the convergence tolerance $\varepsilon = 5 \times 10^{-5}$.

The radiant energy flux at wavelength λ emitted by a black body at temperature T is given by

$$q = \frac{2hc^2}{\lambda^5 (e^{hc/k\lambda T} - 1)}$$

where h is Planck's constant, c is the speed of light, and k is Boltzmann's constant. At 1000°K, this equation simplifies to

$$q = \frac{3.742 \times 10^5}{\lambda^5 (e^{0.001439/\lambda} - 1)}$$

Step 1: Calculate the integral from the elementary trapezoid rule.

$$q(0.5) = 0.41547$$
$$q(2.0) = 0.001625$$
$$T_{1,1} = [(a - b)/2] \cdot [f(a) + f(b)]$$
$$= (1.5/2)(0.41547 + 0.001625) = 0.20855$$

Step 2: Halve the step size and find q at the midpoint of the interval $[a, b]$.

$$q(1.25) = 0.009883$$

Estimate the integral by the composite trapezoid rule

$$T_{2,1} = h[f(a)/2 + f(b)/2] + f(a + h)]$$
$$= 0.75(0.41547/2 + 0.001625/2 + 0.009883) = 0.16439$$

Step 3: Perform the Richardson extrapolation.

$$T_{2,2} = T_{2,1} + (T_{2,1} - T_{1,1})/(4^1 - 1)$$
$$= 0.20855 + (0.20855 - 0.16439)/3 = 0.11492$$

Note that the black-body radiation law is strongly concave upwards on the interval $[a, b]$. Therefore, the trapezoid bounded by $\lambda = a$, $\lambda = b$, and the secant line from $q(a)$ to $q(b)$ includes a sizable region above the curve (Fig. 5.8). The integral is reduced by halving the step size and is further reduced by the Richardson extrapolation.

Step 4: Compare $T_{2,2}$ with $T_{1,1}$. As the difference exceeds ε, repeat

$q(\lambda)$

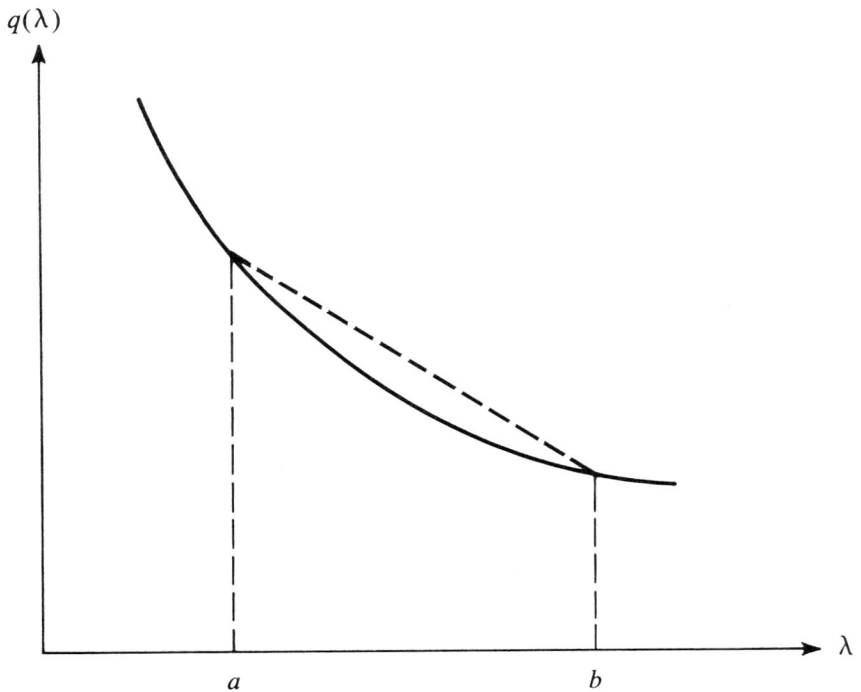

Fig. 5.8. Because the secant line lies substantially above the curve for $q(\lambda)$, trapezoidal integration will result in excessive error.

steps 2 and 3, computing the third line of the Romberg tableau. This yields an estimate of 0.07642 for the integral. As the difference between $T_{3,3}$ and $T_{2,2}$ exceeds ε, repeat the procedure again.

After five interval halvings the tableau has the form

0.20855

0.16439   0.11492

0.10022   0.07882   0.07642

0.07733   0.06970   0.06909   0.06897

0.07058   0.06833   0.06824   0.06822   0.06822

0.06879   0.06820   0.06819   0.06819   0.06819   0.06819

As $T_{6,6} - T_{5,5} = 3 \times 10^{-5} < \varepsilon$, the total radiant energy flux to four decimal places is 0.0682 cal/sec.

chapter 6

Solution of Ordinary Differential Equations

6.1 SOLUTION BY TAYLOR SERIES

There are many processes encountered in science or engineering whose dynamics are specified by an equation of the form

$$F\left(x, y, \frac{dy}{dx}, \frac{d^2y}{dx^2}, \ldots, \frac{d^ny}{dx^n}\right) = 0$$

where $y = f(x)$. Such an equation is called an "ordinary differential equation" of order n. If $y = f(\mathbf{x})$, $\mathbf{x} = (x_1, x_2, \ldots, x_m)^T$, the equation

$$F\left(x_1, \ldots, x_m, y, \frac{\partial y}{\partial x_1}, \ldots, \frac{\partial^n y}{\partial x_1^n}, \ldots, \frac{\partial y}{\partial x_m}, \ldots, \frac{\partial^n y}{\partial x_m^n}\right) = 0$$

is called a "partial differential equation" of order n. Only ordinary differential equations will be considered here.

Suppose we have the second-order equation

$$y'' + 50\, e^{yy'} + \cos x = 0$$

By substituting $z = y'$, the above equation reduces to two simultaneous first-order equations

$$y' = z$$
$$z' = -50\, e^{yz} - \cos x$$

which can be solved for y and z at various values of x by the methods outlined in this chapter. As this process can be extended to still higher derivatives, only first-order equations will be considered here.

Boundary Values and Simulation

The differential equation

$$y' + 2y = 0$$

has the general solution

$$y = Ce^{-2x}$$

where C is an arbitrary constant and

$$y' = -2Ce^{-2x} = -2y$$

In order to find a unique solution more information must be supplied. For an nth order equation, n conditions, normally n values of y at specified x values, are required. Substitution of these x and y values into the analytical solution permits the calculation of C. If all n y values are specified for the same x value, the mathematical problem is called an "initial value problem." If more than one x value is involved, the problem is a "boundary value problem."

Rarely is the differential equation describing the behavior of a physical process sufficiently simple to permit its analytical solution. Instead, the value y_0 of y at some x value x_0 is specified, and the initial value problem is solved by using y', the local slope of the unknown function $y(x)$, to extrapolate $y_0 = y(x_0)$ to $y_1 = y(x_1) = y(x_0 + h)$ by numerical integration. The same operations can be performed with x_1 and y_1 as were done with x_0 and y_0, thereby extrapolating the solution to (x_2, y_2). This procedure can be repeated until an array of closely spaced ordered pairs (x, y) describing the curve of y vs. x over some interval of interest is obtained (Fig. 6.1). If there is more than one variable, there will be one differential equation $y'_i = f_i(x, y)$ for each variable. The above procedure would then be applied to each equation in turn at every extrapolation step, generating a curve of y_i vs. x for each variable.

A common application is when x is time (t) and x_0 is $t = 0$. The variable y describes the state of the physical system, and the function $y' = f(t, y)$ models the dynamics of the physical events occurring. The variable y is generated time point by time point from the initial time of the event to the terminal time. In this manner, the behavior of the real physical system is simulated by the mathematical model.

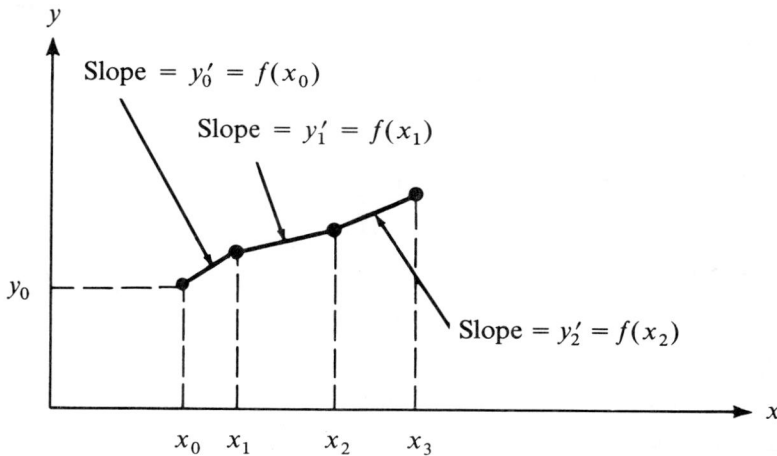

Fig. 6.1. Solution of a differential equation by repeated extrapolation of the function value.

Taylor Series Expansion

Suppose the differential equation to be solved can be written in the form

$$y' = f(x, y)$$
$$y(x_0) = y_0$$

If $x_1 = x_0 + h$ is sufficiently close to x_0, $y(x)$ can be estimated by expanding it about $y(x_0)$ in a Taylor series.

$$y(x_1) = y_0 + hy'(x_0) + \frac{h^2}{2!} y''(x_0) + \dots + \frac{h^n}{n!} y^{(n)}(x_0)$$

The quantity $y(x_1)$ will be referred to as y_1. The approximation error introduced by truncating the infinite Taylor series after $n + 1$ terms is dominated by the next term in the Taylor series. Therefore, an upper bound for the approximation error is

$$e(y_1) = \frac{h^{n+1}}{(n + 1)!} y^{(n+1)}(\xi)$$

where ξ is that point on the interval $[x_0, x_1]$ at which the $n + 1$st derivative is maximal. If the function $y(x)$ is differentiable n times, the Taylor expansion predicts that there will be some h sufficiently small to ensure finding the solution to within the above approximation error.

The various derivatives of y can be evaluated by the chain rule.

$$y' = f(x, y)$$
$$y'' = f'(x, y, y') = f_x + f_y f$$
$$y''' = f'' = f_{xx} + 2f_{xy} f + f_{yy} f^2 + f_x f_y + f_y^2$$

Clearly, unless the function f is very simple, the derivatives can become very complicated and their evalution difficult. This limits the practicality of the Taylor series as a solution method.

Example 6.1:

Given the following differential equation for $y(x)$

$$y' = x(y - 1)$$

and the initial condition

$$y(0) = 2$$

find $y(0.2)$.

Step 1: Find the second and third derivatives analytically.

$$y'' = y - 1 + xy' = y - 1 + x^2(y - 1)$$
$$= (y - 1)(1 + x^2)$$
$$y''' = y'(1 + x^2) + (y - 1)2x = x(y - 1)(1 + x^2) + 2x(y - 1)$$
$$= (y - 1)(x^3 + 3x)$$

Step 2: Evaluate the derivatives at $x = 0$, $y = 2$.

$$y' = 0$$
$$y'' = (2 - 1)(1) = 1$$
$$y''' = 0$$

Step 3: Evaluate the second-order Taylor series. Because y''' is zero, truncating the Taylor series after the second derivative will be as accurate as truncating the series after the third derivative.

$$y(0.2) = y(0) + 0.2y'(0) + (0.2)^2 \, y''(0)/2$$
$$= 2 + 0.2(0) + 0.04(1)/2 = 2.0200$$

The true solution is $y = \exp(x^2/2) + 1$, which is 2.0202 at $x = 0.2$. The approximation error is given by

$$e(y) = \frac{h^4}{4!} y^{(iv)}(\xi)$$

where

$$y^{(iv)} = (y - 1)(x^4 + 6x^2 + 3)$$

In the present case, ξ is the point on the interval $[0, 0.2]$ where the fourth derivative is maximal.

$$e(y) = (0.2)^4 1.0202(0.0016 + 6(0.04) + 3)/24 = 2.2047 \times 10^{-4}$$

which is comparable to the actual error.

6.2 SINGLE-STEP METHODS AND STABILITY

Because of the complexities of evaluating higher-order derivatives, the Taylor series is seldom used for the solution of differential equations. If the infinite series is truncated after the second term, however, the simplified formula is quite manageable.

$$y_{n+1} = y_n + hy'_n = y_n + hf(x_n, y_n)$$

As $f(x, y)$ is known analytically, y' can be evaluated for any (x, y) in the domain of f. Given the initial values (x_0, y_0) the solution $y(x)$ may be extrapolated by small steps h to the terminal value of x. This integration technique is called "Euler's method."

Error of the Euler Approximation

Fig. 6.2 is a graphical representation of Euler's method. Because y' may not be a good estimate of the derivative of the solution function over the entire interval h, the method is generally accurate only for small step sizes. The entire Taylor series is the true solution of the differential equation, and for sufficiently small h each term in the series makes a successively smaller contribution to the solution. The approximation error is therefore dominated by the third term of the Taylor series. An upper bound for the error is given by

$$e_{n+1} = y(x_{n+1}) - y_{n+1} = \frac{h^2}{2} y''(\xi)$$

where ξ is that point on the interval $[x_n, x_{n+1}]$ where y'' is maximal.

Although the approximation error decreases more rapidly than does

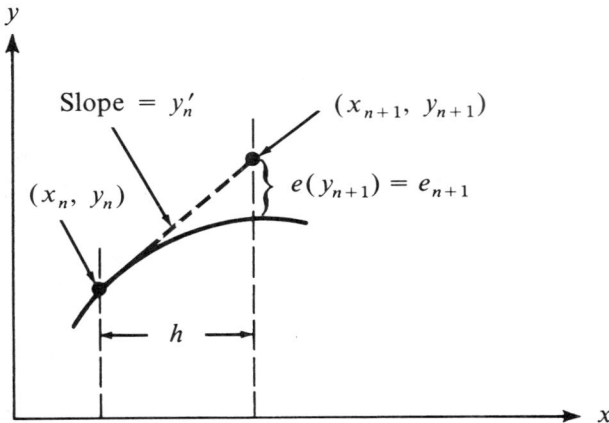

Fig. 6.2. Euler's method for the solution of ordinary differential equations.

the stepsize h, because h must be very small many integration steps are often necessary for solution of the differential equation over the interval of interest. After many steps the accumulated round-off error may produce serious inaccuracy. Suppose that on the interval over which y' is being integrated

$$\left|\frac{\partial f}{\partial y}\right| \leqslant K$$

$$|y''| \leqslant M$$

Then the error can be expressed as

$$e_n \leqslant \frac{hM}{2K} \exp(Khn)$$

Clearly, as h approaches zero (and accordingly, n approaches infinity), e_n approaches zero with the exponential factor approaching unity. Therefore, y_n approaches the true solution $y(x_{n+1})$ linearly with decreasing h. The overall error is $O(h)$ even though the single-step error is $O(h^2)$.

Example 6.2:

$$y' = x(y - 1) \qquad (x_0, y_0) = (0, 2) \qquad h = 0.2$$

$$y_2 = y_1 + hy'(0, 2) = 2 + 0.2(0) = 2$$

Solution by the Taylor series gave $y_2 = 2.0200$, which is close to the correct solution. This discrepancy indicates a serious weakness in Euler's method.

Suppose Euler's method can be used to get a good estimate of y_1. Then the accuracy of the integration can be increased by applying $y' = f(x_1, y_1)$ over the interval $[x_0, x_2]$ of width $2h$ and adding the increment $2hy'$ to y_0 instead of adding hy' to y_1 (Fig. 6.3).

$$y_{n+1} = y_{n-1} + 2hy'_n$$

This is often called the "modified Euler" or "double-interval Euler" method. A better name is the "midpoint rule" because the derivative y' at the middle of the interval is assumed to be a better estimate of the average derivative over the entire interval of width $2h$ than is the derivative at either endpoint.

Expanding the y values at either end of the interval of integration in a Taylor series gives

$$y(x_{n+1}) = y(x_n) + hy'(x_n) + h^2y''(x_n)/2 + h^3y'''(\zeta)/6$$

$$y(x_{n-1}) = y(x_n) - 2hy'(x_n) + h^2y''(x_n)/2 - h^3y'''(\eta)/6$$

where ζ and η are those values on the intervals $[x_{n-1}, x_n]$ and $[x_n, x_{n+1}]$, respectively, where y''' is maximal. Subtracting these two equations yields

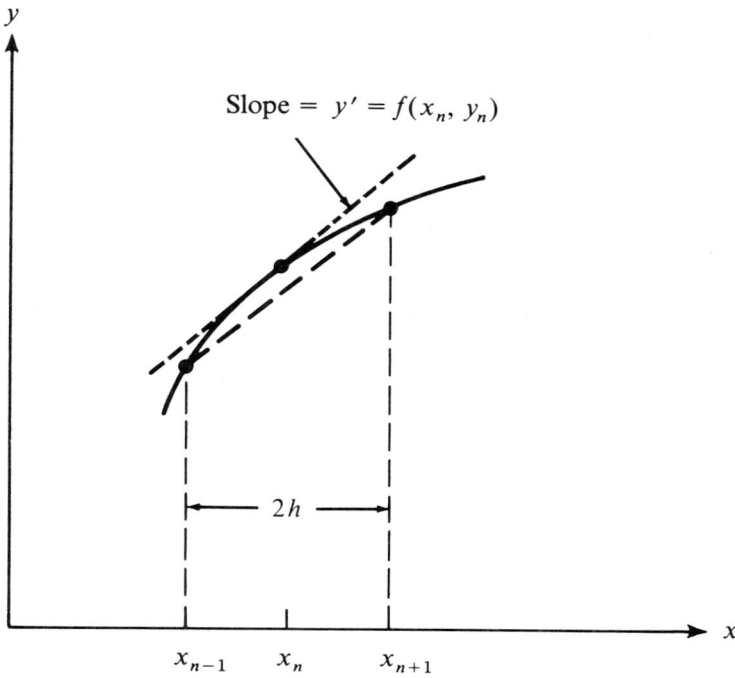

Fig. 6.3. Solution of a differential equation using the midpoint rule.

$$y_{n+1} - y_{n-1} = 2hy'_n + \frac{h^3}{6} [y'''(\zeta) + y'''(\eta)]$$

Because ζ and η are very close numerically, an upper bound for the approximation error of the midpoint rule is

$$e_{n+1} = \frac{h^3}{3} [y'''(\xi)]$$

where ξ is the point on the interval $[x_{n-1}, x_{n+1}]$ where y''' is maximal. This integration rule is more accurate than Euler's method for small h because of its higher-order error term.

Stability

Euler's method and the midpoint rule are called "difference equations," because the difference between y values at the beginning and end of the interval of integration is given as a function of x and y values on the interval. Difference equations generally have analytical solutions of the form $y_n = \alpha^n$. Substitution of this expression into the difference equation gives a characteristic equation in α.

Example 6.3:

Solve the differential equation $y' = -y/L$ (L is a constant called the "relaxation length") using the midpoint rule. Let $x_0 = 0$.

$$y_{n+1} = y_{n-1} - 2hy_n/L$$

Substituting α^n for y_n gives the characteristic equation

$$\alpha^2 + 2h\,\alpha/L - 1 = 0$$

which has solutions

$$\alpha = -\tau \pm \sqrt{1 + \tau^2}$$

where $\tau = h/L$. Therefore, the general solution to the difference equation is

$$y_n = C_1[-\tau + \sqrt{1 + \tau^2}]^n + C_2[-\tau - \sqrt{1 + \tau^2}]^n$$

at $x_n = nh$; C_1 and C_2 are constants.

The analytical solution of the differential equation is

$$y_n = Ce^{-n\tau}$$

where C is a constant. It can be shown by a Taylor series expansion that, for small h, the first term of the general solution approximates the analytical solution. The second term, a "parasitic solution," is proportional to $[-1 - \tau - O(\tau^2)]^n$. Because a number of magnitude greater than unity is being raised to the nth power, no matter how small h is, after a sufficiently large number of steps n the contribution of the second term in the general solution will exceed the contribution of the first term. The midpoint rule is therefore unstable and should be used only with great care.

All higher-order methods of solution of differential equations involve parasitic solutions of their difference equations. To be stable, the parasitic solutions must approach zero with decreasing h faster than does the solution which approximates the analytical solution. The methods described in the following sections either have this stability property or employ a technique to refine an initial estimate of the local solution to compensate for errors.

6.3   RUNGE-KUTTA METHOD

Eulerian methods often require too small a step size to be practical for solution of a differential equation. This behavior arises from their low-order approximation error. Runge-Kutta methods achieve a higher order by utilizing more information about the properties of the function $y' = f(x, y)$ on the interval of a single integration step.

$$y_{n+1} = y_n + h\phi(x_n, y_n, h)$$

where ϕ, the "increment function," is a weighted average of derivative evaluations over the interval $[x_n, x_{n+1}]$.

$$\phi = c_1 k_1 + c_2 k_2 + c_3 k_3 + \ldots$$

The c_i's are the weights and the k_i's are the derivative evaluations. The order of the method equals the number of terms in the increment function. If only one term in the series is retained, c_1 is unity and k_1 is y'_n, namely Euler's method. Second- through fourth-order Runge-Kutta formulas require one evaluation of $f(x, y)$ per term in the increment function. Formulas of fifth or higher order require more derivative evaluations than there are terms in the increment function and are therefore less frequently used.

Derivative Evaluations

The second-order formula will serve as an example of how the derivatives in the increment function are evaluated.

$$k_1 = f(x_n, y_n)$$
$$k_2 = f(x_n + ph, y_n + qhk_1)$$

Note that qhk_1 is an Eulerian estimate of the increment in y needed to reach the point $x_1 + ph$, where the derivative is to be evaluated. Expanding k_2 in a Taylor series and combining terms of like order yields the relationships

$$c_1 + c_2 = 1$$
$$c_2 p = 1/2$$
$$c_2 q = 1/2$$

As there are only three equations constraining the four unknowns, there are an infinite number of choices for the two weights and p and q. If the weights are both set to 1/2 and $p = q = 1$, the formula becomes the trapezoid rule. All higher-order formulas show this same behavior, and convenient integration rules can be derived by judicious selection of the weights and increments in x and y.

One fourth-order Runge-Kutta formula is

$$y_{n+1} = y_n + (h/6)(k_1 + 2k_2 + 2k_3 + k_4)$$
$$k_1 = f(x_n, y_n)$$
$$k_2 = f(x_n + h/2, y_n + (h/2)k_1)$$
$$k_3 = f(x_n + h/2, y_n + (h/2)k_2)$$
$$k_4 = f(x_n + h, y_n + hk_3)$$

There are other fourth-order formulas for other choices of the constants. In this case, k_1 is the derivative evaluated at x_n, the beginning of the interval of integration. K_2 is the derivative evaluated at $x_n + h/2$, the midpoint of that interval. Note that $(h/2)k_1$ is an Eulerian extrapolation of y_n to its value at $x_n + h/2$. Similarly, k_3 is another estimate of the derivative at the midpoint but uses k_2, an estimate of y' at the midpoint, as the derivative in the Eulerian extrapolation of y_n (this is sometimes called the "backwards" Euler method). Finally, k_4 is the derivative evaluated at $x_n + h$, the end of the interval.

Example 6.4:

$y' = -y^2; x_0 = 1; y_0 = 1; h = 0.5$

$k_1 = f(x_0, y_0) = -y_0^2 = -1$

$k_2 = -(y_0 + (h/2)k_1)^2 = -(1 + 0.25(-1))^2 = -0.5625$

$k_3 = -(y_0 + (h/2)k_2)^2 = -(1 + 0.25(-0.5625))^2 = -0.7385$

$k_4 = -(y_0 + hk_3)^2 = -(1 + 0.5(-0.7385))^2 = -0.3978$

$y_1 = y(1.5) = 1 + (0.5/6)(-1 + 2(-0.5625) + 2(-0.7385) - 0.3978)$
$= 0.6667$

The true solution is $y = 1/x$, which, to four decimal places, equals 0.6667 at $x = 1.5$. In contrast, Euler's method with the same step size gives

$$y_1 = y_0 + hy'_0 = 1 = 0.5(1) = 0.5000$$

which is substantially in error.

Step Size Control

To minimize the accumulation of round-off error it is necessary to minimize the number of integration steps taken over the entire interval of solution $[a, b]$ of the differential equation. Because any increase in the step size must not introduce unacceptably large approximation error, a formula for that error is needed. For a Runge-Kutta method of order m the approximation error is $O(h^{m+1})$, but it is given by a very complicated function of the partial derivatives of $f(x, y)$. One way to estimate the error is to perform the computations with an mth-order formula and then repeat them with an $m + 1$st order formula; the difference is the error estimate. This tactic requires an unacceptably large burden of extra computation. However, it can be shown that the first four of the six derivative estimates k_1 to k_6 required for fifth-order Runge-Kutta integration can be used for a fourth-order formula. The difference between the results of the fourth- and fifth-order formulas can be used to control the step size. Discussion of these methods is beyond the scope of this book, but routines implementing them may be found in subroutine libraries such as IMSL.

Another way to estimate the approximation error is to note that for an mth-order formula

$$e_n = \gamma_m h_n^{m+1}$$

after n integration steps. The constant γ_m is generally unknown, but if the two integration steps from x_{n-2} to x_n are repeated using a single step of length $2h$

$$y_n^* = y(x_n) + \gamma_m (2h_n)^{m+1}$$

Comparing this to the results of two steps of length h,

$$y_n = y(x_n) + 2\gamma_m h_n^{m+1}$$

and

$$e_n = \gamma_m h_n^{m+1} = \frac{y_n - y_n^*}{2 - 2^{m+1}}$$

For a fourth-order formula, the constant is given by

$$\gamma_4 = \left| \frac{y_n - y_n^*}{h_n^5 (2 - 2^{m+1})} \right|$$

Frequent recalculation of the error by this method also requires an impractical amount of calculation. There is no guarantee that γ_m will be constant over the entire interval $[a, b]$, but it is unlikely to vary greatly over the span of about ten steps. Let the maximal tolerable error of a single step relative to the fraction of the total interval of integration represented by a single step be denoted by ε. After every (approximately) ten steps, e_n should be recomputed by the double interval technique outlined above and compared to the preset tolerance. If

$$e_n \leq \varepsilon h_n/(b - a)$$

continue with the same step size. Otherwise, as

$$e_n = \gamma_m h_n^{m+1} = \frac{e_{n-1}}{h_{n-1}^{m+1}} h_{n+1}^{m+1}$$

the new step size h_{n+1} is given by

$$h_{n+1} = \left(\frac{\varepsilon h_n^{m+1}}{e_n (b - a)} \right)^{1/m}$$

Similarly, a minimal acceptable error tolerance can be set. If e_n is less than this value, the step size must be increased according to the above formula.

6.4 PREDICTOR-CORRECTOR METHODS

Despite their accuracy Runge-Kutta methods are not practical if the function $y' = f(x, y)$ is very complicated. A fourth-order formula requires four derivative evaluations per integration step, which may impose an excessive computational burden. If a correction can be made to the Eulerian extrapolated value of y_n, it may be possible to compensate for the inaccuracy of Euler's method while retaining its computational simplicity.

Heun's Rule

The trapezoid rule has an approximation error $O(h^3)$, an order higher than Euler's method, but it requires that the derivative at the terminal point of the interval $[x_{n-1}, x_n]$ be known. As y' may be a function of the unknown solution y as well as x, the more accurate trapezoid rule cannot be used by itself. However, once an Eulerian estimate of y_n is available, it can be used to calculate y'_n. When the trapezoid rule is applied, it yields an improved value for y_n, which can be used to calculate a more accurate estimate of y'_n. A second application of the trapezoid rule gives a still-better estimate of y_n, and so on. The iterative refinement of y_n should stop when the difference between two successive estimates is within some preset tolerance. At that point, the approximation error will be within the upper bound for the trapezoid rule. This method is known as "Heun's rule."

Example 6.5:

$$y' = 2x - y; x_0 = 0; y_0 = 1; h = 0.1; \varepsilon = 10^{-4}$$

Step 1: Euler predictor

$$y'_0 = 2(0) - 1 = -1.0$$
$$y_1^{(0)} = y_0 + hy'_0 = 1 - 0.1(1) = 0.90$$

where the superscript indicates the iteration number.

Step 2: Trapezoid corrector, first iteration

$$y'_1{}^{(0)} = 2(0.1) - 0.9 = -0.70$$
$$y_1^{(1)} = y_0 + (h/2)[y'_0 + y'_1{}^{(0)}] = 1 + 0.05[-1.0 - 0.7]$$
$$= 0.915$$

As $y_1^{(1)} - y_1^{(0)} = 0.015 > \varepsilon$, continue the iterations.

Step 3: Second iteration

$$y'_1{}^{(1)} = 2(0.1) - 0.915 = -0.715$$
$$y_1^{(2)} = 1 + 0.05[-1.0 - 0.715] = 0.91425$$

As $|y_1^{(2)} - y_1^{(1)}| = 0.0075 > \varepsilon$, continue the iterations.
    Step 4: Third iteration

$$y'_1{}^{(2)} = 2(0.1) - 0.91425 = -0.71425$$

$$y_1^{(3)} \doteq 1 + 0.05[-1.0 - 0.71425] = 0.9143$$

As $|y_1^{(3)} - y_1^{(2)}| = 0.00005 < \varepsilon$, the iterations may be stopped with the current estimate as the desired solution.

Acceleration of Convergence

It would be ideal if only one iteration of the trapezoid corrector formula were necessary as this would minimize the computation required for the solution of the differential equation over the entire interval of interest. One way to achieve this is to compare the difference between predicted and corrected values of y_n after one application of the corrector formula. If this difference is within the single-step approximation error of the trapezoid rule, continue. Otherwise, set the step size h such that it satisfies the equation for the approximation error

$$\frac{h^3 \, y''' \, (x_n)}{12} = \varepsilon_2$$

where ε_2 is a preset tolerance.

    This tactic ensures convergence after one iteration. If a minimal error ε_1 as well as a maximal error ε_2 are imposed, it is a useful way of selecting the step size. However, it may result in a larger than necessary number of integration steps. Suppose that, after the first integration step, the midpoint rule is used instead of Euler's method as the predictor formula. From the approximation errors of the midpoint and trapezoid rules,

$$y_n^{(pred)} - y(x_n) = -h^3y'''(x_n)/3 + O(h^4)$$

$$y_n^{(corr)} - y(x_n) = h^3y'''(x_n)/12 + O(h^4).$$

Therefore, a weighted average of the predictor's and corrector's values for y_n could result in cancellation of the $O(h^3)$ terms, leaving an approximation error of $O(h^4)$, an order higher than either the predictor or corrector.

$$y(x_n) = (4/5)y_n^{(pred)} + (1/5)y_n^{(corr)} + O(h^4)$$

Only one application of the corrector is necessary before taking this weighted average; the result is superior to iterating the corrector formula. Because Euler's method has an error of $O(h^2)$, this tactic cannot be readily used with the original Heun's rule. Only predictor and corrector formulas of the same order facilitate this method of error reduction.

6.5 MULTISTEP METHODS

The single-step methods for solution of differential equations covered in the last three sections require either a small step size or many derivative evaluations per step to obtain satisfactory accuracy. Although the accuracy of single-step rules can be improved by using the predictor-corrector approach, the result still has a lower-order approximation error than Runge-Kutta formulas. Multistep methods achieve higher order by utilizing information about the behavior of the function $y' = f(x, y)$ at several points on the interval of solution $[a, b]$.

Explicit Formulas

Suppose the value of y is known for a series of equally spaced points x_i, $i = 0, 1, 2,..., n$. There is a unique mth degree interpolating polynomial which includes the points (x_i, y_i), $i = n - m,..., n$. (Note that all of the $n + 1$ points do not have to be used to define the polynomial.) Because y_{n+1} is unknown, an open Newton-Cotes formula of order m must be used to estimate its value. The interpolating polynomial is integrated from x_n to x_{n+1} and the result added to y_n.

$$y_{n+1} = y_n + \int_{x_n}^{x_{n+1}} f(x) \, dx$$

This technique is illustrated for $n = 4$ in Fig. 6.4.

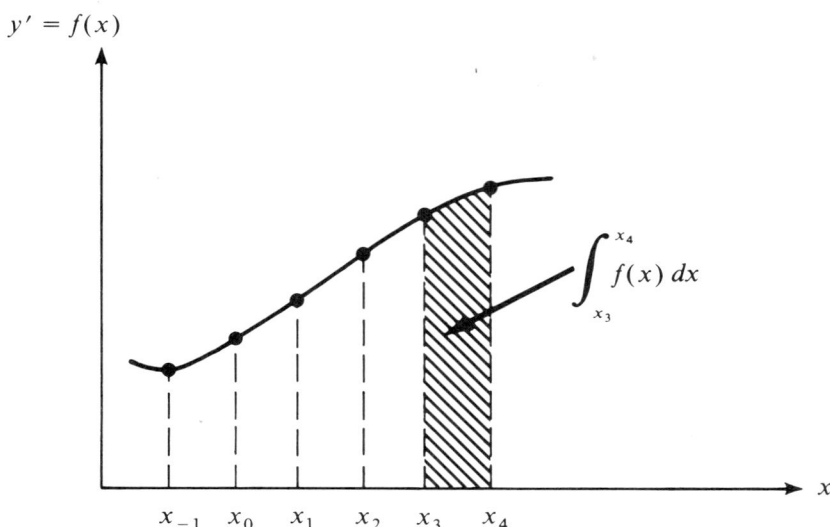

Fig. 6.4. Extrapolation of the function $y(x)$, the solution of the differential equation $y' = f(x)$, from x_3 to x_4.

Replacing $f(x)$ by the expansion for the interpolation polynomial yields

$$y_{n+1} = y_n + \int_0^1 p(x_n + sh)\, ds = y_n + \int_0^1 \sum_{k=1}^m (-1)^k \binom{-s}{k} \nabla^k f_n\, ds$$

$$= y_n + \int_0^1 \sum_{k=1}^m (-1)^k \binom{-s}{k} \Delta^k f_{n-k}\, ds$$

where the step size is given by

$$h = x_{i+1} - x_i$$

The factors $(-1)^k$ are necessary because the value of s is negative for points x_i, $i < n$. Integrating term by term gives the general formula

$$y_{n+1} = y_n + h[\, f_n + \frac{1}{2} \nabla f_n + \frac{5}{12} \nabla^2 f_n + \frac{3}{8} \nabla^3 f_n + \frac{251}{720} \nabla^4 f_n + \ldots\,]$$

This is called an "explicit formula" because it gives y_{n+1} directly as a function of the x and y values of the previous $n + 1$ points.

Denoting $f(x_i, y_i)$ by f_i and expanding the backward differences with $m = 4$,

$$y_{n+1} = y_n + (h/24)(55f_n - 59f_{n-1} + 37f_{n-2} - 9f_{n-3})$$

This is called the "Adams-Bashforth formula." The approximation error for this formula can be obtained by integrating the fifth term in the Gregory-Newton expansion for the interpolating polynomial, as was done for the Newton-Cotes formulas. Substituting for the fourth backward difference and noting that $f^{(iv)} = y^{(v)}$ gives the following upper bound for the approximation error.

$$e_{n+1} = (251/720)h^5 y^{(v)}(\xi)$$

where ξ is the point on the interval $[x_{n-3}, x_n]$ where the fifth derivative is maximal. If the y values for the previous four points are stored in an array rather than recalculated at each integration step, this multistep formula achieves the same degree of accuracy as does the fourth-order Runge-Kutta method but with far less computation.

The closed Newton-Cotes formulas for order greater than two are more accurate than the open formulas of the same order, but they generally cannot be applied by themselves to the solution of differential equations because the function f to be integrated may depend on y as well as on x and y_{n+1} is unknown. If an estimate of y_{n+1} is available (or if y' is a function of x only), y' can be evaluated at x_{n+1} and the closed formulas can be used. Integrating the interpolating polynomial from x_{n-m+1} to x_{n+1} yields the general formula

$$y_{n+1} = y_n + \int_0^1 \sum_{k=1}^m (-1)^k \binom{-s}{k} \nabla^k f_{n+1}\, ds$$

$$= y_n + \int_0^1 \sum_{k=1}^{m} (-1)^k \binom{-s}{k} \Delta^k f_{n-k+1} ds$$

$$y_{n+1} = y_n + h[\, f_{n+1} - \frac{1}{2} \nabla f_{n+1} - \frac{1}{12} \nabla^2 f_{n+1} - \frac{1}{24} \nabla^3 f_{n+1}$$

$$- \frac{19}{720} \nabla^4 f_{n+1} + \cdots]$$

This is called an "implicit formula"; the estimate of y_{n+1} is used to produce an improved value for y_{n+1}.

For $m = 4$, the point x_{n+1} replaces the point x_{n-3} in the Gregory-Newton expansion for the interpolating polynomial and the integration rule becomes

$$y_{n+1} = y_n + \frac{h}{24} (9f_{n+1} + 19f_n - 5f_{n-1} + f_{n-2})$$

This is called the "Adams-Moulton formula." The upper bound for the approximation error is

$$e_n = \frac{19}{720} h^5 y^{(v)}(\xi)$$

where ξ is the point on $[x_{n-2}, x_{n+1}]$ where the fifth derivative is maximal.

Because an implicit rule can begin with a rough estimate of y_{n+1}, it may be necessary to iteratively refine the estimate to obtain the full accuracy of the formula. That is, the improved value for y_{n+1} should be used to reevaluate y'_{n+1}. The implicit rule is then reapplied to further refine the solution. This process is repeated until successive values of y_{n+1} are within some preset tolerance.

Multistep methods, as presented above, have two disadvantages. One is the need for n values of the solution at equally spaced base points for an nth-order formula. For the fourth-order Adams methods outlined here, the fourth-order Runge-Kutta formula is an ideal choice for generating the four starting values. Another problem is that a change in the step size h requires restarting the algorithm with four new points with the new spacing, losing the advantage of retaining the past history of the solution.

6.6   ADAMS PREDICTOR-CORRECTOR METHOD

Unless the initial estimate of y_{n+1} required by the Adams-Moulton formula is reasonably close to the true solution, many iterations may be required to obtain convergence of the iterations of the implicit formula. If this occurred at every integration step, it would involve an unacceptably great amount of computation. The number of iterations can be reduced by using the explicit "Adams-Bashforth formula," whose approximation error is only 14 times greater than that of the Adams-Moulton formula, to obtain the initial estimate. This is the predictor-corrector strategy which was introduced earlier to improve the accuracy of Eulerian methods. Here the explicit formula is used as the predictor and the implicit formula as the corrector.

Algorithm

Given $y' = f(x, y)$ on $[a, b]$, (x_i, y_i), $i = 0,..., 3$, and tolerance ε,

$n = 3$

While $x < b$ do

(Adams-Bashforth predictor formula)

$$y_{n+1}^{(0)} = y_n + \frac{h}{24} (55f_n - 59f_{n-1} + 37f_{n-3} - 9f_{n-3})$$

for $k = 1, 2,...$ until satisfied do

$$y'_{n+1}^{(k-1)} = f_{n+1}^{(k-1)} = f(x_{n+1}, y_{n+1}^{(k-1)})$$

(Adams-Moulton corrector formula)

$$y_{n+1}^{(k)} = y_n + \frac{h}{24} (9f_{n+1}^{(k-1)} + 19f_n - 5f_{n-1} + f_{n-3})$$

If $\left| \dfrac{y_{n+1}^{(k)} - y_{n+1}^{(k-1)}}{y_{n+1}^{(k)}} \right| < \varepsilon$

$x = x + h$; $n = n + 1$; go to next integration step

The values f_{n-2} to f_{n+1} of the function being integrated are used in the next integration step, but the value f_{n-3} is no longer required. Therefore, the new set of four base points required by the predictor formula can be stored in the same locations in a computer program as the old set of base points. This tactic precludes the inefficiency of having to recompute those values.

Convergence

If the step size h is sufficiently small, the corrector will converge within two iterations. In fact, the second iteration should only confirm that the result of the first iteration was sufficiently accurate. The upper bounds for the approximation errors of the two formulas are

$$e(y_{n+1}^{(0)}) = y_{n+1}^{(0)} - y(x_{n+1}) = \frac{251}{720} h^5 y^{(v)}(\xi_1)$$

$$e(y_{n+1}^{(1)}) = y_{n+1}^{(1)} - y(x_{n+1}) = -\frac{19}{720} h^5 y^{(v)}(\xi_2)$$

where ξ_1 is on $[x_{n-3}, x_n]$ and ξ_2 is on $[x_{n-2}, x_{n+1}]$. In general, ξ_1 and ξ_2 are not equal. However, because the width $4h$ of the interval $[x_{n-3}, x_{n+3}]$ is small, $y^{(v)}(x)$ is not likely to vary much on this interval. Therefore, the above two values may be replaced with little error by ξ, which maximizes the fifth derivative on this interval. Taking the difference between the two error terms yields

$$h^5 y^{(v)}(\xi) = \frac{720}{270} (y_{n+1}^{(1)} - y_{n+1}^{(0)})$$

$$y_{n+1}^{(1)} - y(x_{n+1}) = \frac{1}{14} (y_{n+1}^{(1)} - y_{n+1}^{(0)}) = D_{n+1}$$

The approximation error in the corrected value is about 1/14 of the difference between the results of applying the predictor and applying the corrector. If the required accuracy of a single integration step is ε, iteration of the corrector formula can be stopped when

$$|D_{n+1}| < \varepsilon$$

Example 6.6:

$$y' = -y^2; \ y(1) = 1; \ h = 0.1.$$

The single-step tolerance is $\varepsilon = 5 \times 10^{-5}$, that is, the answer is desired to four decimal places. The four starting values for $i = 0,\ldots, 3$ are

x_i	y'_i	y_i
1.0	−1.0000	1.0000
1.1	−0.8265	0.9091
1.2	−0.6944	0.8333
1.3	−0.5917	0.7692

The true solution is $y = 1/x$, and $y^{(v)}(x) = -120x^{-6}$ is maximal at $x = 1$. This predictor-corrector method will be illustrated by a single extrapolation of $y(x)$ from $x = 1$ to $x = 1 + h$.

Step 1: Adams-Bashforth predictor

$$y_4^{(0)} = 0.7692 + \frac{0.1}{24} [55(-0.5917) - 59(-0.6944)$$

$$+ 37(0.8265) - 9(-1)] + \frac{251}{720} (0.1)^5(-120)$$

$$y_4^{(0)} = 0.7144 + e_4^{(0)}$$

The last term is the approximation error

$$e_4^{(0)} = e(y_4^{(0)}) = -4.183 \times 10^{-4}$$

Step 2: Adams-Moulton corrector

$$y'_4{}^{(0)} = -(y_4{}^{(0)})^2 = 0.5104$$

$$y_4{}^{(1)} = 0.7692 + \frac{0.1}{24} [9(-0.5104) + 19(-0.5917)$$

$$- 5(-0.6944) + (-0.8265)] - (19/720) \, 10^{-5}(-120)$$

$$y_4{}^{(1)} = 0.7142 + e_4{}^{(1)}$$

The last term is the approximation error

$$e_4{}^{(1)} = e(y_4{}^{(1)}) = 3.167 \times 10^{-5}$$

which is sufficient to stop the iterations.

Step 3: Because the formula for the fifth derivative of the function $y(x)$ may not be readily computed, for generality the test should be made on the difference function. As

$$D_4 = (0.7144 - 0.7142)/14 = 1.4286 \times 10^{-5}$$

is less than ε, we could stop the iteration here.

Step 4: To test this assertion, perform one more iteration.

$$y'_4{}^{(1)} = -(0.7142)^2 = -0.5101$$

$$y_4{}^{(2)} = 0.7692 + (0.1/24)[9(0.5101) + 19(-0.5917) - 5(0.6944)$$

$$+ (-0.8265)] = 0.7143$$

which equals the true solution to four decimal places.

Step Size Control and Error Reduction

If more than one iteration is required to reduce the error to within the desired tolerance, the step size h must be reduced. Because calculation of the fifth derivative may be too complicated, a common tactic is simply to halve h. Computation is minimized if the step size is as large as is consistent with the single-step tolerance. For example, a step size that gives greater accuracy than does the number of decimal places carried in the calculations will result in many more integration steps than necessary. A convenient way to avoid this problem is to require

$$\varepsilon_1 \leq |D_{n+1}| \leq \varepsilon_2$$

If D_{n+1} falls below ε_1, double h; if D_{n+1} exceeds ε_2, halve h.

The error can be reduced further by noting that the predictor and corrector both have errors of $O(h^5)$. The tactic of taking a weighted average of the predicted and corrected values, as was done for the modified Heun's rule, eliminates the fifth-order term. Because the odd-order derivatives of $f(x, y)$ in the error expression equal zero, the $O(h^7)$ term in the

Newton expansion gives the approximation error. The weighted average for the Adams-Bashforth-Moulton predictor-corrector is

$$y_{n+1}^{(2)} = (251y_{n+1}^{(1)} + 19y_{n+1}^{(0)})/270$$

Therefore, only one application of the corrector formula is ever needed if the step size is properly adjusted. The weighted average is the final value for y_{n+1}.

6.7 BOUNDARY VALUE PROBLEMS

In an earlier section it was shown that a differential equation of order greater than one could be reduced to a system of simultaneous first-order equations.

Example 6.7:

Solve the second-order equation

$$y'' + xyy' = 0$$

on the interval $[a, b]$ with an initial value $x_0 = a$. Let $z = y'$; then $y'' = z'$ and the system of first-order equations to be solved is

$$y' = z.$$
$$z' = -xyz$$

If $y(x_0)$ and $z(x_0) = y'(x_0)$ are known, these two equations can be solved in parallel as normal initial value problems to give a sequence of values for the solution and its derivative on $[a, b]$: $y_i, z_i, i = 1,..., n$.

Shooting Method

However, the slope $y'(a) = z_0$ is often unknown, and the value of $y(b) = y(x_n)$ is known instead. The solution strategy is to assume a value for z_0 and compare the resulting y_n with the known value. If the computed solution is not within a preset tolerance ε of the known solution $y(b)$, modify the estimate of z_0 and try again. If the new result still does not match $y(b)$ within ε, repeat this procedure. Continue to iterate until

$$|y_n - y(b)| \leq \varepsilon$$

This technique is known as the "shooting method"; it is illustrated in Fig. 6.5.

Clearly, a systematic way to adjust z_0 is needed. The most common approach is to define the function

$$g(z_0) = y_n (b, z_0) - y(b) = 0$$

The root of this function is the initial slope $y'(a)$ which will produce $y(b)$ on solution of the system of differential equations. Because $y(x)$, and

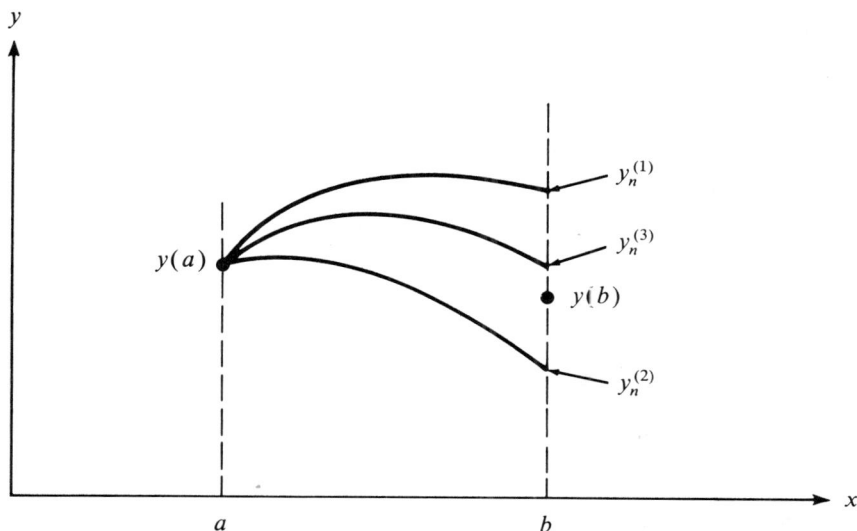

Fig. 6.5. Graphical illustration of the shooting method.

hence $g(z_0)$, are not known analytically, an iterative method is required to find the root.

Begin with two (shrewd) guesses for z_0 and compute the corresponding terminal values $y_n^{(1)}$ and $y_n^{(2)}$. Assuming that neither of these values is fortuitously within ε of $y(b)$, estimate the root of the function g by the secant method.

$$z_0^{(3)} = z_0^{(1)} + \frac{z_0^{(2)} - z_0^{(1)}}{y_n^{(1)} - y_n^{(2)}} (y_n^{(1)} - y(b))$$

Solve the differential equations again and test for convergence. Repeat the procedure as necessary. There is no guarantee that this method will converge, but it is most efficient when it does converge. Note that this method of improving the guess for the initial value of the derivative is simply linear interpolation. Use of higher-order interpolation to refine the estimate of this initial value is a straight-forward modification of the algorithm.

Algorithm

$z_0^{(1)} = s_1$ (Using intuition)

solve the parallel initial value problems over $[a, b]$

$y' = z$

$z' = f(x, y, s_1)$

if $y_n^{(1)} \leq \varepsilon$, output results and stop

    else $z_0^{(2)} = s_2$ (Using intuition)

solve the initial value problems again

if $y_n^{(2)} \leq \varepsilon$, output results and stop

    else for $k = 2, 3,...$ until satisfied do

$$z_0^{(k+1)} = z_0^{(k-1)} + \frac{z_0^{(k)} - z_0^{(k-1)}}{y_n^{(k-1)} - y_n^{(k)}} (y_n^{(k-1)} - y(b))$$

solve the initial value problems

if $y_n^{(k+1)} \leq \varepsilon$, output results and stop

if $k \geq$ maximum iterations, output message and current results

and stop

Finite Difference Method

If the differential equation to be solved is of high order, the above strategy of reduction to a system of first-order equations would necessitate iterative solution of a large number of initial value problems. The attendant computational cost may be prohibitive. Suppose the solution $y(x)$ were known for a number of equally spaced mesh points $x_i = a + ih$, $i = 0,...,$ n, on the interval $[a, b]$ where $a + nh = b$. For sufficiently small h the derivatives in the differential equation could be replaced by their finite difference approximations.

$$y'(x_i) = \frac{y_{i+1} - y_{i-1}}{2h} = f[x_{i-1}, x_{i+1}]$$

$$y''(x) = \frac{y_{i+1} - 2y_i + y_{i-1}}{h^2} = 2! f[x_{i-1}, x_i, x_{i+1}]$$

and so on for higher derivatives (note the use of Newton divided differences).

    If the original differential equation is linear, approximating the derivatives by finite differences results in $n - 1$ linear equations, one for each interior mesh point. In actuality, the solution is only known at the end points of the interval, so the $n - 1$ equations must be solved by Gaussian elimination for the unknown function values at the interior mesh points. This approach involves considerably less computation than does the shooting method for such problems.

Example 6.8:

Suppose a second-order differential equation can be written in the form

$$y'' + f(x)y' + g(x)y = q(x)$$

$$y_0 = a \qquad y_n = b$$

Substituting the finite difference approximations for the derivatives and denoting $f(x_n)$ by f_n, $g(x_n)$ by g_n, and $q(x_n)$ by q_n, produces

$$\frac{y_{i+1} - 2y_i + y_{i-1}}{h^2} + f_i \frac{y_{i+1} - y_{i-1}}{2h} + g_i y_i = q_i, \; i = 1, 2, \ldots, n$$

which simplifies to

$$(1 - f_i h/2)y_{i-1} + (-2 + g_i h^2)y_i + (1 + f_i h/2)y_{i+1} = q_i h^2$$

At $i = 1$ or $n - 1$, $y_0 = a$ and $y_n = b$ in the two equations, respectively. The terms with these quantities may be taken to the right-hand sides of these two equations, giving

$$(-2 + g_1 h^2)y_1 + (1 + f_1 h/2)y_2 = q_1 h^2 - (1 - f_1 h/2)a$$

and

$$(1 - f_{n-1}h/2)y_{n-2} + (-2 + g_{n-1}h^2)y_{n-1} = q_{n-1}h^2 - (1 + f_{n-1}h/2)b$$

The set of simultaneous equations constitutes a tridiagonal matrix problem

$$
\begin{matrix} & \mathbf{A} & & \mathbf{y} & \mathbf{d} \end{matrix}
$$
$$
\begin{pmatrix} b_1 & c_1 & & & \mathbf{0} \\ a_2 & b_2 & c_2 & & \\ & & \ddots & & \\ \mathbf{0} & & & a_n & b_n \end{pmatrix}
\begin{pmatrix} y_1 \\ y_2 \\ \vdots \\ y_n \end{pmatrix}
=
\begin{pmatrix} d_1 \\ d_2 \\ \vdots \\ d_n \end{pmatrix}
$$

$$a_i = 1 - f_i h/2; \; b_i = -2 + g_i h^2; \; c_i = 1 + f_i h/2$$
$$d_1 = q_1 h^2 - (1 - f_1 h/2)a$$
$$d_i = q_i h^2, \; i = 2, \ldots, n-2$$
$$d_{n-1} = q_{n-1}h^2 - (1 + f_{n-1}h/2)b$$

which can be solved by methods previously described.

6.8 COMPUTER PROGRAMS

```
                SUBROUTINE RUNGE(NEQNS, X, H, XSTOP, Y, DERFN)
C*********************************************************************
C* Solution of a set of NEQNS (maximum of 50) first-order ordi-   *
C* nary differential equations on the interval [X, XSTOP] by the  *
C* fourth-order Runge-Kutta method.  H is the step size.  The     *
C* array Y contains the solution values at XSTOP.  DERFN, which   *
C* must be declared EXTERNAL in the calling program, is the name  *
C* of the subroutine which computes the array DY of derivative    *
C* values; its arguments are (X, Y, DY).  X contains the value    *
C* XSTOP on return to the calling program.                        *
C*********************************************************************
```

```
      DIMENSION Y(1), DY(50), YSTORE(50), YO(50)

1     DO 10 I = 1, NEQNS
10      YO(I) = Y(I)
C
C -- Calculate derivatives at start of integration step
C
      CALL DERFN(X, Y, DY)

      DO 20 I = 1, NEQNS
        TEMP = H*DY(I)/2.0
C
C -- Update solution
C
      Y(I) = Y(I) + TEMP/3.0
C
C --   Half-interval Eulerian extrapolation
C
20      YSTORE(I) = YO(I) + TEMP
C
C -- Increment X by half interval
C
      X = X + H/2.0
C
C -- Calculate derivatives at midpoint of integration step
C
      CALL DERFN(X, YSTORE, DY)

      DO 30 I = 1, NEQNS
        TEMP = H*DY(I)
C
C --   Update solution
C
      Y(I) = Y(I) + TEMP/3.0
C
C --   Half-interval backwards Eulerian extrapolation
C
30      YSTORE(I) = YO(I) + TEMP/2.0
C
C -- Calculate improved values of derivatives at midpoint
C
      CALL DERFN(X, YSTORE, DY)

      DO 40 I = 1, NEQNS
        TEMP = H*DY(I)
C
C --   Update solution
C
      Y(I) = Y(I) + TEMP/3.0
C
C --   Extrapolate by midpoint rule
C
40      YSTORE(I) = YO(I) + TEMP
```

```
C
C -- Increment X by half integration step
C
      X = X + H/2.0
C
C -- Calculate derivatives at end of integration step
C
      CALL DERFN(X, YSTORE, DY)

      DO 50 I = 1, NEQNS
C
C --     Update solution
C
50       Y(I) = Y(I) + H*DY(I)/6.0

      IF (X.LT.XSTOP) GO TO 1
      RETURN
      END
```

```
procedure Runge(neqns: integer; var x: real; h, xstop: real; var
  y: vector; procedure derfn(a: real; b: vector; var c: vector) );
{
**************************************************************
* Solution of a set of neqns first-order ordinary differential *
* equations on the interval [x, xstop] by the fourth-order      *
* Runge-Kutta method.  h is the step size.  The data type vector *
* must be defined as array[1..neqns] of real in the calling    *
* program.  y contains the solution values at xstop.  Derfn is  *
* the name of the subroutine which computes the array dy of     *
* derivative values; its arguments are (x, y, dy).  x contains  *
* the value of xstop on return to the calling program.          *
**************************************************************
}
var
  temp: real;
  y0, ystore, dy: vector;
  i: integer;

begin
  while x < xstop do
    begin
      for i := 1 to neqns do
        y0[i] := y[i];

      {Calculate derivatives at start of integration step}

      derfn(x, y, dy);

      for i := 1 to neqns do
        begin
          temp := h*dy[i]/2.0;

          {Update solution}
```

```
    y[i] := y[i] + temp/3.0;

    {Half-interval Eulerian extrapolation}

    ystore[i] := y0[i] + temp
  end;

{Increment x by half integration step}

x := x + h/2.0;

{Calculate derivatives at midpoint}

derfn(x, ystore, dy);

for i := 1 to neqns do
  begin
    temp := h*dy[i];

    {Update solution}

    y[i] := y[i] + temp/3.0;

    {Half-interval backwards Eulerian extrapolation}

    ystore[i] := y0[i] + temp/2.0
  end;

{Calculate improved values of derivatives at midpoint}

derfn(x, ystore, dy);

for i := 1 to neqns do
  begin
    temp := h*dy[i];

    {Update solution}

    y[i] := y[i] + temp/3.0;

    {Extrapolation by midpoint rule}

    ystore[i] := y0[i] + temp
  end;

{Increment x by half integration step}

x := x + h/2.0;

{Calculate derivatives at end of integration step}

derfn(x, ystore, dy);
```

```
        for i := 1 to neqns do

        {Update solution}

        y[i] := y[i] + h*dy[i]/6.0
     end  {of while}
end;
```

```
        SUBROUTINE ADAMS(NEQNS,X,H,XSTOP,DYO,DY1,DY2,DY3,Y,DERFN)
C*********************************************************************
C* Solution of a set of NEQNS (maximum of 50) first-order         *
C* differential equations on the interval [X, XSTOP] by the       *
C* Adams-Bashforth-Moulton predictor-corrector method.  H is the  *
C* integration step size.  DYO, DY1, DY2, and DY3 contain the     *
C* history of the derivatives of Y, the vector of the solutions.  *
C* DERFN, which must be declared EXTERNAL in the calling program, *
C* is the name of the subroutine which evaluates the derivatives; *
C* its arguments are (X, Y, DY).                                  *
C*********************************************************************

        DIMENSION DYO(1), DY1(1), DY2(1), DY3(1), Y(1),
     1  YPRED(50), YCORR(50), DY(50)
C
C -- Adams-Bashforth predictor
C
1       DO 10 I = 1, NEQNS
10        YPRED(I) = Y(I) + (H/24.)*(55.*DY3(I) - 59.*DY2(I)
     1               + 37.*DY1(I) - 9.*DYO(I))
C
C -- Calculate derivatives from predicted values
C
        DERFN(X, YPRED, DY)

        DO 20 I = 1, NEQNS
C
C --     Adams-Moulton corrector
C
        YCORR(I) = Y(I) + (H/24.)*(9.*DY(I) + 19.*DY3(I)
     1               - 5.*DY2(I) + DY1(I))
C
C --     Solution is weighted average of predictor and corrector
C
        Y(I) = (251.*YCOR(I) + 19.*YPRED(I))/270.
C
C --     Update history of derivatives
C
        DYO(I) = DY1(I)
        DY1(I) = DY2(I)
        DY2(I) = DY3(I)
20      DY3(I) = DY(I)
C
C -- Increment X
C
```

```
      X = X + H

      IF (X.GE.XSTOP) GO TO 2
        IF ((XSTOP - X).LT.H) H = XSTOP - X
        GO TO 1

2     RETURN
      END
```

```pascal
procedure Adams(neqns: integer; var x: real; h, xstop: real;
        var dy0, dy1, dy2, dy3, y: vector;
        procedure derfn(a: real; b: vector; var c: vector) );
{
**************************************************************************
* Solution of a set of neqns first-order differential equations  *
* on the interval [x, xstop] by the Adams-Bashforth-Moulton       *
* predictor-corrector method.  H is the integration step size.    *
* dy0, dy1, dy2, and dy3 contain the history of the derivatives    *
* of y, the vector of the solutions.  The data type vector must   *
* be defined as array [1..neqns] of real in the calling program.  *
* Derfn is the name of the procedure which evaluates the          *
* derivatives; its arguments are (x, y, dy).                      *
**************************************************************************
}
var
  ypred, ycorr, dy: vector;
  i: integer;

begin
  while x < xstop do
    begin

      {Adams-Bashforth predictor}

      for i := 1 to neqns do
        ypred[i] := y[i] + (h/24.)*(55.*dy3[i] - 59.*dy2[i]
                  + 37.*dy1[i] - 9.*dy0[i]);
      for i := 1 to neqns do
        begin

          {Adams-Moulton corrector}

          ycorr[i] := y[i] + (h/24.)*9.*dy[i] + 19.*dy3[i]
                    - 5.*dy2[i] + dy1[i]);

          {Solution is weighted average of predictor and
           corrector}

          y[i] := (251.*ycorr[i] + 19.*ypred[i])/270.0;

          {Update history of derivatives}

          dy0[i] := dy1[i];
```

```
            dy1[i] := dy2[i];
            dy2[i] := dy3[i];
            dy3[i] := dy[i]
          end;

      {Increment x}

      x := x + h;
      if ((xstop − x) < h) h := xstop − h
    end {of while}
end;

          SUBROUTINE BNDVAL(NPTS, XO, XN, Y, EPS, F, G, Q)
C******************************************************************
C* Solution of the second−order boundary value problem          *
C*      Y" + F(X)Y' + G(X)Y = Q(X)                               *
C* using the finite differences method with NPTS (maximum of 50) *
C* mesh points.  XO = X(1) and XN = X(NPTS).  Y(1) and Y(0) are  *
C* known; this subroutine determines the solution at the interior*
C* mesh points.  The user−supplied functions F, G, and Q must be *
C* declared EXTERNAL in the calling program.  EPS is the smallest*
C* tolerable diagonal element for the tridiagonal matrix to be   *
C* considered nonsingular.                                       *
C******************************************************************

      DIMENSION Y(1), A(50), B(50), C(50), D(50)

C
C −− Calculate step size
C
      H = (XN − XO)/(NPTS − 1)
      MESH = NPTS − 2
C
C −− Evaluate tridiagonal matrix and constant vector
C
      DO 10 I = 1, MESH
        TEMP = F(X)*H/2.
C
C −−     Subdiagonal elements
C
        A(I) = 1. − TEMP
C
C −−     Diagonal elements
C
        B(I) = −2. + G(X)*H**2
C
C −−     Superdiagonal elements
C
        C(I) = 1. + TEMP
C
C −− Constant vector
C
10        D(I) = Q(X)*H**2
```

```
C
C -- Add end conditions
C
      D(1) = D(1) - A(1)*Y(1)
      D(MESH) = D(MESH) - C(MESH)*Y(NPTS)
C
C -- Solve equations and store solution in Y
C
      CALL TRIDIAG(MESH, A, B, C, D, EPS)
      DO 20 I = 1, MESH
20       Y(1 + I) = D(I)

      RETURN
      END

procedure BoundVal(npts: integer; x0,xn: real; var y: vector;
            eps: real; function f(val: real): real; function
            g(val: real): real; function q(val: real): real);
{
**************************************************************************
* Solution of the second-order boundary value problem                   *
*       y" + f(x)y' + q(x)y = q(x)                                       *
* using the finite differences method with npts mesh points.            *
* x0 = x(1) and xn = x(npts).  y(1) and y(0) are known; this            *
* procedure determines the solution at the interior mesh points.        *
* The data type vector must be defined as array [1..npts] of            *
* real in the calling program.  f, g, and q are user-supplied           *
* functions.  Eps is the smallest tolerable diagonal element for        *
* the tridiagonal matrix to be considered nonsingular.                  *
**************************************************************************
}
var
  a, b, c, d: vector;
  temp, h,: real;
  i, mesh: integer;

begin

  {Calculate step size}

  h := (xn - x0)/(npts - 1);
  mesh := npts - 2;

  {Evaluate tridiagonal matrix and constant vector}

  for i := 1 to mesh do
    begin
      temp := f(x)*h/2.0;
      a[i] := 1. - temp;          {Subdiagonal elements}
      b[i] := -2. + g(x)*sqr(h); {Diagonal elements}
      c[i] := 1. + temp;          {Superdiagonal elements}
      d[i] := q(x)*sqr(h)         {Constant vector}
    end;
```

```
{Add end conditions}

d[1] := d[1] - a[1]*y[1];
d[mesh] := d[mesh] - c[mesh]*y[npts];

{Solve equations and store solution in y}

tridiag(mesh, a, b, c, d, eps);
for i := 1 to mesh do
  y[1 + i] := d[i]
end;
```

6.9 EXAMPLE PROBLEM

A classical model in ecology is the Lotka-Volterra equations for the temporal variation of the populations of a predator species (P) and its prey species (N).

$$\frac{dP}{dt} = akNP - dP$$

$$\frac{dN}{dt} = rN - kNP$$

where

$\quad r =$ fractional reproductive rate of prey
$\quad k =$ fractional kill rate by predators
$\quad a =$ fraction of killed prey assimilated by predators
$\quad d =$ fractional death rate of predators

For a particular ecological model, the parameters are

$$r = 0.2 \qquad k = 0.005 \qquad a = 0.15 \qquad d = 0.3$$

and the initial populations are

$$P(0) = 50 \qquad N(0) = 1000$$

The first five steps of the solution of the differential equations will be calculated with the Adams-Bashforth-Moulton predictor-corrector using a step size of 0.01 time units.

First Integration Step

Use the self-starting Runge-Kutta method to generate the second of the four derivative values required by the Adams-Bashforth formula. From the two Lotka-Volterra equations, the derivatives at the beginning of the integration step are

$$k1 = dP(0)/dt = 22.50 \qquad k1 = dN(0)/dt = -50.00$$

Save these results; they will be needed for the next integration step. Extrapolating a half step to $t = 0.005$ with the Euler formula gives the populations at the midpoint of the step.

$$P(0.005) = P(0) + 0.005 \cdot dP/dt = 50.1125$$
$$N(0.005) = N(0) + 0.005 \cdot dN/dt = 99.75$$

Substituting into the differential equations gives derivatives at the midpoint of the integration step.

$$k2 = dP(0.005)/dt = 22.5412$$
$$k2 = dN(0.005)/dt = -50.5499$$

Using the backwards Euler formula gives another estimate of the populations at the midpoint of the step.

$$P(0.005) = 50.1127 \qquad N(0.005) = 999.7473$$

Substituting into the differential equations gives improved values of the derivatives at the midpoint of the integration step.

$$k3 = dP(0.005)/dt = 22.5412$$
$$k3 = dN(0.005)/dt = -50.5508$$

Extrapolating across the entire integration step using the midpoint rule gives populations at the end of the step.

$$P(0.01) = 50.2254 \qquad N(0.01) = 999.4945$$

Substituting into the differential equations gives derivatives at the end point of the integration step.

$$k4 = dP(0.01)/dt = 22.5824$$
$$k4 = dN(0.01)/dt = -51.1012$$

Taking a weighted average of the four derivatives over the interval of integration and using it in the Euler formula gives

$$P(0.01) = P(0) + (0.01/6) \cdot (k1 + 2 \cdot k2 + 2 \cdot k3 + k4)$$

and similarly for $N(0.01)$.

$$P(0.01) = 50.2254 \qquad N(0.01) = 999.4945$$

Second and Third Integration Steps

Use the Runge-Kutta method again to generate the third and fourth points required by the Adams predictor. The results are:

$$t = 0.02 \qquad P = 50.4516, \; dP/dt = 22.6646$$
$$N = 998.9780, \; dN/dt = -52.2048$$
$$t = 0.03 \qquad P = 50.6787, \; dP/dt = 22.7465$$
$$N = 998.4504, \; dN/dt = -53.3108$$

Fourth Integration Step

Use the Adams-Bashforth predictor formula first. Let's call the interval of width $4h = 0.04$ a "frame."

$$P(0.04) = P(0.03) + (0.01/24) \cdot (55 \cdot 22.7465 - 59 \cdot 22.6646$$
$$+ \; 37 \cdot 22.5824 - 9 \cdot 22.5) = 50.9066$$
$$N(0.04) = N(0.03) + (0.01/24) \cdot (55 \cdot (-53.3108) - 59 \cdot (-52.2048)$$
$$+ \; 37 \cdot (-51.1012) - 9 \cdot (-50.0) = 997.9118$$

Substituting into the differential equations gives the derivatives at $t = 0.04$.

$$dP/dt = 22.8282 \qquad dN/dt = -54.4190$$

Save these values for use in the next integration step. Now use the Adams-Moulton corrector formula. The integration frame now moves off the initial point and encompasses the point computed with the predictor formula.

$$P(0.04) = P(0.03) + (0.01/24) \cdot (9 \cdot 22.8282 + 19 \cdot 22.7465$$
$$- \; 5 \cdot 22.6646 + 22/5824) = 50.9066$$
$$N(0.04) = N(0.03) + (0.01/24) \cdot (9 \cdot (-54.419) + 19 \cdot (-53.3108)$$
$$- \; 5 \cdot (-52.2048) - 51.1012) = 997.9117$$

Taking the weighted average of the predicted and corrected values,

$$P(0.04) = 50.9066 \qquad N(0.04) = 997.9117$$

The derivatives of P and N at $t = 0$ are no longer needed. Save the derivatives at $t = 0.01, 0.02, 0.03$, and 0.04 and use them in the predictor formula in the next integration step. Note that the derivative at $t = 0.0$ is not needed for the next step. Repeating the above calculations for the new four-point frame gives

$$P(0.05) = 51.3648 \qquad N(0.05) = 996.8011$$

The predictor-corrector formula is reapplied as many times as is necessary to reach the terminal time of the simulation of the ecological system.

Should the predicted and corrected values differ by more than 14 times the desired precision, it will be necessary to reduce the step size. If the predicted and corrected values differ by less than the desired tolerance, the step size may be increased. Once the new step size is selected, however, the Runge-Kutta method must again be used three times to generate starting values of the derivatives at correctly spaced time points.

chapter 7

Statistical Methods

7.1 RANDOM NUMBERS

Modeling Measurement Errors

When scientists and engineers measure various quantities in their laboratories or plants, the results invariably include uncertainties due, for example, to small errors made in reading values from a scale, transient fluctuations in voltage in the measuring device, or minor variations in the fabrication of the items being tested. Because these uncertainties do not arise from systematic differences in the construction of the materials used in the test or the manner in which the test is conducted, the uncertainties are called "random errors." These errors are as likely to be negative as positive. Therefore, if a sufficient number of objects or sufficient replicate measurements are made, their average value should be close to the true value of the quantity being measured, the "expectation value."

Commonly, the scientist or engineer constructs a mathematical model which reflects his hypothesis regarding the properties of the physical system he is examining and which predicts the expectation value of his measurement. This model can be used to:

1. test the significance of the observed deviations
2. identify quantitative relationships among the variables in the model

3. predict the outcome of a future measurement or test and estimate its reliability
4. design new experiments or tests to obtain better information about the system under study.

Distributions of Random Variables

Although most people have an intuitive idea of what randomness means, it is important to define the term explicitly to avoid misapplication of statistical methods. The universe of possible measured values for a particular quantity is the "population" of measurements, and the set of measurements actually obtained is a "sample" from that population. The variable in the mathematical model which corresponds to the measured quantity is called a "random variable." The probability that a random variable will have the same value as that obtained empirically equals the fraction of individual measurements in the population which have the observed value, that is, the frequency at which the measured value appears in the population. The analytical expression for the probability is called the "frequency function" or "probability density function." Depending on the nature of the quantity being measured, the frequency function is either continuous or discrete.

In order to use a mathematical model to test hypotheses regarding measured quantities, a frequency function representing the expected distribution of measurements must be selected. Care must be taken that the function chosen faithfully reflects the properties of the random variable.

Example 7.1:

What is the probability that a chord drawn parallel to one edge (of length e) of an equilateral triangle will have a length no greater than half the length of the edge? The answer depends on the random method of selecting the chord.

Suppose the altitude (of length h) intersecting the specified edge is constructed, a point on the altitude is selected at random, and a chord perpendicular to the altitude at the selected point is constructed. If, as shown in Fig. 7.1, the distance d from the point to the apex of the triangle $\leq h/2$, the chord's length will be $\leq e/2$. Should N points on the altitude be chosen at random, dN/h points would be expected to lie on the segment of length d. Therefore, setting $d = e/2$ gives the desired probability.

$$P\{d : d \leq e/2\} = \frac{h/2}{h} = 0.5$$

Suppose instead that a point anywhere inside the triangle is selected at random and the chord passing through the point and parallel to the specified edge is constructed as shown in Fig. 7.2. The desired probability

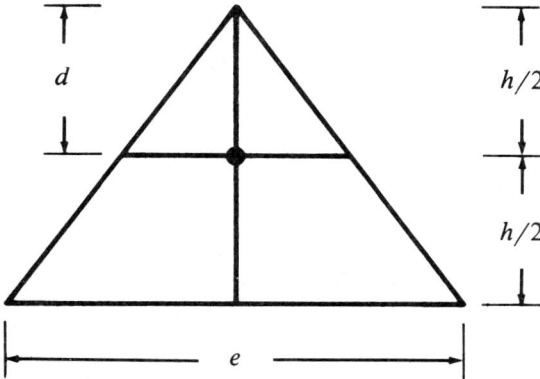

Fig. 7.1. Construction of a chord parallel to an edge of an equilateral triangle by selecting a point on the triangle's altitude.

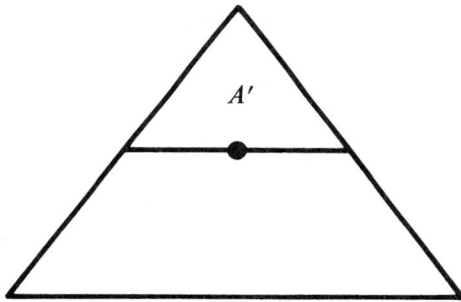

Fig. 7.2. Construction of a chord parallel to an edge of an equilateral triangle by selecting a point anywhere within the triangle.

is the ratio of the area A' of the equilateral triangle whose base is $e/2$ to the area A of the triangle whose base is e.

$$P\{A': A'/A \leq 0.5\} = \frac{0.5(e/2)(h/2)}{0.5\ eh} = 0.25$$

The probabilities obtained by these two methods are different because the points used in the two constructions were selected from different populations.

Generation of Random Numbers

The above example indicates the importance of selecting a random number from the population whose frequency function corresponds to the probability of observing a particular value. Selecting a random number from most of the important frequency functions can be accomplished by selecting from the uniform distribution on the interval $[0, 1]$; the result can be transformed to have the properties of the desired distribution. The most popular approach is the "linear congruential method."

Algorithm

Start with x_0, the so-called "seed"

On the nth call to the random number generator calculate $x_{n+1} = ax_n + c$

return (x_{n+1}/m)

The integers a, c, and m must be selected with care to ensure that successive values of x_n lie on the interval $[0, 1]$, do not have a systematic relationship, and do not follow a periodic sequence. Some empirical rules have been found for the selection of these three parameter values. The following rules presume that the computing machine being used employs binary arithmetic.

1. Choose a such that a mod 8 = 5
2. m = maximal integer value for the computer used; usually 2^k or 2^{k-1} (k is the number of bits per word), depending on whether the last bit of the word is a digit or a sign bit
3. $\sqrt{m} < a < m - \sqrt{m}$
4. Choose an odd value for c
5. $c/m \approx 0.211$

Statistical Models

A statistical model is an equation which implies a particular "error structure" for a set of random variables. For example, a series of laboratory measurements for a quantity x may be represented by the statistical model

$$x_i = \langle x \rangle + \varepsilon_i$$

where $\langle x \rangle$ is the expectation value of x and ε_i is the error of the ith measurement. This is a very simple model implying that there is only one factor which introduces error into the measurements. If there were two sources of error, for example, an unsteady power supply and errors in reading voltages from an instrument's scale, a second error term would have to be included.

$$x_i = \langle x \rangle + \varepsilon_i + \eta_i$$

This model is based on the assumption that the two sources of error are independent.

The statistical methods to be outlined in the remainder of this chapter are valid only for uncorrelated random variables. That is, each random variable must be an independent sampling from a particular population. This property permits simple tests which compare the random sample to the underlying universal population implied by the statistical model.

7.2 RANDOM SAMPLING

The mathematical models constructed by scientists and engineers often require simulating their measurements by selecting a series of values x_i for the random variables in their models' equations. If these random numbers are drawn from the same frequency distribution function $P(x)$ as is the sample of the population of measurements, then the method of generation of the random numbers faithfully models the method of measurement. Some common frequency functions are the Poisson distribution for discrete random variables and the exponential and Gaussian distributions for continuous random variables. Because the random variable must have some value, the sum of the probabilities of selecting x from $P(x)$ is one.

$$\int_a^\infty P(x)dx = 1$$

where a is 0 or $-\infty$, depending on the range of possible values for the random variables. Therefore, these frequency functions are said to be "normalized," which is why the Gaussian distribution is often called the normal distribution.

Binomial Distribution

Consider a population whose individuals can be classified according to whether they possess or do not possess a particular attribute. If a fraction q of the population possesses the desired attribute, the probability that r objects in a sample of n objects will possess the attribute is given by the binomial distribution.

$$P(r) = \binom{n}{r} q^r (1 - q)^{n-r}$$

The expectation value of a random variable distributed according to this distribution is called the "mean" and is given by

$$\mu = \sum_{i=0}^{n} iP(i) = nq$$

The "standard deviation," σ, is a measure of the degree to which the individuals in the population spread about the mean. It is given by the following formula for its square, the "variance."

$$\sigma^2 = nq(1 - q).$$

The binomial distribution is valuable for testing whether an hypothesis should be accepted or rejected. However, most scientific and engineering models include random variables that can have a range of values rather than satisfying a binary condition. Therefore, other distributions derived from the binomial distribution are more commonly used.

Sampling from the Poisson Distribution

Suppose a set of i integers are to be drawn from a population consisting of n non-negative integers. The probability of drawing a particular set is given by the binomial distribution. As n becomes infinite, the distribution of the random variable i can be shown to approach

$$P(i) = e^{-\mu} \mu^i/i!$$

where μ is the mean value of the population of n individuals. This is the frequency function for the Poisson distribution. It is important in assessing the reliability of counting discrete events, such as radioactive decay.

Algorithm

To select a non-negative integer i from the Poisson distribution with mean μ:

$p = e^{-\mu}$

$q = 1$

$i = -1$

while $q > p$

    select random number v from the uniform distribution

    $q = qv$

    $i = i + 1$

exit with current value of i

Sampling from the Gaussian Distribution

The random variables in most mathematical models assume continuous rather than discrete values. Suppose x is such a variable and is clustered about the population mean with (positive or negative) deviations d_i. Further suppose that x can be expanded about the mean as a power series in d_i and that terms in d_i^2 remain finite as the sample size n becomes infinite whereas terms with higher powers of d_i approach zero much more rapidly. It can be shown that the probability of selecting a particular x under these conditions is given by

$$P(x) = \frac{1}{\sqrt{2\pi}} \exp\left[-\left(\frac{x-\mu}{\sigma}\right)^2\right]$$

where μ is the population mean and σ is the standard deviation. This is the Gaussian or normal distribution.

There has been much controversy over the applicability of the Gaussian distribution to all experimental errors. Because empirical values far from the mean occur infrequently, the properties of the measurement method far out on the "tails" of the distribution are difficult to examine. Rarely does an experimenter perform sufficient replicate measurements to verify that the experimental errors follow a Gaussian distribution. However, it is certain that this distribution is qualitatively correct for measurement errors, and for practical purposes it may be treated as quantitatively correct.

The equation

$$y = (x - \mu)/\sigma$$

transforms the random variable x, normally distributed with mean μ and standard deviation σ, into the random variable y, normally distributed with mean zero and standard deviation one, commonly denoted as $N(0, 1)$. Because y can always be transformed back to x, the following algorithm for selecting a value from $N(0, 1)$ is completely general.

Algorithm

do

  select random numbers v_1 and v_2 from the uniform distribution
  $v_1 = 2v_1 - 1$
  $v_2 = 2v_2 - 1$
  $s = v_1^2 + v_2^2$
  while $s \geq 1$ (Ensure that the point (v_1, v_2) is within the unit circle)

$$x = v_1 \sqrt{\frac{-2 (\ln s)}{s}}$$ (Transform to the normal distribution)

Sampling from the Exponential Distribution

Some mathematical models include continuous random variables that assume only non-negative values. The exponential distribution

$$P(x) = e^{-x}$$

for x on $[0, \infty]$ is an important frequency function for such variables. For example, the distance travelled by a molecule in a gas or a subatomic particle in a reactor prior to a collision follows this distribution.

Algorithms

To sample from the exponential distribution, first version:

> select random number v from the uniform distribution
>
> $x = -\ln v$

Because calculating the logarithm is slow, a second version is supplied.

> $x = 0$
> for $i = 0,\dots$ until satisfied do
> > select random number v_i from the uniform distribution.
> > if $v_i > v_{i-1}$
> > > if i is even, $x = x + 1$
> > > else exit with $x = x + v_i$

7.3 TESTING HYPOTHESES

A statistical hypothesis is an assertion that a random variable has a particular probability distribution. Although statistical hypotheses may be quite complex, only simple hypotheses will be discussed here; for complex statistical testing the reader is referred to program packages such as BMD and SAS. Testing an hypothesis involves calculating the probability that the random variable would deviate from the value predicted by the presumed underlying distribution. If that probability is less than some confidence level, most often 0.01 or 0.05, the hypothesis is accepted. If the calculated probability exceeds the confidence level, the hypothesis is rejected.

Comparing a Sample to a Population

A common hypothesis is that the collection of values for a random variable obtained by a mathematical model or an experiment fits a particular probability density function.

Example 7.2:

A sequence of 200 random numbers was generated with the linear congruential random number generator

$$x_{i+1} = (ax_i + c) \bmod m$$

where $a = 2,147,437,301$, $c = 453,816,981$, and $m = 2^{32}$. The hypothesis to be tested is that these 200 numbers are uniformly distributed on the interval [0, 1]. Suppose each random number is assigned to one of ten "bins," depending on its first digit (0 to 9). Each bin should contain 20 numbers if the distribution is completely random. The distributions actually obtained for two values of the seed (x_0) are given in the following table.

bin	$x_0 = 1$	$x_0 = 12345$
0	19	17
1	21	21
2	22	22
3	20	16
4	24	24
5	12	22
6	22	20
7	24	22
8	17	21
9	19	15

The χ^2 test gives the goodness of the fit of such results to the expected distribution. The χ^2 statistic is given by

$$\chi^2 = \sum_{i=1}^{n} \frac{(x_i - \mu_i)^2}{\mu_i}$$

where x_i is a value of the random variable whose distribution is being tested, μ_i is the expected value of the variable, and n is the number of comparisons being made. In the above x_i is the number of random numbers in bin i, μ_i is the expected number of numbers in that bin (20), and $n = 10$ bins. The values of χ^2 for the seeds 1 and 12345 are 5.8 and 4.0, respectively.

This statistic has its own frequency function which depends on n, the number of comparisons of actual and expected values of the random variable. The probability that a given value of χ^2 will be exceeded by chance has been tabulated for many values of $n - 1$, the number of "degrees of freedom" of the distribution. For nine degrees of freedom there is a probability of only 0.05 that χ^2 will exceed 16.9 by chance. As the actual values of the statistic are less than this value, the hypothesis that the two sequences of random numbers fit the uniform distribution on [0, 1] should be accepted.

Testing the Value of a Statistic

The average of the results of a scientific experiment often must be compared to the expected value of the quantity being measured. Because it is unlikely that the measured and theoretical values will agree exactly, it is necessary to determine if the discrepancy is due to random errors of measurement or if it is due to a systematic difference between theoretical preconceptions and actuality. Suppose that a large number of replicate measurements were found to be normally distributed with a standard deviation σ. Is the observed mean value μ of a subsequent experiment involving only a few replicate measurements a reasonable estimate of the theoretical value μ_0 given this known experimental error? To put it more rigorously, is the observed mean value μ a good estimate of the mean of a population distributed as $N(\mu_0, \sigma)$?

The z-statistic is defined as

$$z = \frac{(\mu \cdot \mu_0)\sqrt{n}}{\sigma}$$

where n is the number of estimates that produced the mean μ. This statistic is normally distributed with a mean of zero and a standard deviation of one. There are tables of the probability that a particular value of z is exceeded (i.e., the area under the normal curve of error between that value of z and ∞). Denote the desired confidence limit by α and the value of z at which the above probability equals α by z_α. If the calculated value of z exceeds z_α, then μ is significantly greater than μ_0. If z is less than $-z_\alpha$, then μ is significantly smaller than μ_0. If $|z|$ exceeds $z_{\alpha/2}$, then one of the above conditions applies. The first two of the above cases are called "one-tailed" tests and the third case is called a "two-tailed" test, because they refer to the areas under "tails" of the bell-shaped normal curve of error. The two-tailed test is most often used, but care should be taken that the correct table of z values is being used.

The distribution of the random variables constituting experimental measurements is usually unknown, and only a small sample from that distribution is available. In such cases the standard deviation σ in the above formula should be replaced by s, the root-mean-square deviation of the replicate measurements from their mean. Because the sample size is small, s is only an approximation to the true standard deviation and the formula yields a random variable called Student's t statistic instead of z.

$$t = \frac{(\mu \cdot \mu_0)\sqrt{n}}{s}$$

Student's t can be shown to be distributed as χ^2 and be a close approximation to the normal distribution for moderate to large values of n, the sample size. Values of t for several confidence limits have been tabulated for many degrees of freedom. For a given confidence level α, if the calculated value of t exceeds t_α (or is less than $-t_\alpha$), μ is significantly greater (or less) than μ_0. If $|t|$ exceeds $t_{\alpha/2}$, one of the above two cases applies. Care must be taken to use either the one-tailed or two-tailed table of statistics as appropriate.

Example 7.3:

A student has made several measurements of the density of water at 25°C: 0.987, 0.991, 1.005, 0.993, 1.007, 0.995. The true value is known to be 0.997 to three decimal places. Is the student's result acceptable at the 0.05 confidence level?

The mean value of the student's density measurements is $\mu = 0.996$ and the root-mean-square deviation is $s = 0.00765$. The t statistic equals 0.312 to three decimal places. The table of two-tailed t values gives a value of 2.571 at the 0.05 confidence level. This means that there is a probability of only 0.05 that the tabulated t value would be exceeded by chance. Because the calculated t value does not exceed the tabulated value, the probability that the discrepancy between the theoretical and measured densities reflects the experimental error exceeds 0.95. The student can accept his result as not significantly different from the known density.

A scientist frequently knows from experience the standard error associated with a particular kind of measurement and wishes to determine if several replicate measurements are representative of the precision he has come to expect from such an experiment. That is, he wishes to determine if the root-mean-square deviation s of his measurements from their mean value is significantly different from the known standard deviation σ. If s is significantly greater than σ, the experiments in question are less precise than expected from experience.

This determination can be made using a χ^2 test.

$$\chi^2 = \frac{(n-1)s^2}{\sigma^2}$$

As before, care must be taken to use the one-tailed or two-tailed table of χ^2 values as is appropriate for the test to be made.

Comparison of Two Populations

Suppose scientists in two laboratories measure the viscosity of a fluid a large number of times. The scientists at the first laboratory find their measurements normally distributed with a mean of μ_1 and a standard deviation of σ_1. Those at the second laboratory find their measurements normally distributed with a mean of μ_2 and a standard deviation of σ_2. The laboratory chiefs need to know if the means of the two populations are significantly different.

As the two populations each are normally distributed, a linear combination of them (such as their difference) is also normally distributed. Therefore, the z statistic can be used to test if the difference between the two means is significantly different from zero. Substituting into the formula for z yields

$$z = \frac{\mu_1 - \mu_2}{\sqrt{\dfrac{\sigma_1^2}{n_1} + \dfrac{\sigma_2^2}{n_2}}}$$

where n_1 and n_2 are the sizes of the two populations to be compared. As above, the calculated z value is compared with that for the desired confidence limit from tables for one-tailed or two-tailed tests.

Most often the standard deviations are not known because only a small sample has been taken from the universe of possible measurements. In this case the true means and standard deviations of the two populations are unknown because the sample size is too small to make that determination. As before, σ_1 and σ_2 are replaced by s_1 and s_2, respectively, and Student's t statistic is computed instead of the

$$t = \frac{\mu_1 - \mu_2}{\sqrt{\dfrac{s_1^2}{n_1} + \dfrac{s_2^2}{n_2}}}$$

z statistic. The calculated value of t is compared to the tabulated value for v degrees of freedom at the desired confidence limit. The number of degrees of freedom is the integer closest to the quantity

$$v = \frac{\left(\dfrac{s_1^2}{n_1} + \dfrac{s_2^2}{n_2}\right)^2}{\dfrac{\left(\dfrac{s_1^2}{n_1}\right)^2}{n_1 + 1} + \dfrac{\left(\dfrac{s_2^2}{n_2}\right)^2}{n_2 + 1}} - 2$$

The above test assumes that the two populations of measurements are distinct. To test that the two samples, in fact, do come from the same population calculate the t statistic

$$t = \frac{\mu_1 - \mu_2}{s\sqrt{\dfrac{1}{n_1} + \dfrac{1}{n_2}}}$$

where s, a weighted estimate of the standard deviation of the underlying population, is given by

$$s = \sqrt{\frac{(n_1 - 1)s_1^2 + (n_2 - 1)s_2^2}{n_1 + n_2 - 2}}$$

where $n_1 + n_2 - 2$ is the number of degrees of freedom of the t distribution.

The ratio of the estimates of two sample variances tests that the samples are both representative of the same population. The ratio

$$F = \frac{s_1^2}{s_2^2}$$

has its own frequency function, which is tabulated for several degrees of freedom in each sample. The table is generally repeated for a few different confidence limits. By convention the larger variance is placed in the numerator. The calculated F ratio is compared to the tabulated value at $n_1 - 1$ numerator and $n_2 - 1$ denominator degrees of freedom at the desired confidence limit α. If the calculated value of F exceeds its tabulated value, there is a probability of less than α that the discrepancy between the variances could have arisen by chance and the two samples do not reflect the same population variance.

7.4 TESTING VARIABILITY

A scientist or engineer frequently needs to estimate the inherent variability of his measurements. If the relative variability is large, his experimental observations may be unreliable. This property was reflected in the tests of hypotheses regarding sample means or standard deviations described in the previous section. The variability of a sample mean, for example, reflects the variability of the population from which the sample was drawn. Because the variance of the underlying population is generally unknown, it must be estimated from the range of the observed or measured quantities.

Analysis of Variance

Suppose n "replicate" measurements were made of a quantity observed in a particular experiment. Suppose, further, that the same experiment was performed a total of m times but one experimental condition, called a "factor," was varied in each repetition or "class." The experimenter wants to know how much of the total variability in his measurements arises from random experimental error and how much arises from the variation between classes. In other words, the hypothesis to be tested is that there is no difference between different classes, each one is an independent sample from the same population.

The statistical model for the above set of experiments is

$$x_{ij} = \mu + \delta_i + \varepsilon_{ij}$$

where μ is the true mean of the population, δ_i is the variation owing to the measurement's being in class i, and ε_{ij} is the experimental error of measurement x_{ij}. The strategy, therefore, is to isolate the variance arising from replication and the variance among classes (which unavoidably includes replication variance) and compare the two with an F test. If the calculated value of F does not exceed the tabulated value at the desired confidence limit for the appropriate degrees of freedom, the hypothesis is accepted (that is, $\delta_i = 0$ for all i). Otherwise, the hypothesis is rejected in favor of the conclusion that there is a significant difference among classes.

According to the above statistical model, the deviation of any measurement from the overall mean may be written as the sum of its deviation from its class mean and the deviation of that class mean from the overall mean.

$$x_{ij} - \bar{x} = (x_{ij} - \bar{x}_i) + (\bar{x}_i - \bar{x})$$

where the overbar indicates a mean value. Squaring both sides, summing over classes i and replications j, and simplifying yields the following equation for the sum of the squared deviations of each measurement from the overall mean.

$$\sum_{i=1}^{m} \sum_{j=1}^{n} (x_{ij} - \bar{x})^2 = \sum_{i=1}^{m} \sum_{j=1}^{n} (x_{ij} - \bar{x}_i)^2 + n \sum_{i=1}^{m} (\bar{x}_i - \bar{x})^2$$

This statistic has $N - 1$ degrees of freedom where $N = m \times n$. However, all sources of variation are confounded in this statistic, hence the need to separate the variance into its component parts.

The first summation on the right-hand side is the sum of squared deviations of the measurements from their respective class means. When divided by $N - m$ degrees of freedom it yields an estimate of the variance σ^2 of the population of possible measurements. The second summation on the right-hand side is n times the sum of squared deviations of the class means from the overall mean. When divided by $m - 1$ degrees of freedom it yields an estimate of n times the variance due to classification plus σ^2. The ratio of these two variances constitutes an F test of the hypothesis that the variance due to classification is zero.

Example 7.4:

A manufacturer of flint glass uses the refractive index of replicate samples of glass from a particular batch for quality control. Four batches of glass gave the following values for measurements of the refractive index.

	batch number			
replication	1	2	3	4
1	1.598	1.599	1.594	1.593
2	1.598	1.594	1.560	1.597
3	1.599	1.599	1.595	1.599
4	1.595	1.598	1.561	1.594
5	1.599	1.594	1.598	1.594

The manufacturer must determine if the product's quality is consistent, that is, if the variation between batches is comparable to the variation obtained with replicate measurements within batches.

Each batch is a class in the analysis of variance. The overall mean refractive index is 1.593, and the class means for batches one through four are 1.598, 1.597, 1.582, 1.595, respectively. The sum of squares among classes is 8.3×10^{-4} with three degrees of freedom, giving a mean square estimate of 2.767×10^{-4} for the variance. The sum of squares within classes is 1.406×10^{-3} with 16 degrees of freedom, giving a mean square estimate of 8.788×10^{-5} for the variance.

The F ratio for these two estimates of the sampling error is 3.149. The tabulated F value at 0.05 confidence is 8.69, that is, there is a probability of no greater than 0.05 that the value of 8.69 will be exceeded by chance if the classification variance is zero. Because the F ratio is less than the tabulated value, the hypothesis should be accepted. The overall sum of squares is 2.422×10^{-3} with 19 degrees of freedom, giving the best estimate of 1.129×10^{-2} for the standard deviation σ of the underlying population.

Note that the statistical test makes no claim regarding the correctness of the mean value obtained. The refractive index of properly fabricated flint glass is 1.592, close to the mean value observed in the above measurements. However, this measurement is easily made with higher accuracy than the standard deviation of 0.01129 suggests. Therefore, the manufacturer must conclude that either the tests are being conducted improperly or the control of the manufacturing process is uneven.

Multifactor Statistical Models

A simple extension of the one factor model with replication leads to equations for the analysis of variance for models with two or more varying factors. Although the analysis of such models is beyond the scope of this work, it is important to understand their implied statistical "design" because of its influence on the resulting equations. If all factors are varied independently and all combinations of factors are treated systematically, the model is called a "factorial design." If values for the several factors are selected at random for each experiment (but not for each replication of an experiment), the model is called "randomized blocks." Although each individual observation must be independent of the rest, the factors may be hierarchically nested. That is, a group of factors may represent special cases of another factor. Because these statistical tests were originally designed to analyze agricultural experiments, they were given names like "split plot" and "split split plot" models. Analysis of variance in multifactor experiments requires careful scrutiny of the experimental design to determine the proper statistical model to use.

7.5   CLASSIFICATION OF OBSERVATIONS

Scientists often wish to classify a set of observations into one of a number of possible groups. For example, in order to optimize the refining process a technician in an ore smelting plant may need to identify the geological origin of a particular batch of ore as evidenced by an assay for the desired metal and for several impurities. A biologist may wish to assign a recently discovered animal to one of several genera depending on its morphological and biochemical qualities. Such determinations can be made if the mean values of the properties to be tested are known for the several classes to which the observations to be classified may belong.

Discriminant Analysis

Denote by R the range of values that can be assumed by a random variable x. Two populations of random variables x_1 and x_2 have respective probability density functions $p_1(x)$ and $p_2(x)$ and (possibly overlapping) ranges R_1 and R_2 contained in R. How could an arbitrary measurement x be assigned to one of these two populations? Making replicate measurements and comparing their mean or variance as described in the previous section would only tell if there was a statistically significant difference between the calculated and expected values. It is conceivable that the means are sufficiently close or that the standard deviations are sufficiently large for the measurement to fit both distributions.

Consider an experiment in which p properties given by

$$x_i, i = 1,..., p$$

are measured. Assume that the populations to which this set **x** of measurements can belong are normally distributed and each population has the same covariances between pairs of properties but different means. The ratio of the probabilities of observing **x**, assuming that it belongs to the first or the second population, is

$$\frac{p_1(x)}{p_2(x)} = \exp \left\{ -\frac{1}{2} [(\mathbf{x} - \boldsymbol{\mu}_1)^T \mathbf{V}^{-1}(\mathbf{x} - \boldsymbol{\mu}_1) - (\mathbf{x} - \boldsymbol{\mu}_2)^T \mathbf{V}^{-1}(\mathbf{x} - \boldsymbol{\mu}_2)] \right\}$$

where $\boldsymbol{\mu}_i$ is the vector of mean values of the properties in the ith population and $\mathbf{V}$ is the matrix of covariances of the properties.

Denote the ratio of probabilities by k. Taking the logarithm of both sides of the above equation and rearranging yields

$$\ln k = \mathbf{x}^T \mathbf{V}^{-1}(\boldsymbol{\mu}_1 - \boldsymbol{\mu}_2) - \frac{1}{2}(\boldsymbol{\mu}_1 + \boldsymbol{\mu}_2)^T \mathbf{V}^{-1}(\boldsymbol{\mu}_1 - \boldsymbol{\mu}_2)$$

If the right-hand side of this equation is greater than or equal to the value of $\ln k$ calculated from the *a priori* probabilities, the measurements x should be assigned to the population in range R_1. Otherwise, they should be assigned to the population in range R_2. If there are more than two populations and their associated subranges in the sample space R, A set of measurements $\mathbf{x}$ should be assigned to the population i for which

$$\mathbf{x} \mathbf{V}^{-1} \boldsymbol{\mu}_i - 0.5\, \boldsymbol{\mu}_i \mathbf{V}^{-1} \boldsymbol{\mu}_i$$

is greatest. (Note that interchanging the order of the $\mathbf{x}$ and $\boldsymbol{\mu}$ vectors has no effect on the result.) The above expression is known as the "discriminant function."

In general the probability density functions for the populations are not known; only estimates of their means and variances are available. In that case $\ln k$ cannot be calculated, and the right-hand side of the equation for this quantity equals a random variable u. The expectation value $\langle u \rangle$ can be shown to be

$$\langle u \rangle = \frac{1}{2}(\boldsymbol{\mu}_1 + \boldsymbol{\mu}_2)^T \mathbf{V}^{-1}(\boldsymbol{\mu}_1 - \boldsymbol{\mu}_2) = \frac{1}{2}\alpha$$

with a variance of

$$V(u) = (\boldsymbol{\mu}_1 + \boldsymbol{\mu}_2)^T \mathbf{V}^{-1}(\boldsymbol{\mu}_1 - \boldsymbol{\mu}_2) = \alpha$$

The quantity $\sqrt{\alpha}$ is the "distance" between the two populations. This result indicates that u is distributed as $N(0.05\,\alpha, \alpha)$ if x is distributed as $N(\boldsymbol{\mu}_1, \mathbf{V})$ and distributed as $N(-0.5\,\alpha, \alpha)$ if x is distributed as $N(\boldsymbol{\mu}_2, \mathbf{V})$. The set of measurements $\mathbf{x}$ can be assigned to the population in R_1 or R_2, depending on the value of α.

Classification Error

The probability of misclassifying x is given by the integral of the Gaussian frequency function over the range selected from the value of α. For example, suppose the estimate $\boldsymbol{\mu}_2$ is selected, implying the range R_2, extending from the value of c to ∞ (Fig. 7.3). The function $p_1(x)$ must be integrated over R_2 to obtain the probability that the correct estimate is actually μ_2.

$$\int_c^\infty \frac{1}{\sqrt{2\pi\alpha}} \, e^{-(z-\alpha/2)^2/2\alpha} \, dz$$

The values of this integral (and for integrals from $-\infty$ to c) are tabulated for many values of c. Fig. 7.3 shows how c can be selected as the point where the curves for the two frequency functions intersect. This is the simplest choice, but others are possible.

Computational Approach

The first phase of discriminant analysis is to use preliminary data to calculate the means of the properties in each population and to construct the covariance matrix. This matrix has elements which are the covariances between pairs of properties over the entire sampling range.

$$V_{pq} = \frac{\sum_{i=1}^{m} n_i \sum_{k=1}^{n_i} (x_{ipk} - \mu_{ip})(x_{iqk} - \mu_{iq})/(n_i - 1)}{\sum_{i=1}^{m} n_i}$$

where m is the number of populations in the sample space R and n_i is the number of replicate measurements of properties p and q in population i.

$p(x)$

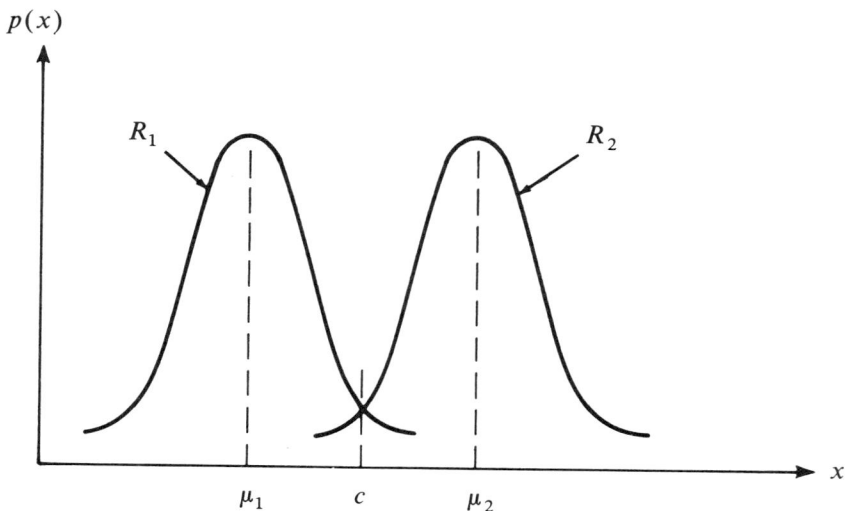

Fig. 7.3. Probability density functions for two populations in the sample space R. The value $x = c$ divides R into regions R_1 and R_2.

Note that the same number of replications is required for the measurement of each property in a given class, but there may be a different number of replications in each class. The quantity V_{pq} is a weighted average of the covariances in each class. If the number of replications is the same for each class, all the weights are one and only the second summation in the numerator need be evaluated.

The means and the pooled covariances are used to calculate the constant vector

$$\gamma_i = V^{-1}\mu_i$$

and the quantity

$$\delta_i = 0.5\ \mu_i V^{-1}\mu_i = 0.5\ \mu_i\gamma_i$$

for each class. The covariance matrix does not actually have to be inverted; γ_i may be obtained by solving the simultaneous equations

$$V\gamma_i = \mu_i$$

For a given set of measurements x the discriminant function is evaluated from

$$d_i = x\gamma_i - \delta_i$$

and the observations assigned to the population for which d_i is maximized. Most often there are several observations to be classified. Storing γ_i and δ_i minimizes the amount of computation for the classification of each new set of measurements.

7.6 MONTE CARLO INTEGRATION

Many numerical problems are very difficult, or even impossible, to solve in closed form because the function to be manipulated is extremely complicated or is given by a table of values rather than by an equation. Evaluating a definite integral or solving a differential equation are typical examples. Often, however, it is possible to simulate the process represented by the function as a stochastic process by assigning some probability that a particular functional value will be observed. A random number is selected from the appropriate distribution and used to compute the value of the desired function. If the function is in tabular form, interpolation between entries in the table will be necessary. The sum of successive trials, perhaps weighted by their probability of success, is an approximation to the solution. Of course, the more trials that are attempted, the better will be the approximation.

Searching a Sample Space

To integrate the function $f(x)$ over the interval $[a, b]$ find some value M such that $f(x) < M$ over the entire interval. Then select a random number

v from the uniform distribution on $[0, 1]$, multiply by M, and determine if $f(v)$ falls below the curve for $f(x)$ or above it. Score one point if the $f(v) \leq f(x)$. Fig. 7.4 illustrates this process. Repeat this procedure a large number of times.

Let S be the number of "successes" (points falling below the curve) in T trials. The estimated probability of success is

$$\frac{S}{T} = \frac{\text{Area under curve}}{\text{Total area of rectangle}} = \frac{\int_a^b f(x)\,dx}{M(b - a)}$$

After a minimal number of trials, say 100, the value of the integral calculated from the above equation can be compared to the value computed at the previous trial. When the value of the integral does not change by more than a preset tolerance between successive trials, the process may be terminated. An upper limit should be set for the number of trials to ensure termination of the procedure.

Algorithm

Given are $f(x)$, a, b, M, mintrials, maxtrials, toler, and a random number generator to select v_i from the uniform distribution on $[0, 1]$.

$T = 0$

$S = 0$

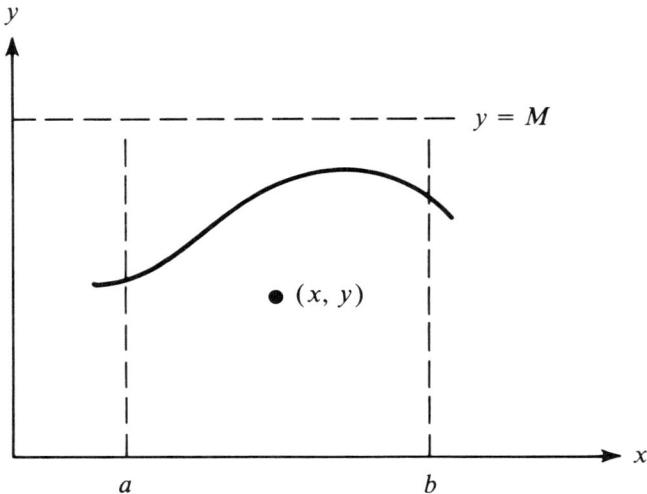

Fig. 7.4. Monte Carlo integration. Many points like (x, y) are selected at random, and the integral approximated by the fraction of the points falling below the curve.

while $T <$ maxtrials

    $T = T + 1$

    $x = a + v_1(b - a)$

    $y = v_2M$

    if $y \leqslant f(x)$

        $S = S + 1$

        if $T \geqslant$ mintrials, integral$_s = SM(b - a)/T$

    if integral$_s -$ integral$_{s-1} \leqslant$ toler, stop

This algorithm can be extended to handle multiple integrals by searching a volume of space rather than an area. Thus, a function $f(x, y)$ may be integrated over x and y by selecting random values of x and y which designate a point in the volume bounded by $x = a$, $x = b$, $y = p$, $y = q$, $f(x, y) = 0$, and $f(x, y) = M$. Even higher dimensional integrals may be evaluated by this method.

Example 7.5:

Integrate $\sin x$ from $x = a = 0$ to $x = b = \pi$. As the maximal value of $\sin x$ on this interval is one, choose that value for M to minimize the search area. The analytical solution is $\cos 0 - \cos \pi = 2$.

Solution

The results for the first three trials are tabulated below. In the first trial $\sin 2.9685 = 0.1722$, which is less than the random number 0.8448 obtained for y. Therefore S remains zero, and $\pi S/T = 0$ is the first approximation to the integral. The second trial gives a value of y which is less than $\sin x$, so S is one and the new approximation to the integral is $\pi/2$.

T	x	y	S	Integral
1	2.9685	0.8448	0	0.0000
2	2.2346	0.7539	1	1.5708
3	1.9689	0.5740	2	2.0944

After 100 trials the approximation to the integral is 2.004, which is close to the analytical value of 2.

Statistics of Monte Carlo Integration

Let I denote the value of an integral determined by searching a volume V with random numbers. As shown above, the expectation value of the integral is

$$\langle I \rangle = \alpha$$

which is approximated by SV/T after a large number of trials. The expectation value of the variance of the integral, that is, the variance of the population of estimates of the integral, is

$$\alpha^2 = \left\langle \left(\frac{SV}{T} - \alpha \right)^2 \right\rangle = VI - \alpha^2$$

Substituting for the mean value (permissible after a large number of trials) gives the standard deviation

$$\sigma = \frac{V}{T} \sqrt{S(T - S)}$$

It can be shown that the probability that the calculated integral is more than m standard deviations from its expectation value is constant.

$$P\{|I - \alpha| > m\sigma\} < 1/m^2$$

Therefore, the only way to improve the accuracy of the integration is to minimize σ. Because the ratio S/T approaches a constant with an increasing number of trials, the only way to minimize σ is to minimize V, the volume of the search space. That is, M should be chosen to be as small as possible.

Comparison with Polynomial Methods

Evaluation of an n-dimensional integral over an interval divided into N subintervals requires N^n function evaluations. For example, the composite trapezoid rule has an error proportional to h^3 where h is the mesh size. For simplicity let the interval of integration be one, that is,

$$Nh = 1$$

(This tactic merely converts the independent variable to relative units and does not result in any loss of generality.) The uncertainty in the value of the integral is

$$e = K/N^3$$

where K is a constant.

After q function evaluations using the Monte Carlo method the integral has a probability of 0.9 of being within the interval $[I - 2\sigma, I + 2\sigma]$ where σ^2 is the variance of the population of estimates. The uncertainty in the value of the integral actually obtained is

$$e = K'/\sqrt{q}$$

If q equals N^n, Monte Carlo integration is more accurate than the composite trapezoid rule when

$$\frac{K}{N^{n/2}} < \frac{K'}{N^3}$$

Ignoring the difference between the constants K and K', the above condition is met when n is greater than six. Frequently, fewer than N^n trials are required for high dimensional integrals, emphasizing the superiority of the Monte Carlo method for such problems.

7.7 COMPUTER PROGRAMS

```
                    SUBROUTINE STATS(N,X, MEAN, STDDEV)
C***********************************************************
C*                                                        *
C*  Calculation of the mean and standard deviation of a   *
C*  set of N observations.                                *
C*                                                        *
C***********************************************************

      REAL MEAN

      DIMENSION X(1)
C
C -- Calculate mean
C
      MEAN = 0.0
      DO 10 I = 1,N
   10    MEAN = MEAN + X(I)
      MEAN = MEAN/N
C
C -- Calculate standard deviation
C
      STDDEV = 0.0
      DO 20 I = 1,N
   20    STDDEV = STDDEV + (X(I) - MEAN)**2
      STDDEV = SQRT(STDDEV/(N - 1))
      RETURN
      END

procedure stats(n: integer; x: vector; var mean, stddev:
                real);
{
***********************************************************
*                                                        *
*  Calculation of the mean and standard deviation of a   *
*  set of N observations.  The data type vector must be  *
*  defined as array[1..n] of real in the calling         *
*  routine.                                              *
*                                                        *
***********************************************************
}
var
  i: integer;

begin

  {Calculate mean}
```

```
  mean := 0.0;
  for i := 1 to n do
    mean := mean + x[i];
  mean := mean/n;

  {Calculate standard deviation}

  stddev = 0.0;
  for i := 1 to n do
    stddev := stddev + sqr(x[i] - mean);
  stddev := sqrt(stddev/(n - 1))
end;
```

```
                        FUNCTION RANDOM(X)
C***************************************************************
C*                                                            *
C*  Select a random number from the uniform distribution   *
C*  on [0,1].  The computer is assumed to have a 32-bit     *
C*  word size with one sign bit for integers.  X is the     *
C*  seed (default value is 1) and stores the accumulated    *
C*  integer in the linear congruential random number        *
C*  generator                                                *
C*                                                            *
C*    X = A*X + C                                              *
C*                                                            *
C*  The value of X must not be changed between               *
C*  successive calls to RANDOM.                              *
C*                                                            *
C***************************************************************

        INTEGER X, A, C
        REAL M
        DATA X,A,C,M /1, 2147437301, 453816981, 2147483648./

        X = A*X + C
        RANDOM = X/M
        RETURN
        END
```

```
function random(var x: integer): real;
{
***************************************************************
*                                                            *
*  Select a random number from the uniform distribution    *
*  on [0,1].  The computer is assumed to have a 32-bit      *
*  word size with one sign bit for integers.  x is the      *
*  seed (default value is 1) and stores the accumulated     *
*  integer in the linear congruential random number         *
*  generator                                                 *
*                                                            *
*    x = a*x + c                                              *
*                                                            *
*  The value of x must not be changed between               *
```

```
*  successive calls to random.                              *
*                                                           *
*************************************************************
}
const
  x = 1;
  a = 2147437301;
  c = 453816981;
  m = 2147483648.0;

begin
  x := a*x + c;
  random := x/m
end;
```

```
              SUBROUTINE ANOVA(NCLASS,NREPL,CMEAN,CVAR,SVAR)
C*************************************************************
C*                                                         *
C*   One-way analysis of variance.  NCLASS and NREPL are   *
C*   the number of classes and replicate observations.  X  *
C*   is the array of observations packed by class and the  *
C*   replications entered consecutively.  CMEAN and SMEAN  *
C*   are the class and overall sample means, respectively. *
C*   CVAR and SVAR are the variances between and within    *
C*   classes, respectively.                                *
C*                                                         *
C*************************************************************

      INTEGER DFCLASS, DFTOT
      DIMENSION X(1), CMEAN(1)
C
C -- Calculate class means and overall mean
C
      SMEAN = 0.0
      DO 20 I = 1,NCLASS
        CMEAN(I) = 0.0
        DO 10 J = 1,NREPL
          CMEAN(I) = CMEAN(I) + X(I*J)
  10      SMEAN = SMEAN + X(I*J)
  20    CMEAN(I) = CMEAN(I)/NREPL
      SMEAN = SMEAN/(NCLASS*NREPL)
C
C -- Calculate number of degrees of freedom
C
      DFCLASS = NCLASS - 1
      DFTOT = NCLASS*NREPL - 1
C
C -- Compute variances
C
      SVAR = 0.0
      CVAR = 0.0
      DO 30 I = 1,NCLASS
        CVAR = CVAR + (CMEAN(I) - SMEAN)**2
```

```
        DO 30 J + 1,NREPL
  30      SVAR = SVAR + (X(I*J) - CMEAN(I))**2
        CVAR = CVAR/DFCLASS
        SVAR = SVAR/DFTOT
C
C -- Output means and variances
C
        WRITE 1000
1000  FORMAT(5X,'Analysis of variance"//
     1 'Class',9x,'Mean'/)
        WRITE 2000, (I, CMEAN(I), I = 1,NCLASS)
2000  FORMAT(1X,I2,2X,1PE12.4)
        WRITE 3000, CVAR, DFCLASS, SVAR, DFTOT
3000  FORMAT((/' Variance among classes =',1PE12.4,
     1 ' at',I3,' degrees of freedom'/
     2 ' Variance within classes =',1PE12.4,' at', I3,
     3 ' degrees of freedom')
        RETURN
        END

procedure anova(nclass, nrepl: integer; var cmean: vector;
                var smean, cvar, svar: real);
{
**************************************************************
*                                                          *
*   One-way analysis of variance.  nclass and nrepl are    *
*   the number of classes and replicate observations.  x   *
*   is the array of observations packed by class and the   *
*   replications entered consecutively.  cmean and smean   *
*   are the class and overall sample means, respectively.  *
*   cvar and svar are the variances between and within     *
*   classes, respectively.  The data type vector must be   *
*   defined as array[1..nclass] of real in the calling     *
*   routine.                                               *
*                                                          *
**************************************************************
}
var
  i, j, dfclass, dftot: integer;

begin

  {Calculate class means and overall means}

  smean := 0.0;
  for i := 1 to nclass do
    begin
      cmean[i] := 0.0;
      for j := 1 to nrepl do
        begin
          cmean[i] := cmean[i] + x[i*j];
          smean := smean + x[i*j]
        end;
```

```
      cmean[i] := cmean[i]/nrepl
    end;
  smean := smean/(nclass*nrepl);

  {Calculate number of degrees of freedom}

  dfclass := nclass - 1;
  dftot := nclass*nrepl - 1;

  {Compute variances}

  cvar := 0.0;
  svar := 0.0;
  for i := 1 to nclass do
    begin
      cvar := cvar + sqr(cmean[i] - smeana);
      for j := 1 to nrepl do
        svar := svar + sqr(x[i*j] - cmean[i])
    end;
  cvar := cvar/dfclass;
  svar := svar/dftot;

  {Output means and variances}

  writeln('     Analysis of variance');
  writeln;
  writeln(' Class        Mean');
  writeln;

  for i := 1 to nclass do
    writeln(i:3,'    ',cmean:12);
  writeln;
  writeln(' Variance among classes =',cvar:12,
          ' at',dfclass:3,' degrees of freedom');
  writeln(' Variance within classes =',svar:12,
          ' at',dftot:3,' degrees of freedom')
end;


        SUBROUTINE DISCRM(NCLASS, NOBS, NREPL, X, G, D)
C****************************************************************
C*                                                            *
C*  Compute the discriminant function vector.  NCLASS,        *
C*  NOBS, NREPL are the number of classifications (max =      *
C*  50), the number of observations for each experiment       *
C*  (max = 50), and the number of replications of each        *
C*  experiment, respectively.  X(class, observation,          *
C*  replication) is the array of observations.  Call          *
C*  this routine once to compute the G and D vectors.         *
C*  Then call CLASS to classify each new set of               *
C*  observations.                                             *
C*                                                            *
C****************************************************************
```

```
      INTEGER P, G, TOTOBS
      DIMENSION X(50,50,1), NREPL(50), CMEANA(50,50),
     1 V(50,50), G(50,50), D(50)
      DATA EPS /1.E-20/
C
C -- Compute means of observations and total number of
C    replications
C
      TOTOBS = 0
      DO 30 J = 1,NCLASS
        TOTOBS = TOTOBS + NREPL(J)
        DO 20 I = 1,NOBS
          CMEAN(I,J) = 0.0
          DO 10 K = 1,NREPL(J)
   10       CMEAN(I,J) = CMEAN(I,J) + X(J,I,K)
   20     CMEAN(I,J) + CMEAN(I,J)/NREPL(J)
   30   CONTINUE
C
C -- Calculate the symmetrical covariance matrix
C
      DO 60 P = 1,NOBS
        DO 60 Q = P,NOBS
          V(P,Q) = 0.0
          DO 50 I = 1,NCLASS
            DO 40 K = 1,NREPL(I)
   40         V(P,Q) = V(P,Q) + (X(I,P,K) - CMEAN(P,I))*
     1                          (X(I,Q,K) - CMEAN(Q,I))
   50       V(P,Q) = V(P,Q)*NREPL*I)/(NREPL(I) - 1)
          V(P,Q) = V(P,Q)/TOTOBS
   60     V(Q,P) = V(P,Q)
C
C -- Solve the equation V*G = CMEAN for the G vectors by
C    the Gaussian elimination routine in Chapter 3
C
          CALL GAUSS(NOBS, NCLASS, V, CMEAN, EPS)
C
C -- Compute the dot products of G vectors and means
C
      DO 80 J = 1,NCLASS
        D(J) = 0.0
        DO 70 I = 1, NOBS
   70     D(J) = D(J) + CMEAN(I,J)*G(I,J)
   80   D(J) = 0.5*D(J)

      RETURN
      END

              SUBROUTINE CLASS(NCLASS, NOBS, OBS, G, D)
C***************************************************************
C*                                                           *
C*  Classify new set of observations of NOBS quantities      *
C*  (max = 50) stored in OBS array.                          *
C*                                                           *
C***************************************************************
```

```
      DIMENSION OBS(50), G(50,50), D(50), DISCR(50)
C
C -- Compute discriminant vector
C
      DO 20 J = 1,NCLASS
        DISCR(J) = 0.0
        DO 10 I = 1,NOBS
  10      DISCR(J) = DISCR(J) + OBS(I)*G(I,J)
  20    DISCR(J) = DISCR(J) - D(J)
C
C -- Output discriminant vector
C
      WRITE 1000
1000  FORMAT(5X,'Discriminant functions'//
     1 'Class  Discriminant'/
      WRITE 2000, (I, DISCR(I), I = 1,NCLASS)
2000  FORMAT(I4,2X,1PE12.4)
      RETURN
      END
```

```
procedure discrm(nclass, nobs: integer; nrepl: ivector;
                 X: dataset; var G: nxm; var d: vector);
{
****************************************************************
*                                                              *
*   Compute the discriminant function of vector.  nclass,      *
*   nobs, nrepl are the number of classifications (max =       *
*   50), the number of observations for each experiment        *
*   (max = 50), and the number of replications of each         *
*   experiment, respectively.  X(class, observation,           *
*   replication) is the array of observations.  Call           *
*   this routine once to compute the G and d vectors.          *
*   Then call class to classify each new set of observa-       *
*   tions.  The data types ivector and vector must be          *
*   defined as array[1..nobs] of integer and array             *
*   [1..nclass] of real, respectively, in the calling          *
*   routine.  The type dataset must be defined as array        *
*   [1..nclass,1..nobs,1..nrepl] of real and the type          *
*   nxm must be defined as array[1..nobs,1..nclass] of         *
*   real in the calling program.                               *
*                                                              *
****************************************************************
{
const
  eps = 1.E-20;

type
  nxn = array[1..nobs,1..nobs] of real;

var
  i, j, k, p, q, totobs: integer;
  Cmean: nxm;
  V: nxn;
```

```
begin

  {Compute means of observations and total number of
   replications}

  totobs := 0;
  for j := 1 to nclass do
    begin
      totobs := totobs + nrepl[j];
      for i := 1 to nobs do
        begin
          Cmean[i,j] := 0.0;
          for k := 1 to nrepl[j] do
            Cmean[i,j] := Cmean[pi,j] + X[j,i,k];
          Cmean[i,j] := Cmean[i,j]/nrepl[j]
        end
    end;

  {Calculate the symmetric covariance matrix}

  for p := 1 to nobs do
    for q := 1 to nobs do
      begin
        V[p,q] = 0.0;
        for i := 1 to nclass do
          begin
            for k := 1 to nrepl[i] do
              V[p,q] := V[p,q]+(X[i,p,k] − Cmean[p,i])
                *(X[i,q,k] − Cmean[q,i]);
            V[p,q] := V[p,q]*nrepl[i]/(nrepl[i] − 1)
          end;
        V[q,p] := V[p,q]
      end;

  {Solve the equation V*G = Cmean for the G vectors by the
   Gausssian elimination procedure in Chapter 3}

  Gauss(nobs, nclass, V, Cmean, eps);

  {Compute dot products of G vectors and means}

  for j := 1 to nclass do
    begin
      d[j] := 0.0;
      for i := 1 to nobs do
        d[j] := d[j] + Cmean[i,j]*G[i,j];
      d[j] := 0.5*d[j]
    end
end;

procedure class(nclass, nobs: integer; obs: rvector;
                G: nxm; d: vector);
{
```

```
******************************************************************
*                                                                *
*   Classify new set of observations of nobs quantities          *
*   (max = 50) stored in obs array.  The data type               *
*   rvector must be defined as array[1..nobs] of real in         *
*   the calling program.                                         *
*                                                                *
******************************************************************
}
var
  i, j: integer;
  discr: vector;

begin

  {Compute discriminant vector}

  for j := 1 to nclass do
    begin
      discr[j] := 0.0;
      for i := 1 to nobs do
        discr[j] := discr[j] + obs[i]*G[i,j];
      disc[j] := discr[j] - d[j]
    end;

  {Output discriminant vector}

  writeln('      Discriminant functions');
  writeln;
  writeln(' Class  Discriminant');
  writeln;
  for i := 1 to nclass do
    writeln(i:4,'     ',discr[i]:12)
end;
```

7.6   EXAMPLE PROBLEMS

Example 7.6:

Two laboratories, using different scintillation counters, measured the intensity of 662 keV γ rays from Cs^{137}. The pulse heights of counts of radioactivity in a typical scintillation counter are normally distributed with a mean of H and a standard deviation given by

$$\sigma = H \sqrt{\frac{13.15}{Eq}}$$

where E is the energy of the radiation in keV and q is the efficiency of the scintillation phosphor. Let $h_{1/2}$ be the pulse height with a probability of observance equal to half the probability of observing the peak pulse height. The uncertainty in the radioactivity measurement is approximated by

$$2|H - h_{1/2}| = 2.36\ \sigma$$

The two laboratories, using the phosphors NaI ($q = 30$) and anthracene ($q = 15$), each made 16 measurements centered on 662 keV and obtained peak count rates of 3120 and 2250 cpm, respectively. Are these two measurements equally reliable, that is, is there a statistically significant difference between the estimated experimental uncertainties in the observations from the two laboratories?

Solution

Clearly, the two measurements represent sampling from entirely different populations with different distributions of pulse heights. An F test for the equality of the variances is certain to show a significant difference owing to the different amounts of Cs^{137} in the two experiments. Therefore, the measurements must be put on a common basis by dividing by the peak count rate H.

The expected variance of the pulse heights relative to the peak pulse height for the first laboratory's measurements is

$$\frac{\sigma^2}{H^2} = \frac{13.15}{662 \times 30} = 6.624 \times 10^{-4}$$

corresponding to a relative standard deviation of 2.57%. The expected relative variance for the second laboratory's measurements is 1.3248×10^{-3}, corresponding to a relative standard deviation of 3.64%. Multiplying by 2.36 gives measurement errors of 6.07% and 8.59%, respectively.

The F statistic is given by

$$F = \frac{0.0859^2}{0.0607^2} = 2.0027$$

The tabulated F statistic for 15 degrees of freedom in each variance is 2.40 at the 0.05 confidence level. As the calculated value of F is less than the tabulated value, the hypothesis that the two variances are equivalent is accepted and the results from the two laboratories are equally reliable.

Example 7.7:

A zoologist has discovered a population of snails which he believes comprises two separate species. He wishes to know to which species a snail from a nearby pond belongs. The length of the shell, the length of the muscular foot, and the weight of the snail for each of four individuals in each species were measured. The data and the mean values of these three properties for each species are listed in the following table.

Species	Shell Length, cm	Foot Length, cm	Weight, g
1	1.85	2.03	1.70
	1.91	1.86	1.65
	1.93	2.12	1.81
	2.16	1.95	1.74
	$\mu_1 = 1.96$	1.99	1.73
2	2.31	2.04	2.05
	2.50	2.20	2.13
	1.96	2.08	1.97
	1.95	1.97	1.81
	$\mu_2 = 2.18$	2.07	1.99

The individual to be classified has a shell length of 2.03 cm, a foot length of 1.98 cm, and a weight of 1.94 g.

Solution

Because the same number of replicate measurements were made for both species, the weights in the equation for the pooled covariances are all one and it is not necessary to weight the species covariances before pooling. The covariance matrix is

$$\begin{pmatrix} 0.0920 & 0.0162 & -0.2809 \\ 0.0162 & 0.0216 & -0.0540 \\ -0.2809 & -0.0540 & 2.6556 \end{pmatrix}$$

Solution of the two equations

$$\mathbf{V}\gamma_i = \mu_1, \ i = 1, 2$$

by Gaussian elimination gives the vectors

$$\gamma_1 = (20.671, \ 105.14, \ 4.027)^T$$

and

$$\gamma_2 = (18.247, \ 109.32, \ 4.535)^T$$

with corresponding constant terms δ_i of 128.36 and 137.55, respectively. The discriminant functions for the two species are

$$d_1 = \mathbf{x}_1\gamma_1 - \delta_1 = 129.6$$
$$d_2 = \mathbf{x}_2\gamma_2 - \delta_2 = 124.7$$

Because the discriminant function d_1 is larger than d_2, the new individual should be classified as belonging to species 1.

PROGRAM LIBRARIES

EISPACK (EIgenSystem PACKage): A collection of Fortran subroutines for the solution of eigenvalue-eigenvector problems. These programs are machine-independent, very reliable, and efficient. The documentation guides the user in selection of the appropriate routines. The package features many diagnostics for error detection. The package includes routines for real and complex, symmetric and nonsymmetric, general and Hermitian, and tridiagonal matrices. To obtain a copy contact: National Energy Software Center, Argonne National Laboratories, 9700 Cass Ave., Argonne, IL 60439.

IMSL (International Mathematical and Statistical Library): A very large collection of Fortran programs for the solution of linear and nonlinear systems, optimization, solution of differential equations, and statistical calculations. Versions are available for a variety of computers. To obtain a copy contact: IMSL, Inc., GNB Building, 7500 Bellaire Blvd., Houston, TX 77036.

LINPACK (LINear simultaneous equations PACKage): Machine-independent Fortran routines for the solution of systems of linear equations, including linear least-squares problems. The programs are highly efficient and reliable. They can handle real, complex, and double precision arithmetic. To obtain a copy contact: National Energy Software Center, Argonne National Laboratories, 9700 Cass Ave., Argonne, IL 60439.

PORT: A reasonably portable collection of Fortran programs for the solution of the standard problems in numerical analysis. It includes some routines for memory management that are useful in other contexts as well. To obtain a copy contact: Bell Telephone Laboratories, Murray Hill, NJ 07974.

BIBLIOGRAPHY

Mathematics

Bodewig, A., *Matrix Calculus,* North Holland, Amsterdam, 1952.
Davis, P. J., *Interpolation and Approximation,* Dover, New York, 1975.
Oden, J. T., *Applied Functional Analysis,* Prentice-Hall, Englewood Cliffs, N.J., 1979.
Wilf, H., *Mathematics for the Physical Sciences,* Wiley, New York, 1963.

Numerical Analysis (without programming)

Acton, F. S., *Numerical Methods that Work,* Harper and Row, New York, 1970.
Atkinson, K. E., *An Introduction to Numerical Analysis,* Wiley, New York, 1978.
Dahlquist, G., and A. Bjork, *Numerical Methods,* Prentice-Hall, Englewood Cliffs, N.J., 1974.
Fox, L., *An Introduction to Numerical Linear Algebra,* Oxford University Press, Fair Lawn, N.J., 1965.
Hamming, R. W., *Introduction to Applied Numerical Analysis,* McGraw-Hill, New York, 1971.
Henrici, P., *Elements of Numerical Analysis,* Wiley, New York, 1964.
Ortega, J. M., *Numerical Analysis—A Second Course,* Academic Press, New York, 1972.
Ralston, A., and P. Rabinowitz, *A First Course in Numerical Analysis,* McGraw-Hill, New York, 1978.

Stummel, F., and K. Hainer, *Introduction to Numerical Analysis,* Scottish Academic Press, Edinburgh, 1980.

Traub, J. F., *Iterative Methods for the Solution of Equations,* Prentice-Hall, Englewood Cliffs, N.J., 1964.

Wilkinson, J. H., *The Algebraic Eigenvalue Problem,* Oxford University Press, Fair Lawn, N.J., 1965.

Numerical Analysis (with programming)

Atkinson, L. V., and P. J. Harley, *An Introduction to Numerical Methods with Pascal,* Addison-Wesley, Reading, Mass., 1983.

Carnahan, B., H. A. Luther, and J. O. Wilkes, *Applied Numerical Methods,* Wiley, New York, 1969.

Conte, S. D., and C. deBoor, *Elementary Numerical Analysis—An Algorithmic Approach,* McGraw-Hill, New York, 1980.

Forsythe, G. E., M. A. Malcolm, and C. B. Moler, *Computer Methods for Mathematical Computation,* Prentice-Hall, Englewood Cliffs, N.J., 1977.

Forsythe, G. E., and C. B. Moler, *Computer Solution of Linear Algebraic Systems,* Prentice-Hall, Englewood Cliffs, N.J., 1967.

Pizer, S. M., and V. L. Wallace, *To Compute Numerically—Concepts and Strategies,* Little, Brown, Boston, 1983.

Rice, J. R., *Matrix Computations and Mathematical Software,* McGraw-Hill, New York, 1981.

Wilf, H., and A. Ralston, *Mathematical Methods for Digital Computers,* Wiley, New York, 1960.

Young, D. M., and R. T. Gregory, *A Survey of Numerical Methods,* Addison-Wesley, Reading, Mass., 1972.

INDEX